Shooter's Bible

GUIDE TO OPTICS

The Most Comprehensive Guide Ever Published on
Riflescopes, Binoculars, Spotting Scopes, Rangefinders, and More

Thomas McIntyre

SKYHORSE PUBLISHING

Skyhorse Publishing books may be purchased in bulk at special discounts for sales promotion, corporate gifts, fund-raising, or educational purposes. Special editions can also be created to specifications. For details, contact the Special Sales Department, Skyhorse Publishing, 307 West 36th Street, 11th Floor, New York, NY 10018 or info@skyhorsepublishing.com.

Skyhorse® and Skyhorse Publishing® are registered trademarks of Skyhorse Publishing, Inc.®, a Delaware corporation.

Visit our website at www.skyhorsepublishing.com.

10 9 8 7 6 5 4 3 2 1

Library of Congress Cataloging-in-Publication Data is available on file.

ISBN: 978-1-61608-632-9

Printed in China

CONTENTS

It is as likely to use a "pair of binoculars" as it is to pedal a
"pair of bicycles." The word is binocular.

Acknowledgments

I am deeply obliged to a great number of people for help and assistance in the production of this book. First of all to the optics manufacturers and their sales, marketing, press-relations, and advertising departments and agencies for graciously providing me with the detailed information and high-quality images of their products that I sought for this book. To Ed Beattie and Doug Howlett for their generous contributions from their fields of expertise. I would also like to thank Leroy Van Buggenum of Story, Wyoming, who shares an interest in the testing and using of sporting optics, and with whom I have been able to exchange ideas about what was good and what was bad in riflescopes, binoculars, spotting scopes, reflex sights, and rangefinders. To my long-time editor Jay Cassell of Skyhorse Publishing, who brought this book project to me and who was unfailingly encouraging when I, more than once, wanted to throw my hands up in defeat at the enormity of the enterprise. And to my wife, Elaine, who was both a vital extra set of eyes in reviewing all the material in this book, helped directly with the editing, and who kept the train reliably on the tracks as I focused on completing this work—I would say more, but not here. And to the likes of Lippershey, Metius, Janssen, Porro, Chapman, James, Malcolm, Zeiss, Swarovski, Redfield, Leupold, Weaver, and many, many others who invented, designed, innovated, constructed, and refined the art of shooting optics to bring us to the extreme level of performance, clarity, and excellence we enjoy today.

Thomas McIntyre
Sheridan, Wyoming
December 1, 2011

Foreword

uns are relatively simple, straightforward, unsophisticated, and easy to understand. Their forms and cosmetics change, but the basic machinery remains unchanged year to year. Sports optics, on the other hand, are complex, sophisticated, and change in fundamental ways at a dizzying pace. Three of the categories of equipment covered in this book did not even exist a generation ago.

Choosing a binocular (not binoculars, as Mr. McIntyre notes) or rifle scope used to be sublimely simple. When I started shooting back in the 50s, you got a Weaver scope or, or if you wanted something better, a Lyman or a Stith Bear Cub or a Bausch & Lomb. Zeiss made scopes, as did Hensoldt, but few were adventurous enough to try them. As for binoculars, B&L was the consensus choice, and there were Zeiss and Leitz (not Leica) binoculars that made it here after World War II.

In the 60 years that have passed, a number of things have changed. Asian and European manufacturers have discovered that the United States has millions of shooters and hunters who will cheerfully spend large sums of money—in some cases, very large sums of money—to get an optical edge. That is because shooting has gained increasing sophistication with longer and longer ranges being involved, and because hunting has become a much different enterprise from what it once was. Licenses are often hard to get, trophy animals are less common and very expensive, and travel is de rigeur, and costs big bucks.

Our once casual sport is now quite serious. In 1987, Bausch & Lomb came out with a binocular called the Elite. It was a superb instrument and it was the first to break the $1,000 barrier. B&L thought it would sell mostly to birders (who would, and still will, go to almost any optical lengths to differentiate the likes of a dunlin from a sanderling sandpiper) in limited numbers. But hunters and shooters got wind of how good the Elite was, and B&L found itself unable to keep up with the demand, price be damned. Now, it is possible to spend more than three times that on a binocular, and a surprising number of people do it.

The other thing that happened was computers. Calculating the lens profiles of optical instruments used to be a lengthy and laborious process, requiring many, many hours of tedious calculation. But, enter the computer and, as one optics company executive told me, "You program it for what you want, leave it running overnight, and in the morning you've got your profile." New designs that once took years to develop now take months.

Let us now talk about people, who still take nine months to produce, and in particular, the author of this book, Tom McIntyre. I've known Tom for a good many years, and this is what I can tell you about him: He has a ton of hunting experience. You name it and he's been there and shot it. He knows a great deal about optics. He is a fanatic about testing. (He once dragged me into a subzero locker to see how some scope stood up to real cold and damn near froze me to death.) He is gifted with an abundance of common sense. And he writes good. I do not trust the optics nonsense that I read on the Internet, which can be measured only by the metric ton, or hear at the range, but I do trust Tom.

If you're looking to buy an optical sight, or a binocular, or a spotting scope, you are entering a world where it is easy to go wrong. There is a great deal of advice around, and most of it is bad. But not what lies between these covers. And that is why you should trust Tom, too.

David E. Petzal
Field Editor
Field & Stream **magazine**

Introduction

ptical illusions are perceptions different from objective reality, and the exact opposite of what the shooter and hunter wants to see through the optical devices he uses. Hunters and shooters use optical devices like riflescopes, binoculars, spotting scopes, and rangefinders to identify their targets, measure the distance to those targets, and to line up their firearms on those targets. They employ these devices to show them the way things actually are "out there." For shooters and hunters, their optics are their gauges of objective reality.

While 103 editions of the *Shooter's Bible* have reliably presented galleries and the data of the firearms that are the primary tool of shooters and hunters, there has not existed until now a book dedicated to that other essential component of shooting and hunting—optics. For those of us who know, appreciate, and are fascinated by fine optics, this was an obvious gap. The effort to fill that gap is this book.

The *Shooter's Bible Guide to Optics* reviews the broad spectrum of optical devices of use to hunters and shooters. Hundreds of models of the optics that hunters and shooters need, want to see, and wish to learn about are presented here in a concise, uniform format that will act as a vital tool for the optics consumer and user. For each model the varied configurations it is made in are listed; the specific data, including prices and websites for the manufacturers, for each model are given; and along with an objective written description, the detailed image of the model is shown in full-color. In addition, this book includes a glossary of all the terms and jargon that so often leave optics users perplexed; and the chapters in the book will lead the reader through some of the basic techniques for the effective uses and proper care of optics, so that reader will be able to get the most out of the optics he already owns or will buy.

The famed American rifleman Colonel Townsend Whelen once said, "Only accurate rifles are interesting." Similarly it is only the robust, precise, clear, bright optics that are of any true interest. And it is hoped that those are exactly the optics to which this book will be a guide.

The right optics are the fundamental management tool the shooter and hunter can possess for confronting the greatest challenge he faces: distance. Whether at the shooting bench, on the rolling high plains of pronghorn or prairie-dog country, or across a wide deep canyon from a bare rocky sheep ridge, the shortest distance between two points is a good riflescope. Or binocular. Or spotting scope. Many of those, and other quality optics as well, will be found in these pages.

How to Buy Optics

Whether a piece of shooting optics is purchased new or used, traded for, or passed along, several factors determine its worth (if not necessarily the exact figure you should pay for it). Here, then, are some considerations.

Let the Optics Match the Shooting: Before buying anything, careful consideration should be given to how the optics will be used. If, for example, you are not going to be shooting prairie dogs or 800-meter targets to any extent, you probably don't require the services of a 20X riflescope. On the other hand, a spotting scope is almost always of use; but the kind you might want, for instance only to see where your bullets are grouping in the 10-ring at two-hundred yards from the shooting bench, is quite different from what you need to recognize a 15-inch pronghorn or a

≫ The advantage of shopping for optics in a store, rather than in a catalog or on the internet, is that you have the chance to pick up the scope, binocular, or spotting scope and get the actual feel of it in your hand; plus, you get to look through it with your own eyes.

39-inch Dall sheep at over 1500 yards in the field. Is a 15X binocular something you must carry around your neck all day, or will an 8x42 mm get the job done? Will you be shooting at ranges at which you have to have a rangefinder? What about reticles: thick, thin, or "busy"? A rimfire scope will not likely be adequate for a magnum rifle, while a 50 mm scope is not something you might need on a .22—although field-target shooters regularly mount 50x56 mm scopes on .17-caliber air rifles. Should you put a $1000 scope on a $250 rifle, vice versa? Do you need to pay more than twice as much for the slight optical improvement between a $900 binocular and a $2000 one? All questions to ponder, even though none changes the fact that if you absolutely cannot live without some piece of optics, and you can afford it, you're probably going to buy it.

Price: An optical device can carry a variety of price tags. The first is MSRP ("manufacturer's suggested retail price"). This is the price at which the manufacturer states that the product should be sold. In fact, it exists to allow retailers to show consumers how much of a bargain the retailers are offering with their own price compared with the maker's. Never, under any circumstances, pay full retail.

Next is the MAP ("minimum advertised price"), and it is a figure approved by the manufacturer that retailers may show in their published or broadcast advertising. Obviously MAP will be less than MSRP, sometimes considerably. Its function is to enable small-shop owners to compete with the big-box stores, which could always undercut the "little guy" if permitted to blazon "low-low prices" set at a level so far beneath the floor established by the MAP that small-volume retailers could never hope to receive a decent return from their far fewer number of sales.

Third is the real-world price. This is the average price a consumer can expect to pay when purchasing a binocular from a retailer, whether a shop, big-box store, or a catalog. This price will sometimes appear in printed reviews of an optical device (though not in advertising) and it can fluctuate from retailer to retailer, depending on how much profit retailers hope to make. As a rule, though, it will not be too far from the MAP, but can sometimes be significantly different. To reiterate, a real-world price below the MAP cannot be publicly advertised. A shooter has to walk into the store to find out what is actually written on the sticker.

The Internet auction price is a fourth possibility. Fine-quality optics have a lengthy shelf life, and ones made ten or even twenty years ago, although they may lack some of the more advanced antireflective coatings or newer glass—and as long as they have not been abused—can continue to function quite satisfactorily today. A hidden treasure to be on the lookout for is any really top-brand binocular that has been refurbished and carries a factory warranty.

Here are some factors a shooter should consider when deciding that the price he is paying for an optical device is right:

Glass: Most optical devices are no more than a convenient way of carrying around a lot of glass lenses and keeping them aligned and in focus. Top-quality glass with the best low-dispersion and antireflective coatings will have the highest value, and probably carry the highest cost. Look for terms such as "fully multi-coated" (rather than merely "fully coated" or "multi-coated") "ED," "HD," and "BaK-4" prisms as marks of glass quality.

Light Transmission: Exit pupil, twilight factor, and field of view are important considerations, but ultimately what matters is how much clear, reflection-free light reaches the shooter's eye through any optical device. If an optics manufacturer can guarantee anywhere from 90 to 92 percent transmission of light through an optical device, that is about as good as it gets. (Please see "Light Transmission" in the Glossary for further discussion of this topic.)

Housing: Quality optics will almost always have housings made of single metal or a metal alloy. Some high-end spotting scopes may be mono-block construction, even if angled or "folded." The goal is to make a housing that is strong and light. Optics like binoculars and spotting scopes ought to be rubber armored to protect the housing and to prevent noise from their swinging against hard surfaces during a stalk.

Waterproof and Fogproof: Shooting can be a far-from-fair-weather pursuit, so shooting optics should be able to stand up to the elements. "Waterproof" is understandable enough, and the technical data for an optical device will state a guarantee that it will remain free of any leakage when submerged to a particular depth, such as "down to 5 meters," if it calls itself waterproof. "Fogproof" guarantees that the optical device, if subject to sharp changes in temperature, will not have condensation form within it; condensation is also capable of leading to corrosion. Fogproofing is obtained by replacing all the atmospheric air and any attendant moisture that may have entered an optical device on dust during the assembly process with the pure, dry, nearly inert nitrogen gas or the even less reactive "noble gas" argon. Some manufacturers claim that argon is superior to nitrogen because even as a monatomic gas, as opposed to diatomic nitrogen, argon is much larger and so will escape (and all purging gases, over time, escape) more slowly from the optics housing than will nitrogen, maintaining fogproofing better and longer.

Warranty: Possible warranties that can be carried by any optical device can include "no-fault" ones that cover the device for its entire lifetime without question. Others are "limited lifetime" warranties in that they cover the device for defects in materials and manufacture, but not against damage, intentional or unintentional. Some cover the mechanics of the device for life but the electronics for only one or two years. A warranty may be for a set number of years or may only cover the device while it is the property of the original owner. Or it may be transferrable to a future owner. The type of warranty carried by a device should be a consideration for a shooter looking to purchase any optics, new or used, especially if the shooter hopes to use the optics for any amount of time.

Pick it Up: Features such as eyecups, focus mechanism, weight, interpupillary distance for binoculars, and so on all need to be evaluated by a hands-on inspection of any optics device in order for a shooter to find one that he really wants to lay out the money for. When buying an optical device start by looking through it in the light inside the store. Try reading a product label at 30 feet by indoor light. This is a good initial yardstick for appraising optical quality. Next take it outside and find a high-contrast image, such as a leafy tree, and place the image in the center of the device's field of view against the sky. A shooter should then look for green or violet color fringing at the edges of the image to determine how much chromatic aberration the device has—the less fringing the better. Similarly, he can look for the amount of spherical aberration, or blurring, at the edges of the viewing field. Finally, with binocular devices, a shooter should visually examine the collimation, or the alignment between the two barrels of the binocular—do they point and focus on the same place? Severe collimation defects, such as double images, would be immediately detectable during a brief viewing through a binocular, with more minor, though finally no less annoying, ones probably becoming apparent only after the purchase and some extended use in the field. Potential collimation problems are a factor a shooter wants to consider when weighing an optical device's warranty—will the manufacturer repair this defect six months or a year from the date of purchase?

The Art and Science of Successful Glassing: The Key to Successful Mountain and Plains Hunting

ongtime licensed professional outfitter and guide, and lifelong hunter, **Ed Beattie** has been an international hunting and fishing consultant since 1988 and today is the manager of Cabela's Outdoor Adventures. Beattie has hunted and fished throughout the American West, Alaska, Canada, Mexico, Central America, South America, Africa, Asia, and Europe. An accomplished mountain hunter, Beattie has achieved the coveted Grand Slam of North American wild sheep and is officially registered as a "Grand Slammer" by the Grand Slam/Ovis Club. His wife, Wendy, is from a fourth-generation Wyoming ranching family; and his two sons, both hunters, are completing their college educations. With Beattie's vast hunting and guiding experience, he seemed the perfect person to write about the "art and science of glassing."

It was thirty years ago, but I vividly remember my first experience with someone who was a genuine expert at using optics to locate game. In early October of 1982 we were guiding mule-deer hunters in the mountains of south-central Wyoming. I had received my first Wyoming professional guide's license back in 1976 while still in college and an outfitter's license in 1979, so I already had several years of professional hunting under my belt.

As the outfitter-of-license and general manager for a substantial group of landowners in southern Wyoming, among my responsibilities was the recruitment and management of a large staff of guides, cooks, wranglers, and other staff. I had just hired a new guide out of Arizona who came highly recommended by one of our regular hunting clients. Jay had been guiding sheep, elk, mule deer, and antelope hunters for many years and arrived at our headquarters a week before the season opened. He made good use of his time, spending every day out scouting and learning the country that we hunted.

I was impressed with Jay's work ethic and how serious he was about preparing to hunt in a new area, but I was even more impressed with his gear. Everything from his 4x4 truck to his personal saddle and tack were top of the line and maintained in perfect condition. It was his collection of optics, though, that really caught

my attention. Most of my guides were local cowboys; and like me, they utilized an assortment of cheap binoculars and spotting scopes. When Jay started pulling optics out of various packs and duffle bags, I couldn't believe it. He had two matching 10x42 Leica binoculars, another 15x60 Leica (that could be mounted on a tripod), and a 20-60X Zeiss spotting scope. To say the least, I felt a little under-gunned with my old beat-up Leupold binocular and Bushnell spotting scope!

Opening day of the mule deer season arrived, and I assigned Jay to guide a couple of hunters from Pennsylvania. I was also guiding out of that same camp and would take a longtime client who had booked a 1x1 trophy hunt. Following a good breakfast, all of the guides and hunters headed out of camp before daylight; and because we had several hundred-thousand acres to hunt, we all went in different directions. My client and I were hunting from horseback, and we rode to the summit of a high peak behind the base camp.

Jay and his clients were hunting by truck in some of our lower country. As I was glassing back from the top of the peak, I saw Jay's truck perched on a high ridge that served as a divide between two drainages. Wanting to check out the "new guy," I got my spotting scope out of the saddle bag and focused it on the truck. It was a crew-cab pickup (fairly unusual back then); and I could see that both hunters and their guide were still inside. And it seemed as though spotting scopes or big binos were mounted on three of the four windows. I had never seen so many sets of optics—all on window mounts—and all being used at the same time. The sun was coming up fast; and since I wanted to check out some high basins before the deer bedded down, my client and I got back on our horses and rode on along a high mountain rim, halting to glass quickly a basin or a big draw as we went.

My hunting client and I covered a lot of country that day, using both the horses and our own legs to work the upper slopes and high basins of the big mountain. We spotted a bunch of deer and elk—including some very respectable bucks—but nothing that we wanted to take. Late afternoon found us riding back down the mountain toward camp, and I stopped at the same vantage point that we had used in the morning and

⌃ The author glassing open country in the West. Optics not only let you find animals at a distance, but let you evaluate them so you can determine if they are worth pursuing.

from where I had seen Jay's truck parked below on the distant ridge. I glassed the ridge and couldn't believe that Jay's truck was still sitting in the same spot where I had seen it at the start of the day. Had he and his hunters been sitting there since sunup? Our hunting areas included some of the best ranches in southern Wyoming; and if you totaled it all up, we had over a million acres to hunt. Why would a guide stay in one spot all day?

As my client and I continued our ride down to camp, I was mentally preparing myself to deal with some very disgruntled clients. I was certain they were going to be angry about being stuck in a parked pickup all day and request that I assign a different guide to them for the rest of their hunt. That would be a problem, as all of our camps were full with hunters and all of my regular guides were booked. There was no such thing as cell phones back then, so I was thinking that I would have to drive into town and see if I could talk my father-in-law (a local rancher) into helping us out and guiding for a few days. This wasn't going to be fun; but as the outfitter and manager, it was one of my responsibilities. I couldn't afford a guide who wouldn't guide.

Dinner came and went in the cook tent, with all of the hunters and guides in attendance—except Jay and his clients. This wasn't unusual: If a kill was made late

⌄ With binoculars, spotting scope, and riflescope, this black-tailed deer hunter is prepared for any eventuality.

in the day, it was common for the hunters and their guide to be late for dinner. Still, I was starting to get concerned and thinking that maybe I should get in my truck and head out to see if these guys needed help, when Jay's truck rolled into camp. I walked out to the vehicle and prepared myself for a potentially stressful conversation. But as I approached the back of the truck, I could see a massive set of deer antlers rising above the tailgate. One of the hunters jumped out of the truck with a flashlight and shined it on one of the biggest mule-deer bucks I had ever seen.

"Look what I got!" he said with delight.

I'd been ready to be chewed out by a couple of frustrated hunters; and instead here was an absolutely magnificent buck, well over 30-inches wide with deep front and back forks, along with great mass and good brow tines. The other hunters and guides started to gather around the back of the truck, and we had flashlights playing over the deer like prison break as we broke out the measuring tape. After deductions, I unofficially scored the buck at 197-plus. Back then it took 195 for a typical mule deer to make the all-time Boone and Crockett Records, and we all soon realized that we were looking at a possible book buck.

To say the least, Jay's clients were ecstatic and very happy with the guide I had assigned to them. As the hunt continued, we were all filling out our clients and it was a happy camp. Later in the week, Jay's other client took a big non-typical buck, with lots of extra points, including matching double drop tines. His clients were extremely pleased and rebooked for the next season before leaving camp. Naturally, they requested Jay to guide them again; and I told them that if Jay were available, they could count on it.

We finished up that first hunt and had a couple of days before our next group of hunters arrived. I decided to get to know the new guide better and offered to show Jay some new country and help him scout some of our other ranches. Jay learned the new ranches and some great country to hunt, but I learned something far more valuable. I used those two days to pick Jay's brain and experience about the right way to use quality optics as a hunting tool as valuable as a good rifle or a well-broken-in pair of boots. This was my introduction to a skill set that has served me well as a hunter and a professional guide, outfitter, and hunting consultant ever since, a skill I call the "Art & Science of Glassing."

Recalling those two days, the key thing that I learned from Jay was how important proper glassing skills are to mountain and plains hunting, and that you can't spend too much time behind your optics. Jay taught me to slow down and not be so concerned about covering lots of country and "seeing what was in the next draw." I learned to be thorough and methodical when glassing for game. I became more stealthy and cognizant of never sky-lining yourself on a ridgeline. Jay showed me how to set-up in the right spot and then spend the required amount of time to cover properly all of the country that could be seen from there. I discovered how much game was missed and overlooked by moving too quickly and thinking the next basin would hold the trophy you were after. Fundamentally, I learned how to be more patient,

⌄ The author with his desert-bighorn ram from Mexico, the fourth sheep of his Grand Slam, and the result of careful glassing.

⌃ A guide scans distant terrain for trophy Dall sheep that cling to the steep slopes.

focused, and skillful as a mountain hunter who used optics as his key tool.

While you need lots of practice to fine-tune your glassing skills, here are the basics I learned from Jay and that I have picked up on my own and refined over the years:

It is not possible to "over-glass." The golden rule is to glass, glass again, and then glass some more!

Even if you are using a guide, do not rely on him to spot all of the game. Even if he is much better at it than you, another set of eyes is a big help. If your guide is glassing, then you should be too. Always try to take advantage of every opportunity for spotting game. Some of the best trophies that I have ever taken were spotted by me first and then pointed out to my guide.

Acquire the best equipment you can afford, period. No doubt about it quality optics are expensive, but they are worth it. For mountain and plains hunting, you are much better off with a $500 rifle and a $1000 binocular than vice-versa. Most professional guides and experienced hunters will have the following optics gear as a minimum: a high quality binocular in something like 10x42; another binocular (that can be mounted on a tripod or window mount) in either 15- or 20-power; and a variable-power spotting scope in something like 15-45- or 20-60-power, with both tripod and window mounts. Whenever possible, always try to glass from a tripod or window mount, as the steadiness will make you much more effective. High-quality, fluid-head

tripods are expensive, but they really are worth it. A rangefinder is also important; and if you don't have a binocular with a built-in rangefinder, then find a separate one of high quality.

Vary the speed of your glassing with the time of day. During early morning and late afternoon hours–when game is active–you can move your glasses fairly quickly as you look for game that is on its feet, either feeding or moving. Glass much slower during late morning or midday hours, as the game tends to bed and is much more difficult to spot.

Develop a system for methodical glassing, so that you can be certain not to overlook anything. This can be left to right; up and down; or a grid-pattern approach–but utilizing some sort of a system is much more efficient than haphazard glassing.

Look for parts of the animal and not the whole animal: the tips of antlers sticking up above the brush; the flick of an ear; the yellowish-white rump-patch of a mule-deer buck in sagebrush.

Look for things that appear out of place, such as a horizontal line among mostly vertical objects. This could be the outline of an animal in a background of timber. Always check out that distant lump in an otherwise smooth and open grassy meadow, or that bump on a clean ridgeline. Many times it will just be a rock or a stump, but you need to check it out.

If possible, always try to locate a good vantage point to glass from. On mountain hunts such places are easy

⌄ The author with a 48-inch Ibex he took in Turkey last fall after long glassing.

to find, but even while on a plains or desert hunt there is usually some piece of ground that is higher than its surroundings. This is where you will want to set up, so keep an eye out for such locations.

Be patient and take your time. You are much better off thoroughly glassing the country you are in than always believing you need to cover more new ground. The most successful trophy hunters and professional guides hunt slowly, thoroughly glassing an area before moving on.

There's a lot of truth to the old saying that "practice makes perfect." Take your optics along on all your outdoor adventures and become familiar with them. Even if you are just looking at birds on a fishing trip, you are getting in valuable practice with your equipment.

Again, as I learned from Jay all those years ago, careful glassing is an essential component of successful open-country hunting. As you become more adept at it and your skill levels increase, so will your hunting success. There is almost nothing more satisfying than spotting a cagey old buck–who is bedded at midday in heavy brush–and all you can see are the tips of his antlers. Once you've done it a few times, you will be well on your way to becoming a better, more optically skilled hunter!

BY ED BEATTIE

How to Use Optics

The basics of optics use involve carrying, focusing, steadying, and maintaining, which includes cleaning.

Carrying: While riflescopes are carried mounted on firearms, means need to be found for carrying other optics, such as binoculars, rangefinders, and spotting scopes, that keeps them secure and accessible. The most fundamental way of carrying a binocular is by a neck strap, and a wider, padded, often neoprene one will be more comfortable than a narrow nylon ribbon. The length of the strap is always somewhat problematic. If the binocular is worn on a long strap, it will swing out and back against a shooter's chest when he is walking, especially on slopes. One solution is to shorten the strap so that the binocular rests high on the chest; when a shooter lifts it to his eyes, the oculars will just clear his chin and nose. This will turn the binocular into much less of a pendulum. Alternatively, a shooter can lengthen the strap far enough to allow him to slip an arm through and have the strap running diagonally across his chest, then tuck the binocular around behind where it will ride on the small of his back without bumping against him and can still be swung back quickly for fast viewing. An alternative to the strap is an elastic harness that will hold the binocular close to the chest, without swinging, while distributing the weight of the binocular through the chest, shoulders, and back and allow it to be brought up easily for viewing. Pouches around the neck or on the belt, are another way of protecting and carrying binoculars and rangefinders; and spotting scopes will sometimes come with soft fitted cases that pad them for carrying in a backpack. And if your binocular or rangefinder is small enough, it can be secured around the neck by a strap and carried in a shirt pocket.

Focusing: Keeping an optical device properly focused is like keeping a knife blade whetted–that's the way they work the best. Riflescopes may have a focus ring on the ocular that is used to make the crosshairs sharp for the shooter's eye. Focusing is accomplished by adjusting the ring until the crosshairs come into their sharpest image, and then focusing just slightly past this point. This insures that the finest focus point has been reached and exceeded; the shooter *then* brings the focus back to its best image. Spotting scopes often have two focus wheels, one coarse to identify the object being viewed and another fine one to bring it into crisp detail. Monocular rangefinders are generally focused by adjusting the ocular. A binocular requires the most complex focusing procedure. A shooter begins by opening the hinge, or bridge, so that the eyepieces are set at the correct interpupillary distance for his eyes. It is then necessary to have the eyecups extended or retracted to the right position to provide the best eye relief and the greatest field of view, with or without eyeglasses. To focus a binocular with a separate dioptric adjustment, it should be held

《 Hold binoculars as steady as possible when focusing the dioptric adjustment.

≫ Shortening the strap in the binocular will help prevent its swinging against your chest when walking.

as steadily as possible while the shooter looks through the eyepiece without the dioptric adjustment. Closing his other eye, he will use the center-focus wheel to bring the image he is viewing into sharp focus, following the method of going past the sharpest focus, then returning to it. (The reverse adjustment should be made slowly until the image just comes into focus again.) Then with that eye closed and the other—the one viewing through the eyepiece with the dioptric adjustment (usually the right one)—open, the dioptric focus ring is adjusted until that eyepiece is, similarly, focused. With both eyes open, the image should be a single sharp circle without any distortion. (Another quality of a binocular to examine is how well the dioptric lens stays in focus without drifting, with some binoculars having locking dioptric focus rings.)

Steadying: Spotting scopes and high-power binoculars need to be attached to tripods or window mounts for proper use. For a lower-power binocular, finding a solid object, like a log or rock, to rest it on, or a flat surface upon which the shooter can place his elbows, will give steadier viewing that simply holding the binocular offhand. If a shooter cannot locate such a surface, he can keep his elbows tucked into his body to form a brace against which his forearms rest. If he has to view while standing, he can use the tension of the neck strap or harness to steady the binocular, and can increase this by wrapping his fingers around the top of the bill of his cap, if he is wearing one, and using upward thumb pressure to sandwich the binocular against the bill's underside while pulling down on the bill with

his fingers. This creates a "push me-pull you" locking tension like that of assuming a two-handed grip on a pistol in which the rear hand is pushing while the front one is pulling, holding everything steady. Lying prone will provide the steadiest viewing position for using a binocular or for aiming with a riflescope. For long-range shooting, a rifle should be supported at two points, at the fore-end and the butt of the stock. Not as steady, but still effective, is a sitting position with the elbows braced against the knees. Short shooting sticks greatly aid in shooting accurately from the sitting or kneeling position and are nearly mandatory if a shooter must fire from a standing position. The key to steady viewing is reducing the amplitude of movement by lowering the viewing height, and the shooter's and the optical device's centers of gravity, as much as possible (stay low to stay steady).

Maintaining: The maintenance of optical devises requires only some common-sense considerations. To begin with: Don't toss your optics onto the dashboard, floorboard, or into the truckbed. Keep your binoculars and spotting scopes in a case as much as possible and have a cover for your riflescope. Use lens covers on both the objectives and oculars. Keep your optics clean. Wipe dirt and dust off the housings with a soft cloth—"microfiber" clothes are the newest technology for this purpose and target oils and

≫ Proper maintenance of optics begins with a lens cleaning kit such as this.

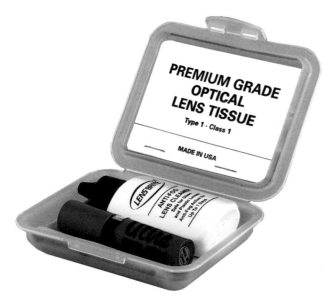

《 When using a spotting scope, a quality tripod that is rock-steady is critical.

⌃ When the lens is free of dust and dirt, use a clean lens cloth and, starting at the center of the lens, use a with light circular motion to clean each lens out to the edge.

⌃ Finally, use a lens tissue and lens-cleaning solution to wipe off any smudges or fingerprints form the lens.

smudges. The proper technique for cleaning lenses starts with a lens brush free of dirt and oils. With the brush gently remove any dust or lint particles from the surfaces of the lenses Alternatively, a spray dust remover can be used over the lenses, being careful to keep the can level while spraying to prevent propellant's getting onto the glass. When the lens is free of dust and dirt, next use a *clean* lens-cleaning cloth (lens-cleaning cloths can be laundered, as long as they are not ironed—they could melt—or washed with fabric softeners that transfer chemicals to the cloth that might then be transferred to the lens surface), such as a microfiber, and start at the center of the lens and with light circular motions clean each lens out to the edge. If fingerprints or smudges still show on the lenses, then use a good-quality lens-cleaning solution and lens-cleaning tissues. Loosely wad a couple of tissues and put a drop or two of solution on the tissues (it's not necessary to overdo it with the solution). Clean in circular motions from the center to the edges as you did with the dry lens cloth. Finally use a second wad of clean dry lens tissues and remove any fluid left on the lenses. (According to lens-cleaning-products manufacturer Peca Products, Inc., www.pecaproducts.com, the use of the second, dry wad of tissues is important because the cleaning fluid releases oils and residue from the lens surface and holds them in suspension until the fluid is removed; if the fluid is left to dry on the optical surfaces, the oils and residues will simply return to the lenses.)

Tactical Sighting Options

*T*he expert eminently qualified to write about tactical-sighting options is **Doug Howlett**, award-winning editor and writer who grew up hunting and shooting. Author of the Shooter's Bible Guide to AR-15s, Doug began his writing career as a newspaper reporter—first in his native Virginia and then in North Carolina—before combining his passion for writing and the outdoors at the National Rifle Association, where he worked as assistant editor of that organization's American Hunter magazine. He has served as editor-in-chief of Turkey Call magazine at the National Wild Turkey Federation, as well as deputy editor at Outdoor Life magazine in New York City. It was on a hunt that he covered for Outdoor Life that he discovered the absolute thrill of hunting with modern tactical rifles. Howlett now lives in Virginia Beach, Virginia, with his wife and three children, where he works as a freelance writer, editor, and digital-media consultant. His home near the coast is but an hour away from his family's 470-acre farm in Southampton County, Virginia, where he spends as much time as possible testing new guns, hunting, and managing the land for whitetails, wild turkeys, and any other wild creature that chooses to call the place home.

The wild popularity enjoyed by tactical, or modern sporting, rifles—led by the reliable and amazingly customizable AR platform—has generated an echo effect well beyond the simple manufacture of the firearms. In many ways, the popularity of these rifles has spawned a phenomenal selection and availability of accessories designed expressly for the tactical market—chief among them being optics.

From companies dedicated to serving the exclusive sighting demands of military and law enforcement teams to decades-old optical stalwarts long rooted in producing top-quality optics for traditional sporting audiences, it seems every manufacturer boasts a proven line of models created for and marketed as "tactical."

So what exactly is a tactical scope or sight?

"The truth is, there is actually very little to discern the two, when discussing tactical verses traditional optics or sights. They both serve the same function," says John Enloe, a longtime lead technical advisor at Aimpoint, one of the leading manufacturers of red dot sights serving both military and civilian markets. Enloe now works as a regional sales manager in government sales for the company. Indeed many of the features originally designed for sporting audiences have been tweaked and improved upon to enhance military applications, while functions developed at the behest of soldiers often trickle across the divide and find themselves incorporated in traditional hunting optics as well.

But in essence, if the military uses it, most civilians want it. Battle-tested products feel the most genuine when it comes to performance—even if the most challenging encounter you ever experience is a paper target blown free from a board.

One military operator described a tactical optic as this: "When talking scopes with magnification, you are generally looking at a model with a low variable magnification in the 1-5X or 2-5X range and with adjustable turrets that have a zero stop as well as a compensator so you can dial the scope in for the range you are shooting or a mildot reticle that allows the same function." Typical features also include illuminated reticles.

Variable power ranges can also roll upward in the 3-9X, 2.5-10X and even 4-12X range, which allows a shooter to dial it down and shoot easily with both eyes open at closer targets, while retaining the ability to crank it out for longer range shooting objectives.

⯆ Any scope used on a tactical rifle can serve as a "tactical" scope, but most models considered tactical typically have lighted reticles, a low variable power for close combat situations, and are easily adjusted with turrets to quickly dial them in for various ranges.
Photo courtesy Doug Howlett

Scopes with higher powers exist in the exclusive realm of long range shooting, whether in military or LE sniping applications, 600-plus yard target competitions, or varmint hunting. Their size and optical power makes them poor choices for dealing with close range targets.

"Optics designed to make shots on human-sized targets at 1000 yards are not practical for most police work or even home defense purposes, where shooting requirements are most often measured in feet instead of yards," says one soldier.

Magnified or Red Dot

For this reason, beyond magnified optics, a favorite tactical-sighting option on both sides of the military and civilian fence has long been the non-magnification red-dot sight such as those made by EOTech, Aimpoint, and others. Red dots possess certain advantages over magnified optics given the uniqueness of tactical applications whether replicated on the range or honed for actual home defense. Because most

scenarios are close range, magnification becomes unnecessary. Optics require eye relief as well, with most shooters naturally closing one eye to sight—something they should never do. Red-dot sights allow for a more natural use with both eyes open, which also broadens a shooters peripheral vision, something that can be crucial in a tactical situation where moving targets and threats and changing situations need to be spotted as quickly as possible.

With both eyes open, a shooter is also able to capture more light in low-light situations, again enhancing his ability to see better the events unfolding before him. Best of all, red dots are zeroed to the gun, not the shooter. When two people shoot a rifle sighted with a magnified scope, it's not unusual for their point of aim to vary just slightly because of the way each aligns his eyes with the crosshairs. With a red dot, it doesn't matter. Wherever that dot is sitting is where the shot is going, even if a shooter's cheek isn't properly aligned along the barrel. This can be a huge benefit should a person find himself in a home-defense situation where nerves and adrenaline are likely to override attention to proper shooting form.

For that reason, many soldiers like to use both a low power variable scope and a red-dot sight co-mounted on the rifle. The smaller red-dot is typically mounted on a side rail or on an angled 45-degree rail attached to the upper of the firearm, which allows simple, close-

⥥ As more hunters use AR-style rifles, they require the same quality optical performance that they have come to count on with traditional optics.

Photo courtesy Doug Howlett

⥥ A red-dot sight is a great alternative or companion to a magnified scope. It provides for optimal shooting at close distances, yet is good for aiming out to 400 yards.

Photo courtesy Doug Howlett

range sighting with a slight cant of the gun. At the very least, they will combine one or the other with fixed or fold-down iron sights, which means, if you're looking to trick your AR out in top tactical form, you'll want to do the same.

"One is none, two are one with sights," says David "Jonzy" Jones, a retired U.S. Navy SEAL who now works for Blackhawk, a company that manufactures a full line of holsters, knives, packs, clothing, slings and other accessories for the tactical market. He always goes with two sighting options—a fold down sight and an optic.

Mounting Your Optic

Because most ARs and other tactical rifles are easily customized with available placement and rows of Picatinny rails, either single or dual sighting is easily achieved. This can be done by utilizing a single straight rail atop the receiver, multiple rails along the top and sides of the rifle, or a straight rail in conjunction with an offset 45-degree angled rail that allows an optic to be mounted on the upper receiver and permits sighting alternately between two devices with the slight roll or twist of the rifle, as noted above. In addition to optics, either magnified or red dot, tactical shooters also have the option of fixed or folding sights and even laser sights.

≫ Sighting in a tactical scope such as this Bushnell Elite is no different from sighting in a traditional optic. You still need a solid rest from which to shoot and then merely adjust the windage and elevation to walk the point of aim to where it needs to be.

Photo courtesy Doug Howlett

When mounting an optic, go with a quality base and rings. You can spend all the money in the world on a quality optic; but if you go cheap on the mount, it will come loose from recoil and handling and your point of aim will move around as if you weren't using any sighting system at all. While the tubular bodies of scopes can vary in diameter by slight degrees when actually measured, most will be either 30 mm or 1 inch, with the overriding amount of U.S.-made scopes falling into the latter category. Choose a base designed for the diameter of your scope and one that can be mounted on a Picatinny rail (in most tactical gun applications).

If an optic will be used in conjunction with steel sights, choose a see-through base that allows an optic to be attached yet won't disrupt the sighting plain between rear and forward sights. If you simply want to elevate the red dot or optic above fixed sights, a mountable riser block might be necessary.

One of Weaver's most popular-selling tactical rings is their two-piece 6-Hole Picatinny Rings, which feature six screws on each ring for optimal clamping and more even distribution of pressure along the exterior barrel of the scope. For tactical applications, particularly where a shooter might want to switch quickly out optics or use the same optic on multiple rifles, rings with a quick-detach lever is the way to go. If you don't plan on moving or switching optics, that will not be as much of a concern.

One-piece mounts that incorporate both rear and forward rings with a single, machined base offer even more security by eliminating alignment issues and reducing points where screws can come loose. Millet's 1-inch to 30 mm mount is a great example of a quality single-piece mount. In fact, during a sight-in session before a Texas hog hunt to test Mossberg's new MMR rifles in conjunction with Bushnell Elite scopes, we pulled a scope from a sighted-in MMR Hunter model and put it atop an MMR Tactical model and needed only a few clicks to bring the scope into alignment on the new rifle. It is this adaptability and functionality that makes using a variety of sighting systems both fun and easy when shooting tactical rifles.

BY DOUG HOWLETT

How to Mount a Scope on a Rifle

*I*t's easy to do if you have quality rings and bases and the right tools. The question of mounting a riflescope yourself is whether you plan on doing it on a regular basis and/or you want to be absolutely certain that the job is done right. If you change out a scope or put a new one on a rifle only every few years, and don't want to invest in some seldom-used tools, then you might as well take it to your trusty gunsmith and have him mount it and bore-sight it for you. You will still have to take the rifle out afterward and sight it in yourself with live fire at a target to make sure it's on. You also need to rely on the gunsmith's having done a proper job of mounting the scope.

If you're going to mount your scope yourself (or even if you're going to have the gunsmith do it), start with good rings and bases. Cheap mounts are no bargain if the screws strip or wallow out before you ever get them torqued or shake loose under recoil. If you have a $1500 rifle and a $600 scope, $100 spent on rings and bases is not an extravagance. Leupold, Burris, Nikon, Redfield, and Weaver are some of the reliable names for rings and mounts, as are Talley (www.talleymanufacturing.com), Conetrol (www.conetrol.com), and Warne (www.warnescopemount.com), among others.

Before anything else, *make certain the rifle is completely unloaded and safe.* Set the rifle up in a solid rest or gun vise; and then, starting with the bases, I like to use a drop of Loctite 243™ blue removable threadlocker on the screws. You really can't overtighten the base screws, short of stripping them; but make sure the screws aren't so long that they screw down through holes tapped into the receiver and interfere with the bolt. The mount manufacturer may have a recommended amount of torque for the base screws, and if you know what it is, then you will need a torque driver to apply the correct number of inch-pounds. Torque drivers can range in price from the relatively inexpen

sive Wheeler FAT Wrench (www.battenfeldtechnologies.com) to Brownell's Magna-Tip adjustable torque handle (www.brownells.com) that lists for $149.00. The more expensive, the more accurate, generally; and it's ultimately a matter of how precise you want to be.

A torque driver is more important for the scope rings. Here the manufacturer should have specific inch-pounds of torque to apply to the screws. Before tightening the screws down, though, it's important first to make sure the rings are properly aligned with each other. For that a set of scope-alignment rods are helpful. These are a pair of pointed metal rods that fit the diameter of the rings and are turned in the rings until the two pointed-ends meet. Then it's a good idea to place the scope in the rings and work the bolt handle to assure that it will clear the ocular bell.

Before tightening the screws in the rings, position the scope to the eye-relief you are most comfortable with that won't "bite" you, that also gives you a full field of view through the ocular. One more consideration is whether the reticle is aligned with the rifle's bore (does the vertical post of the sight run directly perpendicular to the axis of the bore?). If you don't trust your eye to verify this, there are devices that have spirit levels to insure that the scope is square with the bore.

For tightening the rings, knowing the correct torque is vital; and if the manufacturer does not include that information in the product's packaging, do feel free to e-mail him or give him a call to get the exact numbers. For tightening the screws on the rings no Loctite is needed (the spring tension of the rings should be sufficient to keep them tight, and you avoid the possibility of getting goop on the scope). Using your torque driver, tighten the screws to the proper torque the way you would the lug nuts on a wheel: Crisscross back and forth so that the pressure remains evenly distributed throughout the process. With that, the scope should be ready for bore-sighting and zeroing in on a target with live ammunition.

There are greater subtleties to the art of scope mounting; and to discover more of them, I would recommend Chapter 28, "Semi-Pro Scope Mounting," in John Barsness's book *Obsessions of a Rifle Loony* (*www.riflesandreceipes.com*).

≫ Mounting a riflescope requires exactly aligned rings; and to make sure of that, use alignment rods such as these.

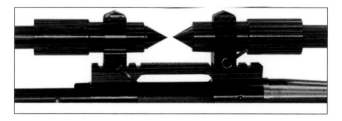

Rangefinding and Long-Range Shooting

One of the primary roles optics have to play in shooting is in making it possible to "break a shot" successfully at extended distances. The inviting challenge of trying to hit an inanimate target at extreme yardages is obvious. And the critical necessity of striking a distant human target in a tactical or combat situation is understood. Yet the justification for shooting an animal that is out of the hearing, scent, and effective visual range of a hunter is not so easily appreciated, or explained, despite its being a tradition woven into the fabric of American history.

Long-range shooting might be thought of as an American invention arising out of the long-rifle hunters of the colonial wilderness and leading to the likes of "Morgan's Sharpshooters" in the Continental Army of 1775 and proceeding on to the "skirmishers" beneath both flags in the Civil War, Sergeant York in World War I (admittedly more crack shooting than long range), US Marine snipers in the Pacific in World War II with their external-adjustment target scopes, Vietnam marksmen like Gunnery Sergeant Carlos Hancock, and the two-man spotter-and-shooter sniper teams deployed throughout Iraq and Afghanistan. Again, the necessity of shooting dangerous humans at long-ranges under warfare or in law-enforcement circumstances is never truly questioned. And nobody objects to firing at steel-plates out at 1000 yards. Yet when it comes to taking shots at a distance at big game, the subject among hunters and non-hunters alike virtually never fails to instigate an argument.

The famed British firearms expert, Major Sir Gerald Burrard, author of *Notes on Sporting Rifles*, perhaps best stated the fundamental animus many hunters, themselves, bear toward long-range shooting at game, when he wrote:

. . . if stalking is regarded as the craft of outwitting in its natural haunts an ever-alert quarry, whose senses of eyesight, hearing and scent are developed to a degree far beyond human experience, what possible satisfaction there is to be derived from a sort of "barrage fire" is beyond my understanding.

And when Major Burrard wrote that, in the 1920s, the state of the art of rifles, sights, and cartridges—especially those designed and built to hit and kill game animals, rather than for the tactical function of hitting and perhaps only wounding an opposing combatant—did indeed make long-range hunting very much a matter of barrage fire. Today, though, not so much.

The question is, Is it a "sporting" proposition to consider taking a shot on big game at extreme long ranges if the conditions dictate? And the answer is that (with strict provisos) considering, setting up, and taking a shot at up to half a mile can be no more of an ethical dilemma than at an eighth of that range.

To make the case, the modern rifle, scope, and bullet, along with advanced technologies like the laser rangefinder, the spotting scope, and ballistics calculator, and all that has been learned over the years about long-range shooting from tactical and benchrest shooters, hunters, and ballisticians (a scientific field that didn't really exist in Burrard's day) make shots (and hits and most importantly, kills) on game at 500, 600, 700, and even 800 yards and beyond not only feasible but effective and ethical, supplying the practiced hunter with another tool in his "possibles" bag. None of that, though, seems to allay the misgivings many hunters, and not a few supposedly expert gun writers, have about the very concept.

The objections raised by numerous writers about the idea of long-range shots at big game seem to follow predictable patterns: Few rifles and scopes, and fewer riflemen, are accurate enough for shots anything beyond 500 yards; benchrest shooting conditions cannot be duplicated in the field; bullets don't have enough accuracy or killing energy at long range; there are too many variables of wind and angles to

⩗ Shooting at 1000-yard targets – more reasonable than ever with the proper optics.

guarantee a killing shot; and hunting is not the same as sniping. All of which contains some truth. But it would be just as true to say that the average pilot in the average airplane cannot fly at supersonic speeds a hundred feet above the ground; therefore, such a feat cannot be done. Except that it is done.

If you do not acknowledge, or at least believe, that the level of competence required to make clean 700 to 800 yard shots on big game is achievable through rigorous study, practice, and the proper use of the right technology, you really ought to have serious doubt, as well, about the possibility of killing game competently at 300, 200, or even 100 yards.

For all of the objections (some not unfounded) to long-range shooting at big game, there are persuasive answers to the contrary.

Rifles are not accurate enough—Some mass-produced rifles might not be accurate enough for shots beyond 400 yards; but even if he's so innocent as to believe that he would never so much as contemplate a shot at game beyond a hundred yards, and so did not require any greater accuracy, why would anybody

⩔ Shooting at a mile is feasible with the right rifle, cartridge, and scope, *and* with the right spotting, measurements, calculations, and rests.

want to own so tedious a rifle as that to begin with (see Col. Whelen)? The secret to a long-range rifle is fine tolerances, stable bedding, and weight. Getting a bore that runs true to the barrel is not as simple as it might seem, even with modern manufacturing techniques. It's also, alas, not that noticeable to most hunters. The foremost argument for using a top-quality, relatively heavy-contour, match-grade rifle barrel is to have a bore that runs down the exact, not almost, center. And precise chambering, rifling, crowning, etc., are also vital. The bedding needs to be dead solid (which probably means some form of pillar bedding and a stock that remains completely inert, no matter the weather— so synthetic rather than wood). Finally, weight: Ultra-light or "mountain" rifles can be supremely accurate; they are just much harder to shoot at extreme long ranges than a heavier rifle. How heavy? Even though military sniping, to say it again, is not hunting (the essential contradiction in the comparison, which boils down to the sniper's being able to settle for wounding while the hunter must know he can kill, is that a soldier in combat is generally obligated to shoot; a hunter is not), a Marine sniper rifle tips the scales at over 16 pounds, for a reason. A sniper needs the rock-steady stability that only weight provides to make mile-long shots. For a hunter who is not a 23-year-old Jarhead, a rifle with an ergonomically designed stock suitable for packing into the hunting field and a scoped weight of around ten pounds is reasonable for making shots even beyond 800 yards. And if even that sounds too heavy, it should be remembered that a hunter can much better stave off fatigue by lightening himself, rather than his rifle.

Bullets aren't accurate enough to kill at long ranges—Hunters too often think of a long-range bullet as something built exclusively for punching through the air; there are hunting bullets, though, specifically made to kill game, and not the air, at long ranges. A well-made hunting bullet will perform (penetrate, expand, create a lethal wound channel, and "upset" in internal organs) within a certain range of velocities. A "tougher" bullet, such as a partition, will have a larger, softer striking surface (the meplat or just the plain old "point") and will need a higher range of velocities (which means either shorter distances or hellacious recoil) to do its job. On the other hand, a true long-range hunting bullet will display features such as a small meplat, a long pointy nose or ogive, boattail, and a high ballistic coefficient; but at terminal velocities down to 2000 feet per second, it will still do what it is supposed to when it hits the animal in terms of expansion and penetration. These facts of ballistics do suggest that a hunter who wants to be able to make a long-range shot may have to rethink his choice of calibers. In general, a 7 mm bullet can outperform a .30 caliber at distance, while producing less recoil. At some long-range-shooting schools (such as Burlington, Wyoming's, Gunwerks Shooting School, www.gunwerks.com) the bullet of choice is a Berger 168 grain VLD hunting bullet chambered for 7 mm Remington Magnum with a very tolerable–in terms of felt recoil–muzzle velocity of 3050 feet per second, which means it will still be traveling at over 1900 feet per second out past 1000 yards. Whatever the caliber, the sine qua non of the long-range hunting bullet, of a hunting bullet at any range, is to deliver a lethal blow to an animal's vital area to insure a one-shot kill. And that is the final verdict on a bullet's suitability for long-range hunting.

A rifle can't be held steady enough—Rifle weight is virtually worthless without the proper rest. And there is, in fact, no way, reliably, to make a long-range shot on big game with only a one-point rest, no matter how sturdy it may seem. Shooting to kill with a long-range hunting rifle means supporting both the fore-end and the butt. Which means having the right equipment in the field, whether a bipod or tripod for the front of the rifle, and something like a sandbag (and small, lightweight, field shooting bags that snap onto a belt can be found—see Holland Field Bags at http://www.dog-gone-good.com) for the rear. More than anything else, though, having proper support means taking the time to stop, think, and prepare before taking the shot.

Scopes are not accurate enough—This is the most optical factor of the equation. Trying to shoot game out to 500 or 600 yards or more with an average 3-9X scope is about like trying to cook a soufflé in an Easy-Bake Oven: It can be attempted, but the results may not be entirely satisfactory. Long-range shots require a high-magnification tactical or target scope with a means of compensating for bullet drop. A compensating reticle is one way of correcting the trajectory of a bullet, but a better way is a target-style elevation turret. There are, of course, a number of assumptions attached to that statement. Most important is assuming that the scope is well-made and exact enough to make compensation adjustments accurate. Then the scope's increments of adjustments must be calibrated to the caliber, weight, ballistic coefficient, and the velocity of the bullet being shot, plus the elevation and the air temperature (seriously). Only with all of that can compensations be dialed into a scope in any meaning-

⩔ Nightforce ZeroStop tactical-style external elevation-adjustment turret.

⩔ A two-point rest is necessary for long-range shooting.

⌃ Spotting for a shooter at long range.

ful way. (All of this is where ballistics calculators, or at least ballistics tables, come into play.)

Range cannot be gauged accurately enough— Before the compensation can be dialed into the elevation of a scope's reticle the exact distance to the target must be known, meaning a precise method of rangefinding must be used.

There are ways of ranging an animal through a riflescope without using a dedicated laser rangefinder. With a duplex reticle the distance, or arc, covered by the stadia, the thin wire, between the picket, the point of the thick post, and the crosshair is often designed to subtend a certain amount of a target at a certain range—data the scope manufacturer can provide, usually in the owner's manual. For example, some reticles are calibrated to the body width of a white-tailed deer (about 18 inches or half a yard from withers to brisket) at 100 yards. If a deer fits fully into the space between the picket and the crosshair it is approximately 100 yards away; if the space is twice as long as the deer is deep, then the buck is 200 yards away, and so on. There are some variable scopes that have range estimators on the variable magnification band—changing the power to bracket a deer between the crosshair and picket will dial up a yardage estimate that can be read on the band.

Another non-laser ranging and holdover system is the mil-dot reticle developed at least in part for Marine snipers in the 1970s. Today, many scope makers offer mil-dot reticles, and they can be added to a scope as an aftermarket option. Although there may be some variations among mil-dot systems, normally the distance between the center points of the dots, at the highest power setting on a variable scope, is 3.6 inches at 100 yards and is used in the following formula

(Height in Yards × 1000) ÷ Number of Mils = Yardage

If a white-tailed buck is bracketed from the withers to brisket by 1½ mils, the range can be calculated as follows

(.5 yard × 1000) ÷ 1.5 = 333 yards

The mil dots can then be used to gauge how much holdover to use for the shot.

Along with mil-dots many scope manufacturers offer proprietary range-compensating reticles. Some let the hunter use hash marks to measure the depth of the game animal and calculate the distance, then has bars for holdover aiming, the indices matched to specific cartridges and loads.

The ultimate means of measuring target distant is to use a laser rangefinder. The type of object being ranged determines the accuracy of the reading. Flat reflective surfaces–the side of a barn, a rock face–can be read at the longest distances, with objects like trees less far, and animals the least distance of all. While a bluff wall might give an accurate reading out to 1500

⌄ For long-range shooting, the Leica CRF 1600 provides the temperature, angle, and atmospheric pressure at the site of the shot. It also has 12 ballistics curves that will match most cartridge trajectories.

yards, a deer with the same laser rangefinder might be measured out to only 500 yards. Practicing with a rangefinder lets a shooter find ways of measuring extreme yardages, such as glassing a large rock next to a buck out past 500 yards.

Wind, angle, spin drift, the Coriolis effect, all of these variable make long-range shooting at game a dubious proposition—For a variety of reasons all these factors, except the wind, while important, do not become critical until ranges considerably beyond 800 yards come into play. Even angle, uphill or downhill, is less critical at long ranges than many hunters are wont to believe. Rather than trying to explain all of the factors here, though, let's just examine the most troublesome one, the wind. One of the purposes of a hunting bullet with a high ballistic coefficient is to let it slip through the air with a minimum of wind drift. But if you know the ballistic characteristics of your bullet, you can, in fact, estimate what the wind will do to it down range and correct your hold on an animal. The question is, how do you dope the wind eight football fields away? A handheld wind gauge, or anemometer, can measure the wind speed where a hunter's standing, but not necessarily where the animal is. So other, natural gauges, like the way the branches of the trees bend out where the animal is, can be used. The best method, though, is to read the mirage through a spotting scope: Focus

≫ Long-range shooting requires the teamwork of two people – the spotter and the shooter.

≫ "Wind doping" with the use of anemometer is essential to long-range shooting accuracy.

on the animal; then turn the scope back, slightly out of focus, and the heat shimmer at the animal will remain visible (and even on a cold day, there is almost always some shimmer at long range). Then you read the shimmer like a clock—straight-up noon, no wind; 1:30, five mph from the left; 10:30, five mph from the right; 3:00 or 9:00, at least 10 mph. Yes, gauging the wind is ultimately a calculation; but then, some calculation is part of any shot at any range, for the hunter who shoots responsibly and competently.

All of the above, it should be noted, can be a daunting task for the lone rifleman. Successfully breaking the long-range shot is, as the professionals know, best accomplished through team effort, bringing a second set of eyes into the equation. A shooter's best friend may be his rifle, but his spotter is a very close second.

The fundamental lesson of long-range shooting at game, when called for, is that it is never a matter of a Hail Mary or laying down a barrage or showing off how "expert" you are. It's a matter of experience, technical knowledge, the right components, exact measurement, calculation, compensation, technique, and practice. And more practice. Which can all be classed under the single heading of "judgment." It comes down to a hunter's having to judge and think before he fires–which should apply to breaking a shot at a living animal at any range, whether 50 feet or half a mile.

Alpen

Alpen Apex XP 2-10x44 Mossy

Alpen Rainier
HD ED 10x42

Established in 1997, Alpen has tried to combine quality and affordability in its sport optics. And this year it has come out with its new Apex XP ("Xtreme Performance") line of mid-priced fully multi-coated riflescopes. The XP series is said to be able to withstand a recoil shock of 1000 g's, so it ought to be capable of surviving magnum-load rifles. Made fully waterproof and fogproof with a one-piece tube construction, the XP includes zero-reset windage and elevation dials. A fast-focus eyepiece is standard with a "bullet-drop-compensating" (BDC) reticle also standard on most models. Side-focus parallax adjustment comes with the scopes, as well. The XP is available in a variety of 1 inch and 30 mm tubes and in such configurations as the 1.5-6x42 mm with a 30 mm tube suitable for turkey hunting and slug guns; a 3 9x40 mm scope with a 1-inch tube and ¼ MOA adjustments, useful for all-around big-game hunting; and a 30 mm 6-24x50 mm long-range and varmint scope with 1/8 MOA click adjustments. The XP also offers several illuminated red-dot reticles models including a 30 mm tube 4-16x56 mm. Sunshades are included with all scopes and a matte-black finish is standard, but there is also a 1-inch 2-10x44 mm in Mossy Oak Break-Up Infinity finish. All the XPs are backed by a "no fault," "no questions asked" Alpen lifetime warranty.

Adding to Alpen's binoculars are expansions of three existing models. The Rainier "bins" now include rubber-armored magnesium-body 8x42 and 10x42 mm HD ED glasses with high-definition extra-low dispersion apochromatic optics. In the Wings line there are two new extra-low-dispersion fogproof and waterproof compacts in 8x20 and 10x25 mm. An on the economical side there is now a 10x50 mm Pro Series Porro-prism wide-angle fixed focus.

The last new addition to the Alpen make is the massive, at least in terms of objective lens, is the Rainier spotting scope in ED HD 25-75x85 mm. The scope uses BaK-4 prisms and fully multi-coated extra-low-dispersion glass in the lenses. www.alpenoutdoors.com

Alpen Apex XP 6-24x50

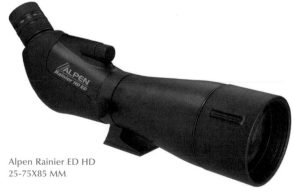

Alpen Rainier ED HD
25-75X85 MM

Brunton

Wyoming's own Brunton brings two new entries to its top line of Icon optics. The first is the new short-bridge, center-focus Icon binocular, in 8x44 mm and 11x44 mm. Both configurations weigh in at under two pounds and use premium SK glass Porro prisms with SHR nano coating, and all air-to-glass surfaces are multicoated with extra-low-dispersion glass used in the objective lens. The lightweight magnesium-alloy frame is rubber-coated. Includes "glare reducing" multi-stop eyecups, neoprene strap, and lens covers. The Icon is tripod adaptable, offers long eye relief, close focus down to three feet, and unconditional lifetime replacement "Halo" warranty. Suggested retail is $2375.

The second Icon offering is a new spotting scope in both angled and straight. Built with an 80 mm objective and available with either 20-60X or wide-angle 20-50X variable eyepiece, it has a water-proof-fogproof polymer frame with body armoring,

Brunton F-ICON844

Brunton F-ICON2060A

super-low-dispersion, fully multi-coated flourite-glass lenses, a locking tripod-mounting ring for multiple viewing positions, 17 mm eye relief, and weighs in at 70 ounces with a 16-inch overall length in straight and 15 in angled. Comes with an "interactive" case, Halo no-question warranty, and a price tag of $3900. www.bruntonhunting.com

BSA

It's hard not to be impressed by the history of BSA, the British Small Arms Company, Limited. Although BSA's optics division was started in 1996, only a year before Alpen was founded, the company's roots go back more than three hundred years to the English court of William and Mary in the late 17th century. It was then that King William III, dependent on military arms purchased from his native Holland and worried both about invasion and the urgent need to shoot Catholics, was told about the skilled gunsmiths of Birmingham; and an order was placed with them for the production of two hundred "snaphance" (an older version of the flintlock) muskets a month at 17 shillings "ready money" apiece. The actual public company was formed in 1861, adopting the symbol of three crossed rifles, or the "Piled Arms" trademark. From the Boer War through World War II BSA was a major supplier of British military weapons including service rifles, Sten guns, anti-tank rifles, and a half-million Browning machine guns carried on Spitfire and Hurricane fighter planes. BSA continues to produce sporting firearms and an expanding line of sports optics. For 2011 BSA has a new moderately

priced Gold Star line of riflescopes in a variety of configurations. These include the 1-6x24 mm for (at 1X) close-range full-view shooting with both eyes open; a 2-12x44 mm for general big-game hunting; and a long-range 4-24x50 mm. All come in black matte and use 1-inch tubes, have fully multi-coated optics, fast-focus eyepiece, side parallax adjustment on some models, a listed 4-inch eye relief, and come with the "EZ Hunter" reticle that is gauged to various points of hold for the trajectories of a range of popular factory calibers from 40-grain .204 Ruger to 225-grain .338 Winchester Magnum. The waterproof and fogproof scopes also include a limited lifetime warranty. www.bsaoptics.com

BSA Gold Star 2-12x44 MM

Burris

The MTAC is the new line of tactical riflescopes being put out by the Burris Company of Greeley, Colorado, meant to meet the needs of tactical and 3-Gun competition shooters. The 30-mm-tube scopes are offered in five configurations. The 1-4x24 mm is designed for close-quarters-combat situations and includes a wide field-of-few illuminated 5.56-7.62 ballistic reticle for AR platforms, and it can be packaged with the FastFire II red-dot reflex sight. The 1.5-6x40 mm also comes with an illuminated reticle and is suitable for longer-range conditions. For true long-range tactical shooters there are the 3.5-10x42 mm, 4.5-14x42 mm, and 6.5-20x50 mm scopes, each with adjustable parallax.

The reticle in all three is the G2B Mil-Dot for range estimation, holdover and holdoff, and precise aiming. The long-range trio also includes the MTAC Mil-Rad finger-adjustable and resettable adjustment knobs for windage and elevation. All five scopes have fourin-ches of eye relief, large exit pupils, index-matched fully multi-coated lenses, and weigh in between 14 and 18 ounces and run 11 to 14 inches in length. Suggested prices are: 1-4x24 mm, $399; 1-4x24 mm with FastFire II reflex sight, $599; 1.5-6x40 mm, $399; 3.5-10x42 mm, $499; 4.5-14x42 mm, $549; and 6.5- 20x50 mm, $699. www.burrisoptics.com

MTAC 1x-4x 24 MM

Bushnell

Bushnell ET10x40 MM

Bushnell Performance Optics has been marketing and manufacturing binoculars, riflescopes, and spotting scopes for some sixty years. And for this year they've taken their top-of-the-line Elite 6500 riflescope and offered it to "personnel" (military, police, and to private shooters who want a high-tech, hard-use scope

and have a $1000 to spend) by giving it a tactical treatment. The fogproof and waterproof Elite Tactical comes in both 1 inch and 30 mm tube diameters and in a variety of configurations from 10x40 mm fixed to 6-24x50 mm variable. Some of the scopes feature 6.5-times magnification range, similar to the Elite

Bushnell

Bushnell ET6-24x50 MM

6500. All come with tactical target-adjustment turrets and non-glare black-matte finish as well as "blacked-out" cosmetics for concealment. All the Elite Tacticals have fully multi-coated (with Bushnell "Ultra Wide Band Coating") optics and RainGuard HD moisture-shedding exterior coating, along with illuminated and non-illuminated mil-dot reticles. They come with a 3-inch sunshade and are covered by Bushnell's limited lifetime warranty. www.bushnell.com

Cabela's

Cabela's has partnered with the Czech optics manufacturer Meopta to make its new Euro line of riflescopes. These one-inch-tube variable scopes are computer-numerically-controlled machined from a single billet of aircraft aluminum and bead blasted before undergoing ELOX (electrolytic oxidation) anodization for a reduced-glare black matte, abrasion-resistant finish. The scopes are available in configurations ranging from 3-9x42 mm to 4-12x50 and 6-18x50 mm, with objectives on the 6-18s equipped with parallax adjustment. Lenses are fully multi-coated, using ion-assisted coatings. The scopes are listed as having 3 ¾ inches of eye relief; fields of view that span from 36.3 feet to 6.1 feet at 100 yards, depending on power setting and objective diameter; have fast-focus eyepieces; and are waterproof and fogproof. Elevation and windage turrets are finger adjustable in ¼ MOA clicks. The Euro scopes also offer two reticle options, the "D" for duplex and for $50 more the "EXT" glass-etched hash-marked "extended range" for individual holds out to 500 yards. The Euro scopes come with Cabela's sixty-day free-trial-period guarantee. www.cabelas.com

Cabela's Euro

NEW PRODUCTS

EOTech

EOTech XPS2-RF

In 1996 EOTech introduced its holographic sighting technology for use in sport shooting and hunting, and in 2001 extended their "holographic weapons sight" (HWS) in military and law-enforcement applications. In 2005, EOTech was acquired by L-3 Communications, and it hasn't lost sight of its roots in hunting and recreational shooting. This year it came out with what it claims to be the first-ever holographic sight designed specifically for rimfire rifles, the XPS2-RF. It's made

EOTech

for small-game hunting, high-speed target shooting, and plinking. Its integrated base mounts to any 3/8 dovetail rails found on most rimfire rifles (but which also means it will not mount on one-inch Weaver-style or 1913 rails). For a shorter sight length and shortened base the HWS uses a single transverse CR123 lithium battery, with an average battery life of 600 hours at the 12-rheostat setting, covered by an O-ring tethered cap. The sight "halo" is 30x23 mm in dimension, and the reticle is a 65 MOA circle with a 1 MOA aiming dot. The sight's water-resistant and comes with a two-year warranty. www.eotech-inc.com

Kowa

Kowa SV42 MM

Kowa YF30-Flat MM

The Torrance, California, headquartered optics company has a couple of the newest binoculars on the market in their YF and SV series. The Kowa SV roof prisms are available in 8x32 mm, 10x32 mm, 8x42 mm, 10x42 mm, 10x50 mm, and 12x50 mm. The lightweight red-accented black rubber-armored housing includes a curved grip area and is nitrogen purged and fully waterproof and fogproof. The lenses are fully multi-coated and phase corrected, and the price at just over $200 is very attractive.

Even more attractive at half that price, and at just a pound in weight a good fit for young hands, are the similarly black-rubber-armored, red-accented Porro prism YF (which is said to stand for "Youth and Family") series binoculars in 6x30 mm and 8x30 mm configurations. In the 8x30 mm the YF offers a nearly four-hundred-foot linear field of view at 1000 yards. Includes palm swells on the housing for grip, twist-up-and-down eyecups, fully multi-coated optics, and they are waterproof and fogproof, being purged with pure dry nitrogen gas. http://www.kowa-usa.com

Kruger

Along with hunting optics, Sisters, Oregon-based Kruger Optical offers optics for tactical applications, including spotting scopes, riflescopes, and the new 1-8x40 mm Dual Tactical Sight Gen II. The DTS uses two different sighting systems through a 38x50.8 mm window, one a 1X reflex sight with a one MOA red dot and a sixty MOA circle. The dot-sight function has six brightness levels with "off" settings between each level. Flipping a lever engages what seems to be a reflex-camera mirror system and turns the sight into a 40 mm scope that can be used at 2X or 8X with a mil-dot ranging reticle. The sight features a patent-pending, extended-range elevation system for long-range impact adjustments, with resettable clicks and a Geneva-style revolution counter, and the locking windage and elevation adjustments are ¼ MOA and independent for both sighting systems. The main rectangular-shaped 10½-inch body of the sight around the mechanics is made from a carbon-fiber composite shell for reduced

Kruger 1-8x40 MM DTS

weight. The DTS mounts on a Picatinny rail, is stated to be waterproof and fogproof, and has a limited lifetime warranty. www.Krugeroptical.com

Leatherwood/Hi-Lux Optics

Leatherwood Hi-Lux
Top Angle Focus

Leatherwood offers affordable riflescopes that are built to withstand tough weather conditions, terrain, and recoil. Features include a revolutionary larger erector housing that allows greater transmission of light through the scope tube, making the ATR scopes brighter. The added room also allows for additional windage and elevation adjustment. Plus the all-new addition of the "Tri-Center" spring tension suspension insures positive scope adjustment and that your scope holds alignment.

New this year is the Top Angle Series 7-30x50 which has a larger diameter turrent housing that offers additional windage-elevation adjustment in . MOA clicks. All surfaces of the lense are fully multicoated. The Top Angle objective lens focuses rather than needing adjustment on the objective lens bell. It comes with a mildot reticle for determining range.

The Malcom Series Long 6x32 in. scope is a modern copy of the Model 1855 W. Malcom riflescopes. It comes with early-style mounts for scoping original and replica 19th century breech loading rifles (Sharps, rolling block, high wall, etc.) or late period long-range

Leatherwood/Hi-Lux Optics

Leatherwood Hi-Lux
Malcolm Long 6 x 32 Inch

Leatherwood Hi-Lux
CMR 1-4X24 MM

percussion muzzleloading bullet rifles. Objective, ocular and internal lenses are fully multi-coated for maximum light transition through a . inch steel scope tube. Interchangable front extension tubes allows this mid 1800s period-correct scope to be mounted on rifles with barrels of 30 to 34 inches.

The CMR (Close Medium Range) Series 1-4x24 scope has all of its surfaces mutli-coated, zero locking turrets, large external target-style windage and elevation adjustment knobs, and Power-ring extended lever handle for power change. It features a fast eye-piece focus, CMR ranging reticle for determining range and also BDC hold over value good for .223, .308, and other calibers. It comes with a green or red illuminated. The Turret is adjustable ½-in. MOA clicks.

The M-1000 Auto Ranging trajectory (ART) 2.5-10x44 scope compensates for the bullet drop automatically by using an external cam system. It can be calibrated for most centerfire rifle cartridges—from .223 to .50 BMG. The shooters sets the multi-caliber cam for the different cartridges being used. The M-1000 scope

Leatherwood/Hi-Lux Toby Bridges High-
Performance Muzzleloading 3-9X40

Leatherwood Hi-Lux M1000 ART

comes with mount and rings. The scope reticle is the "No-Math Mil Dot."

The Toby Bridges High Performance Muzzleloading 3-9x40 scope is designed for in-line ignition muzzleloaders and saboted bullets. It offers multiple reticles for shooting at ranges out to two hundred fifty yards. The scope is shipped with a chart providing points of impact at different ranges when using the longer range cross-bar reticles with different bullets at different velocities. All lens surfaces are mutli-coated for maximum light transmission.

Another retro offering, new this year, is the remake of the 8X USMC sniper scope. The heritage of the Leatherwood/Hi-Lux Malcolm 8X USMC sniper scope dates to the micrometer-click external-adjustment Unertl, Fecker, Lyman, Redfield, and other "target scopes" built between the 1940s and 1970s and once

Leatherwood/Hi-Lux Optics

favored by long-range precision shooters. Mounted on the .30-'06 Springfield Model 1903-A1, these scopes were employed by US combat snipers during World War II and Korea. In the early days of the Vietnam war famed marksman such as the legendary Marine sniper Carlos Hancock, credited with 93 kills, used the original of this scope on a Winchester Model 70, also chambered in '06. Today, an original USMC-marked scope in mint condition might sell for as much as $5000 while a working standard model in very good condition can bring $2000 or more. For the hunter or shooter looking for an age-appropriate scope to outfit his own '03 Springfield, or for those shooting in vintage sniper-rifle competitions, this scope will set them back less than $550, retail. www.hi-luxoptics.com

Leatherwood-Hi Lux 8X
USMC Sniper Scope

Leica

Leica Rangemaster CRF 1600

Shots on big game at extreme distances, from three hundred to beyond eight hundred yards, can with modern rifles, bullets, and scopes be not only feasible but ethical if a shooter really knows what he's doing and if he has a truly reliable laser rangefinder. I was able to personally test Leica's Rangemaster CRF 1600 with a small group of fellow shooters, hunters, and optics users. One of that group found this rangefinder to be "small, compact, and easy to use." In my own unscientific durability test I dropped the CRF ten times from shoulder height onto a carpeted floor with no problem. The CRF provided repeated consistent readings out to 1300 yards at assorted targets (I ranged, off hand, a lone dark-bay horse at seven hundred and seventy-two yards on a bright day). Another tester thought the weight was a good compromise between lightness and the heft to "hold steady." The CR2 three-volt lithium battery is listed at 2000 readings down to 14 degrees Fahrenheit. The display is an easy-to-read auto-regulating (for ambient light) red LED with a listed accuracy within one yard at four hundred yards, two yards out to eight hundred yards, and ± .5 percent beyond eight hundred yards, with measurements in either yards or meters. Measuring speed is .35 seconds. Lenses are fully-multi-coated and treated with moisture-resistant AquaDura. Essential for long-range shooting is the rangefinder's added ability to read temperature, angle, and absolute air pressure in pounds-per-square-inch, all data needed for calculating external ballistics and holdover—for when to shoot and more important, when not. http://us.leica-camera.com/sport_optics/

Leupold

Leupold- VXR 4-12x40 MM

Leupold BX-3 Mojave 8x42 MM

Leupold began manufacturing optical equipment in the form of surveying instruments exactly a century ago and was among the first, if not *the* first, to nitrogen purge riflescopes to prevent internal fogging. Leupold's latest model, the VX-R, is certainly fogproof and waterproof but has more to offer than that. The scope uses a fiber-optic LED illumination system employing the FireDot Reticle System, which is available in FireDot Duplex, FireDot Circle, Ballistic FireDot, and FireDot 4, with the dot within the reticle illuminated while the rest of the reticle is non-illuminated. The VX-R uses what Leupold calls its "Motion Sensor Technology" (MST) that employs a single-touch button to activate the illumination, offering eight different intensity settings, including a high-low indicator. The reticle will automatically switch to "stand-by mode" after five minutes of inactivity, then reactivate whenever the rifle is moved. The VX-R is powered by a CR-2032 coin cell battery. Windage and elevation are adjustable in ¼-MOA finger clicks, and the erector assembly uses twin bias springs. The extended-focus-range eyepiece is one-turn adjustable. The lenses are lead-free glass and the exterior surfaces have an ion-assisted coating to help prevent scratches. The VX-Rs have 30 mm tubes and are available in configurations ranging from 1.25-4x20 mm to 3-9x40 mm "custom dial system" (CDS) that can be matched to your rifle's ballistics, and a long-range 4-12x50 mm. Comes with a limited lifetime warranty on optics and a two-year warranty on electronics.

In binoculars Leupold added the new BX-3 Mojave series of roof-prisms in 8x42, 10x42, 10x50, and 12x50 mm in black or Mossy Oak camouflage. The BX-3's use an open-bridge design and feature cold-mirror coated BaK-4 prisms combined with a fully multi-coated lens system.

Leupold's newest spotters are the SX-1 Ventana line in 15-45x60 and 2-060x80 mm angled and straight scopes. The SX-1 has a "Multicoat 4" lens system.

Leupold SX-I Ventana
15-45x60 MM

Leupold RX 1000i

Leupold Vendetta

Knurling on the black body aids in grip and operation, and the scopes include a retractable sunshade and twist-out eyecups. There is also an available kit with a hard-side carrying case, soft case, and compact adjustable tripod.

There are two new models of Leupold rangefinders. The first is the RX-1000*i* that has maximum range of 1000 yards with a stated accuracy of 1/10th of a yard against all back background colors and textures. With trees the maximum range is seven hundred yards, six hundred yards for wildlife. The "True Ballistic Range" (TBR) feature calculates the shot angle and provides the actual ballistic range to the target, rather than the straight-line distance. The new Vendetta rangefinder is for mounting on bows and is activated by squeezing a pressure pad on the bow's grip, allowing a hunter to range a target with the bow at full draw, minimizing movement. The Vendetta includes the TBR feature, and it provides "laser-dot alignment" to sync to the bowsight's pins. The Vendetta ranges from ten to seventy-five yards and has a one-touch scan mode that lets a hunter range an animal as it's coming toward him. www.leupold.com

Minox

Minox does seem able to blend the look and feel of European optics (although at least some of the mechanical parts are made in a large Asian nation that shall remain nameless) with a reasonable price. In 2010 Minox branched out into riflescopes with its ZA3/7A5 lines, offering three-times and five-times magnification ranges, respectively. This year Minox has added a number of new configurations, including a 30 mm tube in the ZA5 6-30x56 mm SF (side-focus

Minox ZA3

Minox

Minox ZA5

parallax adjustment). Other configurations include the ZA3 3-9x50 mm and ZA5s in 2-10x5o mm, 3-15x50 mm SF, and 1.5-8x32 mm. These are all one-inch-tube matte-black scopes and are available with Plex, German #4, BDC, and XR-BDC for the extreme-range bullet-drop-compensating reticle, and the "Versa-Plex" reticle in the 1.5-8X ZA5. The Versa-Plex combines a circle reticle, like that on a turkey scope, with the duplex crosshairs used for big game. Windage and elevation on the 1.5-8X each have 90 minutes of travel (and range between thirty-six and seventy-two minutes on the other configurations) in finger-adjustable positive ¼ MOA clicks, and the turrets can be reset to zero. The scopes all have a generous rubber-armored well-marked power ring, and a rubber-ringed eyepiece that feels tight but focuses smoothly without the need for a locking ring. Waterproof and fogproof, the ZA3 and ZA5s have limited lifetime warranties. Minox.com

Nikon

Nikon Bolt XR 3x32 MM

Nikon Monarch
3 10x42 MM

Nikon M-223 Laser IRT 2.5-10x40 MM

There are a number of new products from Nikon. Waterproof and fogproof the ProStaff riflescopes are available in 3-9x40 mm black matte with Nikoplex reticle (also in 2-7x32–and in Shotgun Hunter with BDC 200 reticle–4-12x40, and 3-9x50 and in silver, RealTree APG and with BDC reticle). Has multi-coated lenses and comes with ¼ MOA hand-turn reticle adjustments with "Zero-Reset" turrets and a quick-focus eyepiece. The 40 and 50 mm scopes are adaptable for sunshades. Also waterproof and fogproof is the new laser range-finding scope, the M-223 Laser IRT 2.5-10x40 mm. The M-223 provides the equivalent horizontal range to the target, features one-touch laser technology that keeps ranging and displaying distance for twelve seconds with a button push, and has an integral mount for Picatinny rails. There is also a remote control that can be attached to most firearms. With the BDC 600 reticle, circle aiming points and hash marks are available to correspond to the trajectory of the .223 Rem 5.56 NATO round with 55-grain polymer tip bullet at approximately 3240 fps from ranges from one hundred to six hundred yards. Finally there's Bolt XR 3x32 BDC crossbow scope. Fogproof and waterproof the Bolt XR with multi-coated lenses has 3 2/5 inches of eye relief and a quick-focus eyepiece with ±4 diopter adjustment. The BDC 60 reticle has aiming points out to sixty yards based upon velocity of approximately three hundred and five feet-per-second. Adjustment increments are ¼ inch at twenty yards.

Nikon's very newest binoculars are the Monarch 3 All Terrain Binocular (ATB) line, available in 10x42 and 8x42 mm versions. The Monarch 3 features high-contrast, high-resolution optics using fully multi-coated Nikon Eco-Glass lenses and phase-corrected, high-reflective silver-alloy multi-layer prism coatings. The binoculars have long eye relief—24.1 mm in the 8x42 and 17.4 mm in the 10x42—and are fully rubber armored and include flip-down rubber lens covers to protect the 42 mm objective lenses from scratches and dirt. www.nikonhunting.com

Nikon ProStaff 3-9x40 MM

Premier

Premier V8 1-8x24 MM

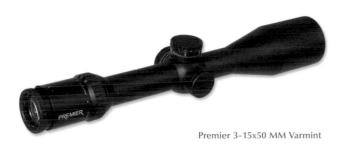

Premier 3-15x50 MM Varmint

Formerly Premier Reticles, German-engineered Premier Optics is known for long-range, tactical sniper scopes. Recently awarded the USMC contract to supply its Heritage 3-15x 50 mm tactical scopes to the Marine Corps Scout Sniper Units worldwide, Premier is making a shift into the hunting and varmint shooting markets. Two of its newest scopes are the Heritage 3-15x50 mm Varmint and the V8 1-8x24 mm Tactical.

The new Varmint comes standard with an exposed double-turn elevator adjustment knob featuring a"1-2" indicator window to display the number of revolutions for ranges out to seven hundred yards or more. Windage adjustment is finger adjustable with a dust cover. The 3-15x50 mm, true five-time magnification ratio. Reticle choices include the XR, A7, and Premier's patented Gen2" Mil-Dot Reticle, or a Custom Ballistic Reticle (CBR).

Premier

Premier's other newly introduced scope is the V8 1-8x24 mm Tactical CQB which includes two sighting systems—when the magnification is set at 3X or lower, a projected red dot appears on the second focal plane.

From 3X to the maximum 8X the illuminated Gen 2 CQB reticle operates from the first focal plane. This makes the dual sighting systems effective from five feet to five hundred yards. www.premieroptics.com

Steiner

New from Steiner, and an expansion from their binocular line, are their Military Tactical scopes, said to have been developed in cooperation with "Special Forces" and international weapons experts. Available in 3-12x50, 3-12x56, and 4-16x50 mm configurations (with a 5-25x56 and a 30 mm tube, true 1X 1-4x24 both scheduled for introduction later in 2011), the Steiners are manufactured from a solid one-piece 34 mm tube of 6061 T-6 aerospace aluminum which offers high strength, good workability, as well as high resistance to corrosion. It uses Steiner HD XP optics with hydrophobic protective coating. Windage and elevation adjustments are .1 mil and guaranteed repeatable with "True-Zero" stop for retune to zero. Has a side-mounted parallax adjustment and a side-mounted illumination control with eleven brightness settings and automatic shutoff. The front-focal-plane scopes use the G2 mildot illuminated reticle, the illuminated

Steiner 4x16-50 MM

stadia subtending 10 mils vertically and horizontally, suitable for both CQB and long-range conditions. The list price is a cool four grand, but "real world" cost is around $2500. www.steiner.binoculars.com

Swarovski

Swarovski CL 8x30 MM

Swarovski's brand-new CL Companion 8x30 mm binocular is anything but dull. The CL is light and compact without falling into the shirt-pocket category. This is a binocular to use all day in the African bush or tote up a sheep mountain with comfort. Having tested it myself, I can see it for tree-stand sitting in the whitetail woods (one of my favorites for that very thing is, in fact, a long-discontinued Swarovski 6x30 mm Porro prism). In a world of same-old black, green, or God help us, camo rubber armor, the binocular's tan color would blend in against a khaki shirt or the gray background above timberline. More important is the technical quality of the binocular with its light-transmitting and scratch-resisting lens coatings, turn-out eyecups, tight diopter adjustment, generous center-focus ring, solid bridge, and grippy ergonomic feel. www.Swarovskioptik.com

Trijicon

Trijicon RM06

Trijicon's noted for its fiber-optic battery-free illuminated-reticle scopes and reflex sights. The new compact, lightweight adjustable LED RMR (Ruggedized Miniature Reflex) red-dot sight, though, is powered by a standard CR2032 lithium battery; battery life is estimated for up to four years and can be left on for 25 days straight. It has eight brightness levels, including a "Super Bright" setting. The housing's an investment-cast aircraft-aluminum alloy with a hard-coat anodized finish. It has windage and elevation adjusters with audible clicks to allow for quick setting. Offered with 3.25 MOA (RM06) and 6.5 MOA (RM07) aiming points. It's waterproof to a pressure of twenty meters; can be mounted on a handgun, rifle, shotgun, or bow; and has a two-year warranty. www.trijicon.com

Weaver

The newest offerings from Weaver this year include the addition of a 2-7x32 mm scope to the 40/44 line. It has fully multi-coated lenses, one-piece one-inch tube construction, and is waterproof and fogproof. The Buck Commander scopes, made with whitetail hunters in mind and bearing the "imprimatur" of Duck, now Buck, Commander Willie Robertson, have a new 2-8x36 mm scope for shotgun and muzzle loader. Also with fully multi-coated lenses with finger-adjustable turrets that can be reset to zero. It's fogproof and waterproof, as well, and has the options of Dual X and Command X ballistic-drop-compensation reticle. For new tactical scopes there's the Tactical 1-5x24 mm for AR platforms. The reticle is an illuminated glass-etched first-focal-plane "close intermediate range tactical" (CIRT) with the crosshairs referenced to 20-inch shoulder width for ranging. The horizontal crosshairs are segmented in milliradians for windage leads, while the ballistic-drop calculations in the vertical crosshairs are matched to the .223 round. The 1-5x24 has a one-piece-construction 30 mm tube, as does the Tactical 3-15x50 mm Illuminated Long-Range Scope. The reticle of the 3-15x50 is the "enhanced mildot ranging" (EMDR), glass etched with first focal plane and "open-center" subtention for target acquisition.

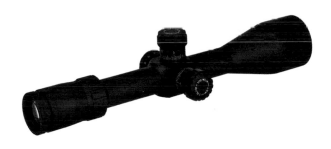

Weaver Tactical 3-15x50 MM

Weaver 40-44 2-7x32 MM

Weaver

Weaver Tactical 1-5x24 MM

The center crosshairs are 15 percent narrower for reduced target subtention–in other words, to cover less of the target at long ranges. Uses mil dots and hash marks for fractions of mils. Like all of the scopes above, the 3-15x50 is waterproof and fogproof; and it has a side-focus parallax adjustment, reset-to-zero external turret adjustments, and ten illumination settings, five red and five green. www.weaveroptics.com

Carl Zeiss Sports Optics

Zeisss DiaLyt 18-45×65 MM Field Spotter

Zeiss has run the table with new entries in spotting scopes, binoculars, and riflescopes. What may be "newest" about the Zeiss DiaLyt 18-45x65 mm Field Spotter is the price tag. At a penny under $1300 it's around a third the cost of Zeiss's DiaScope and weighs in at two-thirds of what the bigger scopes tip the scales at. And for hunting the DiaLyt could be one of the purest, most rugged spotting scopes seen in quite some time. Clearly, the scope speaks "retro" with its straight metal body armored in ribbed black rubber and built-in variable eyepiece—but without the dust or moisture issues of traditional draw-tube scopes. Zeiss's engineering seems to have followed tradition, though, with large full snug-fitting rubber covers for the ocular and objective lenses and with the focus at the objective (in technical terms the "big end"). The scope is designed for rigging with a shoulder strap through the covers so the strap can be removed easily for tripod mounting,

but with the strap and covers remaining attached to the scope. And from a practical hunting standpoint the DiaLyt's 18-45x65 mm configuration is pretty close to ideal for field carrying and spotting, while allaying concerns about exterior covers, lost lens caps, and the wobble of higher magnification that's likely to appear when glassing on the ground rather than from the platform of a vehicle. Built to hunt, the DiaLyt's fully-multi-coated lenses confirm Zeiss's reputation for optical quality. Brand-spanking new is Zeiss's Conquest HD Porro-prism binocular in 8x42 mm and 10x42 mm. Both are retail tagged at just under $1000, continuing what seems to be a price-point theme in its new products. They employ Zeiss T* multi-coating, dielectric coatings on mirrors, and LotuTec water protection on the lenses and promise an extra-wide field of view. The aluminum housings are armored with an ergonomically designed gripping area, and the binoc-

Carl Zeiss Sports Optics

Zeiss Conquest HD 8x42 MM

Zeiss Conquest Duralyt 2-8x42 MM

ular features a large focus wheel and close focus down to eight feet. In new riflescopes, Zeiss is offering the 30 mm-tube Conquest Duralyt. Available in three configurations—1.2-5x36 mm, 2-8x42 mm, and 3-12x50 mm—the Duralyts come with either #60 illuminated or #6 non-illuminated second-image-plane reticles and range in retail price from $1350 in the illuminated 3-12x50 mm to $950 in the non-illuminated 1.2x5x36 mm. The illuminated reticles employ a fine red dot (just 1/3 inch of target coverage at 100 yards at 12X) in the center of the crosshairs, and are push-button activated with automatic shut-off after four hours of uninterrupted use. And the scope body is an anodized gray for a neutral, unobtrusive appearance in the field. www.zeiss.com/sports

CATALOG

BINOCULARS

The concept of joining together two telescopes to create a *binocular* (in the same way two wheels are put together to make a *bicycle*, not a "bicycles" or a "pair of bicycles") is one of the earliest innovations in optics, nearly as old as the telescope itself. The binocular may be the perfect optical instrument because it mimics the vision of paired human eyes, rather than the monocular view through a telescope. The major improvement in the binocular came with the development of the reflective prism–first the Porro prism developed in the mid-19th century by the Italian optics maker Ignazio Porro, then the roof prism after that–which allowed for much greater magnifying power than possible with Galilean "field glasses" without inverting the image.

The binocular is the primary optical device for the hunter, as well as the birder and even the "butterflyer," in identifying what he is hunting for, fulfilling the basic function of bringing the distant close. (Early in *Green Hills of Africa*, Ernest Hemingway describes a scene that would have been possible to witness only through a binocular: "In the glasses it was a rhino, showing very clear and minute at the distance, red-colored in the sun, moving with a quick waterbug-like motion across the hill. Then there were three more of them that came out of the forest, dark in the shadow, and two that fought, tinily, in the glasses, pushing head-on, fighting in front of a clump of bushes while we watched them and the light failed.") The binocular is also a basic tool of the law-enforcement and tactical shooter and spotter, as well as a handy target-spotting device for the precision rifleman.

The type of binocular a shooter chooses depends on how he will apply it. The deep-woods whitetail hunter will vote for a generous exit-pupil (say something in the 6x30 mm range, as an example) for picking out antlers 50 yards away in the shadows, rather than sacrificing it in favor of excessively high magnification, while the Western or plains hunter will need added power, but also a sufficiently large, light-pulling objective (10x40 mm is seldom a wrong choice), to save miles of fruitless hiking. For the birder's needs a close-focus capability is essential, while the butterflyer wants a binocular with *extreme* close focus. And the mountain hunter and tactical shooter may opt for a large binocular, like a 15x56 mm, that can also serve, when mounted on a tripod, as an easy-glassing spotting scope. Ultimately, there may be no single perfect binocular for every specific use, but there are many right ones to consider and choose from, as needs dictate.

Minox BL 15x56 MM

Alpen Optics
www.alpenoptics.com

Alpen Apex 10x42 MM–Mossy Oak

Alpen Pro Series 10x50 MM

Alpen Monocular 8x25 MM

APEX 10X42 MM
(also in 8x32 mm, 10x32 mm, 8x42 mm, 8x42 mm Mossy Oak, 10x42 mm, 8.5x50 mm, 10x50 mm, 12x50 mm, and 8-16x42 mm zoom)
Weight: 22 oz
Length: 6 in
Width: 5 in
Power: 10X
Objective Diameter: 42 mm
Exit Pupil: 4.2 mm
Field of View: 315 ft @ 1000 yds
Twilight Factor: 20.5
Eye Relief: 16 mm
Waterproof: Yes
Fogproof: Yes
Limited Lifetime Warranty
Features: The Alpen® Apex® binocular features fully multi-coated lenses, HR™ metallic prism coatings, and PXA™ phase-correction coatings. Includes BaK-4 roof prisms combined with apochromatic optics and multiple-element eyepieces. The body is rubber armored, 0-ring sealed, nitrogen purged, and has long eye relief and twist-lock eye cups. Imprinted with Mossy Oak camo.
Manufacturer's Suggested Retail Price: $500
Estimated "Real World" Price: . $330

MONOCULAR 8X25 MM
(and in 10x25 mm)
Weight: 5 oz
Length: 4 ¼ in
Width: 2 in
Power: 8X
Objective Diameter: 25 mm
Exit Pupil: 3.1 mm
Field of View: 321 ft @ 1000 yds
Twilight Factor: 14.1
Eye Relief: 18 mm
Waterproof: Yes
Fogproof: Yes
Limited Lifetime Warranty
Features: The Alpen® monocular uses multi-coated lenses, BaK-4 Porro prisms, and multiple-element eyepieces. The body is rubber armored.
Manufacturer's Suggested Retail Price: $75
Estimated "Real World" Price: . . $55

PRO SERIES 10X50 MM WIDE ANGLE FIXED FOCUS
(also in 8x25 mm and 10x25 mm wide angle, 8x25 mm and 10x25 mm long eye relief, 8x42 mm and 10x42 mm long-eye-relief roof prism, 8x42 mm and 10x50 mm wide angle, 7-21x40 zoom)
Weight: 30 oz
Length: 7 in
Width: 8 in
Power: 10X
Objective Diameter: 50 mm
Exit Pupil: 5 mm
Field of View: 342 ft @ 1000 yds
Twilight Factor: 22.4
Eye Relief: 16 mm
Waterproof: No
Fogproof: No
Limited Lifetime Warranty
Features: The Alpen® Pro™ Fixed Focus binocular features multi-coated lenses, BaK-4 Porro prisms, multiple-element eyepieces, long eye relief, and rubber-armored body. The focus is fixed from 80 feet out.
Manufacturer's Suggested Retail Price: $105
Estimated "Real World" Price: . . $70

Alpen Rainier HD ED 10x42 MM

Alpen Teton 8x42 MM

Alpen Shasta Ridge 8.5x50 MM

RAINIER HD ED 10X42 MM

(also in 8x42 mm HD ED and in 8x32 mm and 10x32 mm)
Weight: 29 oz
Length: 7 in
Width: 6 in
Power: 10X
Objective Diameter: 42 mm
Exit Pupil: 4.2 mm
Field of View: 341 ft @ 1000 yds
Twilight Factor: 20.5
Eye Relief: 16 mm
Waterproof: Yes
Fogproof: Yes
Limited Lifetime Warranty
Features: Alpen® Rainier® HD ED binocular has UBX™ fully multi-coated lenses, SHR™ metallic prism coatings, and PXA™ phase-correction coatings. Features BaK-4 roof prisms, high-definition extra-low-dispersion apochromatic optics, and multiple element eyepieces. Has long eye relief, twist-lock eye cups, and rubber-armored open-hinge magnesium body. O-ring sealed and nitrogen purged.
Manufacturer's Suggested Retail Price: **$1645**
Estimated "Real World" Price: $1035

SHASTA RIDGE 8.5X50

(also in 8x26 mm, 10x26 mm, 8x42 mm, 10x42 mm, 10x42 mm Next G 1 camo, and 10x50 mm)
Weight: 30 oz
Length: 7 in
Width: 5 in
Power: 8.5X
Objective Diameter: 50 mm
Exit Pupil: 5.9 mm
Field of View: 294 ft @ 1000 yds
Twilight Factor: 20.6
Eye Relief: 22 mm
Waterproof: Yes
Fogproof: Yes
Limited Lifetime Warranty
Features: The rubber-armored Alpen® Shasta Ridge™ binocular features fully multi-coated lenses and PXA™ phase-correction coatings. Has BaK-4 metallic-coated roof prisms and multiple element eyepieces, along with long eye relief and twist up eye cups. The binocular is o-ring sealed and nitrogen purged.
Manufacturer's Suggested Retail Price: **$250**
Estimated "Real World" Price: . $175

TETON 8X42 MM

(also in 10x42 mm, 8.5x50 mm, and 10x50 mm)
Weight: 26 oz
Length: 7 in
Width: 5 in
Power: 8X
Objective Diameter: 42 mm
Exit Pupil: 5.3 mm
Field of View: 383 ft @ 1000 yds
Twilight Factor: 18.3
Eye Relief: 17 mm
Waterproof: Yes
Fogproof: Yes
Limited Lifetime Warranty
Features: The Alpen® Teton® binocular has fully multi-coated lenses, SHR™ metallic prism coatings, and PXA™ phase-correction coatings. The BaK-4 roof prisms are combined with apochromatic optics and multiple-element eyepieces. Includes long eye relief and twist-lock eye cups. O-ring sealed and nitrogen purged.
Manufacturer's Suggested Retail Price: **$825**
Estimated "Real World" Price: . $540

BINOCULARS

Alpen Optics

www.alpenoptics.com

WINGS ED 8X20 MM

(also in ED 10x25 mm, 8x42 mm, and 10x42 mm, and in 8x42 mm and 10x42 mm)
Weight: 8 oz
Length: 4 in
Width: 2 ½ in
Power: 8X
Objective Diameter: 20 mm
Exit Pupil: 2.5 mm
Field of View: 357 ft @ 1000 yds
Twilight Factor: 12.6
Eye Relief: 16 mm
Waterproof: Yes

Fogproof: Yes
Limited Lifetime Warranty
Features: The Alpen® Wings™ ED Compact binocular features fully multi-coated extra-low-dispersion lenses and PXA™ phase correction coatings on the BaK4 silver-coated roof prisms. With multiple-element eyepieces, long eye relief, and twist up eye cups. O-ring sealed and nitrogen purged.
Manufacturer's Suggested Retail Price: $245
Estimated "Real World" Price: . $170

Alpen Wings ED 8x20 MM

Brunton

www.bruntonhunting.com

EPOCH FULL-SIZE 8.5X43 MM

(also in 10.5x43 mm)
Weight: 25 oz
Length: 5 ⅘ in
Width: 5 in
Power: 8.5X
Objective Diameter: 43 mm
Exit Pupil: 5.1 mm
Field of View: 377 ft @ 1000 yds
Twilight Factor: 19.11
Eye Relief: 19.5 mm locking multi-step
Waterproof: Yes
Fogproof: Yes
Unconditional "HALO" Warranty
Features: The Brunton EPOCH binocular employs a variable-speed focus system that acquires targets from six feet and beyond with minimal wheel turn for close-focus and is also faster from 30 feet to infinity. The Brunton EPOCH's eyecups adjust in tiers, then lock to hold the position. The prism design features SF glass, AL-HR reflective coatings, and five roof-prism set screws.
Manufacturer's Suggested Retail Price: $1395

ICON FULL-SIZE 11X44 MM

(also in 8x44 mm)
Weight: 29 oz
Power: 11X
Objective Diameter: 44 mm
Exit Pupil: 4 mm
Field of View: 314 ft @ 1000 yds
Twilight Factor: 22
Eye Relief: 15 mm
Waterproof: Yes
Fogproof: Yes

Unconditional "HALO" Warranty
Feature: The Brunton ICON binoculars's roof prisms are made from SK glass with SHR nano coating, and the objective lenses are ED glass. Has an interchangeable eyecup system. The rubber-coated magnesium frame uses a short-bridge design.
Manufacturer's Suggested Retail Price: $2375

Brunton Epoch

Brunton Icon

BINOCULARS

C8X21ACP 8X21 MM

(also in 10x25 mm, 12x25 mm, 10x50 mm, and 12x50 mm
Weight: 4.98 oz
Length: 3 ²/₅ in
Width: 2 ¹/₇ in
Power: 8X
Objective Diameter: 21 mm
Exit Pupil: 2.6 mm
Field of View: 408 ft @1000 yds
Twilight Factor: 12.96
Eye Relief: 10.5 mm
Waterproof: Yes
Fogproof: Yes
Lifetime Limited Warranty
Features: The dual-hinged BSA C8X21ACP 8x21 mm is built with a lightweight magnesium housing and includes "Wraparound Comfort Grip." Optics are fully coated. Larger models are tripod adaptable and have wide-angle view.
Manufacturer's Suggested Retail Price: **$29.95**
Estimated "Real World" Price: **$26.95**

BSA C8X21ACP 8x21 MM

ELITE COMPACT 7X26 MM

Weight: 12 oz
Length: 3 ½ in
Width: 4 ¾ in
Interpupillary Distance: 57-79 mm
Power: 7X
Objective Diameter: 26 mm
Exit Pupil: 3.7 mm
Field of View: 363 ft @ 1000 yards
Twilight Factor: 13.5
Eye Relief: 16 mm
Waterproof: Yes
Fogproof: Yes
Limited Lifetime Warranty
Features: The Elite Compact 7x26 mm comes with BaK-4-glass porro-prisms, ED Prime glass, fully multi-coated optics, and RainGuard HD lens coating. Has center focus and twist-up eyecups.
Manufacturer's Suggested Retail Price: **$398.95**
Estimated "Real World" Price: **$249.95**

Bushnell Elite Compact 7x26 MM

BINOCULARS

Bushnell

www.bushnell.com

Bushnell Elite 8x24 MM

Bushnell Fusion 1600 ARC
10x42 MM

Bushnell Legend UHD 10x42 MM

BINOCULARS

ELITE 8X42 MM

(also in 10x42 mm)
Weight: 25.7 oz
Length: 5 ⅝ in
Width: 5 ⅛ in
Interpupillary Distance: 60-75 mm
Power: 8X
Objective Diameter: 42 mm
Exit Pupil: 5.25 mm
Field of View: 330 ft @ 1000 yards
Twilight Factor: 18.3
Eye Relief: 19.5 mm
Waterproof: Yes
Fogproof: Yes
Limited Lifetime Warranty
Features: The roof prisms of the Elite 8x42 mm are BaK-4 glass, phase-coated and treated with Bushnell's XTR process using 60 layers of coating on each prism. The fully-multi-coated ED-glass lenses are also treated with RainGuard HD water-repellent coating. With rubber-armored magnesium housing, scratch-resistant powder coating, center focus, and twist-up eyecups.
Manufacturer's Suggested Retail Price:.................$729.95
Estimated "Real World" Price:.................$479.95

FUSION 1600 ARC 10X42 MM

(also in 12x50 mm)
Weight: 31 oz
Length: 6 ¼ in
Width: 5 ½ in
Interpupillary Distances: 56-72 mm
Power: 10X
Range: 10-1600 yds
Objective Diameter: 42 mm
Display: Vivid Display Technology (VDT)
Speed of Reading: <1 sec
Exit Pupil: 4.2 mm
Field of View: 305 ft @ 1000 yds
Twilight Factor: 20.5
Eye Relief: 18 mm
Waterproof: Yes
Fogproof: Yes
Limited Lifetime Warranty
Features: The Bushnell Fusion 1600 binocular-rangefinder includes fully-multi-coated lenses and BaK-4 glass prisms. Has a built-in ARC bow mode for "shoots-like" horizontal distance; and the ARC rifle mode provides bullet-drop and holdover information, with a Variable Sight-In option. Has Scan, Bullseye, and Brush targeting modes, reading reflective surfaces to 1600 yards, trees to 1000, and deer-sized animals to 500. Lenses are coated with RainGuard HD, and the Fusion is fully waterproof .
Manufacturer's Suggested Retail Price:.................$1435.95
Estimated "Real World" Price:.................$899.99

LEGEND ULTRA HD 10X42 MM

(also in 8x36 mm, 10x36 mm, and 8x42 mm, and in RealTree AP casmouflage)
Weight: 22.5 oz
Length: 5 ½ in
Width: 5 in
Interpupillary Distance: 57-74mm
Power: 10X
Objective Diameter: 42 mm
Exit Pupil: 4.2 mm
Field of View: 340 ft @ 1000 yards
Twilight Factor: 20.5
Eye Relief: 15.2 mm
Waterproof: Yes
Fogproof: Yes
Limited Lifetime Warranty
Features: The BaK-4-glass roof-prism, fully-multi-coated Legend UHD binocular combines premium ED (extra-low dispersion) glass with Ultra-Wide Custom Band anti-reflective coating, as well as RainGuard HD water-repellent coating. Includes center focus, locking diopter, twist-up eyecups, rubber-armored magnesium housing, and "soft-touch" grips.
Manufacturer's Suggested Retail Price:.................$444.95
Estimated "Real World" Price:.................$299.95

Bushnell Outdoor Products

www.bushnell.com

LEGEND ULTRA HD COMPACT 10X26 MM

(also in 8x26 mm)
Weight: 15 oz
Length: 4 in
Width: 4 ¾ in
Interpupillary Distance: 58-74 mm
Power: 10X
Objective Diameter: 26 mm
Exit Pupil: 2.6mm
Field of View: 262 ft @ 1000 yards
Twilight Factor: 16.1
Eye Relief: 14 mm
Waterproof: Yes
Fogproof: Yes
Limited Lifetime Warranty and One Year Money Back Guarantee
Features: The BaK-4-glass porro-prism Legend UHD Compact binocular combines fully-multi-coated ED glass and Ultra-Wide Custom Band anti-reflective coating. The eyecups twist up, and the rubber-armored housing is waterproof and fogproof.
Manufacturer's Suggested Retail Price: **$182.95**
Estimated "Real World" Price: **$109.95**

Bushnell Legend Ultra HD Compact 10x26 MM

Cabela's

www.cabelas.com

ALASKAN GUIDE FULL-SIZE 8X42 MM

(also in 10x42 mm and 12x50 mm)
Weight: 25 oz
Height: 5 ¾ in
Power: 8X
Objective Diameter: 42 mm
Exit Pupil: 5.25 mm
Field of View: 367 ½ ft @ 1000 yards
Twilight Factor: 18.33
Waterproof: Yes
Fogproof: Yes
Limited Lifetime Warranty
Features: Full-sized, phase-coated roof-prism, rubber-armored, closed-bridge binocular with multicoated lenses. Friction center focus and diopter adjustments, twist-up eyecups, lens covers, and a rain-guard cover. Tripod adaptable.
Manufacturer's Suggested Retail Price: **$479.99**
Estimated "Real World" Price: . . . . **$ 479.99**

Cabela's Alaskan Guide Full-Size 8x42 MM

BINOCULARS

Cabela's

www.cabelas.com

Cabela's Porro Prism 8x30 MM

PORRO PRISM 8X30 MM

(also in 10x30 mm)
Weight: 16 oz
Height: 4 ½ in
Power: 8X
Objective Diameter: 30 mm
Exit Pupil: 3.75 mm
Field of View: 387 ft @ 1000 yards
Twilight Factor: 15.49
Waterproof: Yes
Fogproof: Yes
Limited Lifetime Warranty
Features: Traditional porro-prism design, wide-angle viewing and light-weight, compact portability. Premium Bak-4 prisms, fully multicoated lenses, nonslip rubber-armored grip, twist-up rubber eyecups, center-focus wheel, and carry bag and neckstrap included.
Manufacturer's Suggested Retail Price:....................$79.99
Estimated "Real World" Price:....................$79.99

ALPHA EXTREME 8X42 MM CAMO

(also in 10x42 mm and in black)
Weight: 26 oz
Height: 5 ½ in
Power: 8X
Objective Diameter: 42 mm
Exit Pupil: 5.25 mm
Field of View: 390 ft @ 1000 yards
Twilight Factor: 18.33
Waterproof: Yes
Fogproof: Yes
Limited Lifetime Warranty
Features: Fully multicoated with phase correction, center focus ring includes diopter adjustment, open-bridge design in Mossy Oak Treestand camouflage rubber armor and in black.
Manufacturer's Suggested Retail Price:....................$239.99
Estimated "Real World" Price:....................$219.99

XT FULL-SIZE 8X42 MM CAMO

(also in 10x42 mm and 12x50 mm and in black)

Cabela's Alpha Extreme 8x42 MM Camo

Weight: 22.3 oz
Height: 5 ⅖ in
Power: 8X
Objective Diameter: 42 mm
Exit Pupil: 5.25 mm
Field of View: 328.0 ft @ 1000 yards
Twilight Factor: 18.33
Eye Relief: 19 mm
Waterproof: Yes
Fogproof: Yes
Limited Lifetime Warranty
Features: Fully multicoated optics and rubber armored.
Estimated "Real World" Price:....................$289.99

Cabela's XT Full-Size 8x42 MM Camo

Cabela's Alaskan
Guide Compact
10x28 MM

Cabela's European Optics 12x50 MM

ALASKAN GUIDE COMPACT 12X30 MM
(also in 10x28 mm)
Weight: 9.6 oz
Height: 5 ⅕ in
Power: 12X
Objective Diameter: 30 mm
Exit Pupil: 2.5 mm
Field of View: 218 ft @ 1000 yards
Twilight Factor: 18.97
Eye Relief: 11.4 mm
Waterproof: Yes
Fogproof: Yes
Limited Lifetime Warranty
Features: Compact binocular with phase coated prisms, fully multicoated optics, center focus, and rubber armored.
Manufacturer's Suggested Retail Price: **$249.99**
Estimated "Real World" Price: **$249.99**

EUROPEAN OPTICS 12X50 MM
(also in 10x42 mm)
Weight: 37.1 oz
Height: 6 ⅞ in
Power: 12X
Objective Diameter: 50 mm
Exit Pupil: 4.16 mm
Field of View: 273 ft @ 1000 yards
Twilight Factor: 24.49
Eye Relief: 15 mm
Waterproof: Yes
Fogproof: Yes
Limited Lifetime Warranty
Features: Fully "Ion Assisted" phase and multicoated lenses, and half-pentagonal and Schmidt roof prisms, in green rubber-armored, nitrogen-purged and sealed aluminum-alloy

Cabela's Pine Ridge 8x42 MM

body with twist up eyecups and center focus wheel with integrated diopter adjustment.
Manufacturer's Suggested Retail Price: **$949.99**
Estimated "Real World" Price: **$799.99**

PINE RIDGE ROOF PRISM 8X42 MM
(also in 10x42, 12x50 and in camo)
Weight: 21.2 oz
Height: 5 ⅗ in
Power: 8X

Objective Diameter: 42 mm
Exit Pupil: 5.25 mm
Field of View: 330 ft @ 1000 yards
Twilight Factor: 18.33
Eye Relief: 19 mm
Waterproof: Yes
Fogproof: Yes
Limited Lifetime Warranty
Features: Rubber-armored BaK-4 roof-prism binocular with twist-up eyecups and a large, centrally located, grooved focus wheel.
Estimated "Real World" Price: **$199.99**

Konus USA

www.konuspro.com

Konus Emperor 10x42 MM

EMPEROR 10X42 MM

(also in 8x42 mm, 10x50 mm, and 12x50 mm)
Weight: 26.2 oz
Length: 5 in
Width: 4 ⁴/₅ in
Power: 10X
Objective Diameter: 42 mm
Exit Pupil: 4.1 mm
Twilight Factor: 20.5
Field of View: 400 ft @ 1000 yards
Eye Relief: 15.5 mm
Waterproof: Yes
Fogproof: Yes
Warranty: Lifetime Replacement
Features: The Emperor 10x42 mm binocular uses BaK-4 prisms with phase correction and features a light-weight body, fully- multi-coated optics, wide-angle field of view, large eyepieces, and long eye relief. The 42 mm models are rubber armored in hunter-green or gray, while the 50 mm's come in gray only.

Manufacturer's Suggested Retail Price: $259.99
Estimated "Real World" Price: $199.99

Kowa

www.kowa-usa.com

SV42-10 ROOF PRISM 10X42 MM

(also in 8x32 mm, 10x32 mm, 8x42 mm, 10x50 mm, and 12x50 mm)
Weight: 23.6 oz
Length: 6 ¾ in
Width: 5 in
Interpupillary Distance: 58.5-72 mm
Power: 10X
Objective Diameter: 42 mm
Exit Pupil: 4.2 mm
Field of View: 315 ft @1000 yds
Twilight Factor: 20.5
Eye Relief: 15.5 mm
Waterproof: Yes
Fogproof: Yes
Limited Lifetime Warranty
Features: The new lightweight Kowa SV42-10 roof-prism binocular includes fully multi-coated, phase-corrected lenses with highly reflective coating. Has depressions in the rubber armor for all-weather grip and is nitrogen-gas purged.
Manufacturer's Suggested Retail Price: $240
Estimated "Real World" Price: $220

Kowa SV42-10

Kowa YF30-8 Porro Prism

YF30-8 PORRO PRISM 8X30 MM

(also in 6x30 mm)
Weight: 16.7 oz
Length: 6 ⅓ in
Width: 4 ½ in
Interpupillary Distance: 50-70 mm
Power: 8X
Objective Diameter: 30 mm
Exit Pupil: 3.8
Field of View: 393 ft @1000 yds
Twilight Factor: 15.5
Eye Relief: 16 mm
Waterproof: Yes
Fogproof: Yes
Limited Lifetime Warranty
Features: The newly introduced Kowa YF30-8 Porro prism is an economically priced, fully multi-coated binocular. At 16.7 oz it is a good size for a youth binocular. Includes twist up-and-down eyecups. Features red accents on the black rubber-armored housing.
Manufacturer's Suggested Retail Price: $120
Estimated "Real World" Price: $105

BINOCULARS

Kowa

www.kowa-usa.com

Kowa BD42 8x42 MM

Kowa Genesis 10.5x44 MM

BD42 ROOF PRISM 8X42

(also in 10x42 mm and in black)
Weight: 25.7 oz
Length: 5 7/10 in
Width: 5 in
Power: 8X
Objective Diameter: 42 mm
Exit Pupil: 5.25 mm
Field of View: 340 ft @ 1000 yards
Twilight Factor: 18.3
Eye Relief: 18.3 mm

Waterproof: Yes
Fogproof: Yes
Features: Rubber armored binocular uses Kowa's C3 fully multi-coating and phase correction. Close focus down to 6 ½ feet. With twist-up eyecups.
Manufacturer's Suggested Retail Price: **$655**
Estimated "Real World" Price: **$590**

GENESIS 10.5X44 WITH PROMINAR XD LENS

(also in 10x33 mm and 8.5x44 mm)
Weight: 33.9 oz
Length: 6 ½ in
Width: 5 2/5 in
Power: 10.5 X
Objective Diameter: 44 mm
Exit Pupil: 4.2 mm
Field of View: 330 ft @ 1000 yards
Twilight Factor: 21.5
Eye Relief: 16.0 mm
Waterproof: Yes
Fogproof: Yes
Limited Lifetime Warranty
Features: Magnesium-alloy rubber-armored body. Lenses are Kowa Prominar XD glass with "blended C3 coating." Includes locking diopter adjustment.
Manufacturer's Suggested Retail Price: **$1,710**
Estimated "Real World" Price: **$1,540**

Kruger Optical

www.krugeroptical.com

BACKCOUNTRY 10X32 MM ROOF PRISM

(also in 8x32 mm, 8x42 mm, 10x42 mm, and 10x50 mm)
Weight: 15.9 oz
Length: 4 1/3 in
Width: 4 2/3 in
Power: 10X
Objective Diameter: 32 mm
Exit Pupil: 3.2 mm
Field of View: 290 ft @ 1000 yds
Twilight Factor: 17.88
Eye Relief: 18 mm
Waterproof: Yes
Fogproof: Yes

Transferable Limited lifetime Warranty
Features: The Kruger Backcountry binocular offers phase-coated prisms and fully broadband-coated lenses. The binocular is o-ring sealed and nitrogen-filled. Near focus is below one meter with long eye relief and twist-up eyecups. The body is rubber-armored and features a Coolneck™ strap made with breathable materials.
Manufacturer's Suggested Retail Price: **$152.93**
Estimated "Real World" Price: **$129.99**

Kruger Backcountry 10x32 MM

BINOCULARS

Kruger Optical

www.krugeroptical.com

Kruger Caldera 10x42 MM

CALDERA 10X42 MM

(also in 8x42 mm)
Weight: 25.5 oz
Length: 5 ½ in
Width: 5 ¼ in
Interpupillary Distances: 20 mm
Power: 10X
Objective Diameter: 42 mm
Exit Pupil: 4.2 mm
Field of View: 367 ft @ 1000 yds
Twilight Factor: 20.49
Eye Relief: 17 mm

Waterproof: Yes
Fogproof: Yes
Features: Kruger Caldera binoculars use fluorite low-dispersion glass, "BBAR" coatings, and phase-coated Bak-4 roof prisms with highly reflective dielectric mirror coatings. Includes a patented, single-hinge design. Made from cast magnesium, armored in rubber.
Manufacturer's Suggested Retail Price: $470.53
Estimated "Real World" Price: $399.95

Leica Sport Optics

www.leica-sportoptics.com

Leica Duovid 10-15x50 MM

Leica Geovid Laser Rangefinding 15x56 MM

DUOVID 10X-15X50 MM

(also in 8x-12x42 mm)
Weight: 44 oz
Length: 7 ¹/₁₆ in
Width: 4 ³¹/₃₂
Interpupillary Distance: 59-74 mm
Power: 10x │ 15x
Objective Diameter: 50 mm
Exit Pupil: 5-3.3 mm
Field of View: 273-208 ft @ 1000 yds
Twilight Factor: 22.4-27.4
Eye Relief: 14.5 mm
Waterproof: Yes
Fogproof: Yes
Limited Lifetime Warranty
Features: The HighLux System (HLS) phase-coated roof-prism Leica Duovid 10+15x 50 provides two distinct magnifications, rather than a zoom (in which the sharpest images are generally at the low and high ends of magnification). The power is switched by individual rings beneath each eyepiece. The dual-power binocular uses "Automatic Diopter Compensation" when switching between high and low power. The body is die-cast aluminum coated in black rubber armor, and the eyecups slide out to two different click settings. Comes with a tripod adapter and leather carrying case.
Manufacturer's Suggested Retail Price: $3245
Estimated "Real World" Price: $2799

GEOVID LASER RANGEFINDING 15X56 MM

(also in 8x42 mm, 10x42 mm, and 8x56 mm)
Weight (including batteries): 45.9 oz
Length: 7 ⅛ in
Width: 5 ¼ in
Interpupillary Distance: 56-74 mm
Power: 15X
Objective Diameter: 56 mm
Exit Pupil: 7 mm
Field of View: 225 ft @ 1000 yds
Twilight Factor: 28.2
Eye Relief: 15.6mm
Waterproof: Yes
Fogproof: Yes
5-Year Warranty
Features: The Leica Geovid Laser Rangefinding binocular reads distances from 10 to 1400 yards to within 1 yard at 400 yards to within .5 percent beyond 800 yards within 1.4 seconds. The display is a red LED powered by a 3-volt CR2 lithium battery that will read approximately 2000 measurements at an average temperature of 68-degrees F. Has a rubber-armored aluminum die-cast housing and two-click sliding eyecups.
Manufacturer's Suggested Retail Price: $3299
Estimated "Real World" Price: $2999

Leica Trinovid Compact 10x25 MM

Ultravid BL Compact 8x20 MM with leather covering

Leica Ultravid HD 8x32 MM

TRINOVID COMPACT 10X25 MM

(also in 8x20 mm)
Weight: 9.3 oz
Length: 4 ¾ in
Width: 3 ⅝ in
Interpupillary Distance: 32-74 mm
Power: 10X
Objective Diameter: 25 mm
Exit Pupil: 2.5 mm
Field of View: 273 ft @ 1000 yards
Twilight Factor: 15.8
Eye Relief: 14.6 mm
Fogproof: Yes
Limited Lifetime Warranty
Features: A phase-coated roof-prism compact binocular with Leica HDC multi-layer lens coating and a die-cast aluminum housing. Eyecups are extendable and the focusing is internal via a central knob.
Manufacturer's Suggested Retail Price: $499

ULTRAVID HD 8X32 MM

(also in 10x32 mm, 7x42 mm, 8x42 mm, 10x42 mm, 8x50 mm, 10x50 mm, and 12x50 mm)
Weight: 18.9 oz
Length: 4 ⅝ in
Width: 4 ⅝ in
Interpupillary Distance: 52-74 mm
Power: 8X
Objective Diameter: 32 mm
Exit Pupil: 4 mm
Field of View: 404 ft @ 1000 yards
Twilight Factor: 16
Eye Relief: 13.3
Waterproof: Yes
Fogproof: Yes
Limited Lifetime Warranty
Features: The Leica Ultravid HD series of binoculars is made with die-cast magnesium housings, coated in black rubber armor. Has Leica's Aqua Dura lens coating to repel dust, moisture, and fingerprints. The roof prism is phase coated and the lenses are fully multi-coated.
Manufacturer's Suggested Retail Price: $2299
Estimated "Real World" Price: $1899

ULTRAVID BL COMPACT 8X20 MM WITH LEATHER COVERING

(also in 10x25 mm with leather and in 8x20 mm and 10x25 mm with rubber armoring)
Weight: 8.1 oz
Length: 3 ⅝ in
Width: 4 ⅜ in
Objective Diameter: 20 mm
Interpupillary Distance: 34-74 mm
Power: 8X
Exit Pupil: 2.5 mm
Field of View: 341 ft @ 1000 yards
Twilight Factor: 12.6
Eye Relief: 16 mm
Waterproof: Yes
Fogproof: Yes
Limited Lifetime Warranty
Features: The Ultravid BR/BL Compacts use the Leica HighLux System (HLS) phase coating on their roof prisms and HDC multi-coating on the lens elements and Aqua Dura protective outer coating. The housings are aluminum and covered either in leather or rubber.
Manufacturer's Suggested Retail Price: $799

BINOCULARS

Leupold & Stevens Inc

www.leupold.com

BX-3 MOJAVE 8X42 MM

(also in 10x42 mm, 10x50 mm, and 12x50 mm; available in black or Mossy Oak Treestand camo; other Leupold binoculars include the Katmai, Olympic, Olympic Dual Hinge, BX-2 Cascades, BX-2 Acadia, BX-1 Rogue, BX-1 Rogue Compact and BX-1 Yosemite)
Weight: 23.4 ounces
Length: 5 ²/₃ inches
Interpupillary Distances: 58-74 mm
Power: 8X
Objective Aperture: 42 mm

Exit Pupil: 5.3 mm
Field of View: 368 ft @ 1000 yds
Twilight Factor: 18.3
Eye Relief: 19 mm
Waterproof: Yes
Fogproof: Yes
Limited Lifetime Warranty
Features: The BX-3 Mojave features BaK-4 cold-mirror-coated prisms and fully multi-coated lenses. Has twist-up eyecups and advertises a wider field of view "than many competitive models."
Manufacturer's Suggested Retail Price: **$379.99**

Leupold Mojave BX-3 8x42 MM

Minox

www.minox.com

BL 15X56 MM

(also in 13x56 mm, 10x52 mm, 10x44 mm, 8x56 mm, 8x52 mm, 8x44 mm, and 8x33 mm).
Weight: 38.1 oz
Length: 6 ¹³/₂₀ in
Width: 5 ⁷/₁₀ in
Power: 15X
Objective Diameter: 56 mm
Exit Pupil: 3.7 mm
Field of View: 215 ft @ 1000 yards
Twilight Factor: 13.9
Eye Relief: 17.4 mm
Waterproof: Yes
Fogproof: Yes
Limited Lifetime Warranty
Features: Rigid rubber armoring, metal focus wheel with "finger-felt" marker for infinite settting.
Manufacturer's Suggested Retail Price: **$995**
Estimated "Real World" Price: **$829**

Minox BL 15x56 MM

BD 7X28 MM IF

Weight: 10.93 oz
Length: 4 ²/₅ in
Width: 4 ¹/₅ in
Power: 7X
Objective Diameter: 28 mm
Exit Pupil: 4 mm
Field of View: 420 ft @ 1000 yards
Twilight Factor: 14
Eye Relief: 15 mm
Waterproof: Yes

Fogproof: Yes
Limited Lifetime Warranty
Features: Ultra lightweight compact binocular with individual diopter focus adjustment.
Manufacturer's Suggested Retail Price: **$349**
Estimated "Real World" Price: **$299**

Minox BD 7x28 MM IF

BINOCULARS

Minox GmbH

www.minox.com

HG 8X43 MM BR

(also in 10x43 mm, 8x56 mm, 8-5x52 mm, and 8x33 mm)
Weight: 22.9 oz
Length: 6 in
Width: 5 $\frac{1}{7}$ in
Power: 8X
Objective Diameter: 43 mm
Exit Pupil: 5.375 mm
Field of View: 379 ft @ 1000 yards
Twilight Factor: 18.5
Eye Relief: 19.3 mm
Waterproof: Yes
Fogproof: Yes
Limited Lifetime Warranty
Features: German-made lightweight full-sized binocular with 100-percent magnesium body and Schott German optical glass.
Manufacturer's Suggested Retail Price: **$1549**
Estimated "Real World" Price: **$1345**

APO HG 10 X 43 MM BR

(also in 8x43 mm)
Weight: 22.9 oz
Length: 6 $\frac{1}{5}$ in

Minox HG 8x43 MM BR

Width: 5 $\frac{3}{20}$ in
Power: 10X
Objective Diameter: 43 mm
Exit Pupil: 4.3 mm
Field of View: 342 ft @ 1000 yards
Twilight Factor: 20.7
Eye Relief: 16.5 mm
Waterproof: Yes
Fogproof: Yes
Limited Lifetime Warranty

Minox APO HG 10x43 MM BR

Features: Body is 100-percent magnesium and the lenses are apochromatic, made from fluoride-containing Schott glass, for reduced color aberration.
Manufacturer's Suggested Retail Price: **$2179**
Estimated "Real World" Price: **$1899**

Nikon Sport Optics

www.nikonhunting.com/products/binoculars

ACTION 8X40 MM

(also in 7x35 mm, 7x50 mm, 10x40 mm, 10x50 mm, 12x50 mm, 16x50 mm; 8x40 RealTree APG; 7-15x35 mm Zoom and 10-22x50 mm XL; Action Extreme 7x50 mm, 10x50 mm, 12x50 mm, and 16x50 mm; and Action Extreme ATB 7x35 mm and 8x40 mm)
Weight: 26.8 oz
Length: 5 $\frac{3}{5}$ in
Width: 7 $\frac{1}{5}$ in
Power: 8X
Objective Diameter: 40 mm
Exit Pupil: 5 mm
Field of View: 430 ft @ 1000 yards
Twilight Factor: 17.88
Eye Relief: 11.9 mm
Waterproof: No

Fogproof: No
25-Year Limited Warranty
Features: The Action is Nikon's basic series of Porro-prism binoculars, featuring multi-coated optics, aspherical eyepiece lenses, BaK-4 prisms, and a rubber-armored body. The wide variety of models the binocular comes in include the waterproof-fogproof Extreme and the Extreme All Terrain Binocular with Nikon Eco-Glass. The XL Zoom model includes a tripod adapter.
Manufacturer's Suggested Retail Price: **$120.95**
Estimated "Real World" Price: **$84.95**

Nikon Action 8x40 MM

BINOCULARS

Nikon Sport Optics

www.nikonhunting.com/products/binoculars

EDG 7X42 MM

(also in 8x32 mm, 10x32 mm, 8x42 mm, and 10x42 mm)
Weight: 27.7 oz
Length: 5 ⁹/₁₀ in
Width: 5 ³/₅ in
Power: 7X
Objective Diameter: 42 mm
Exit Pupil: 6 mm
Field of View: 419 ft @ 1000 yards
Twilight Factor: 17.14
Eye Relief: 22.1 mm
Waterproof: Yes
Fogproof: Yes
25-Year Limited Warranty
Features: Nikon's top-of-the-line roof-prism binocular, the EDG features extra-low-dispersion fully-multi-coated glass with "field-flattener" lens system, dielectric high-reflective multi-layer phase-coating on the prisms, dual center-focus knob with diopter adjustment, magnesium-alloy rubber-armored body, and horn-shaped detachable ratcheting-adjustment eyecups.
Manufacturer's Suggested Retail Price: **$3280.95**
Estimated "Real World" Price: **$2099.95**

Nikon EDG 7x42 MM

MONARCH 3 10X42 MM

(also in 8x42 mm)
Weight: 24.7 oz
Length: 6 in
Width: 5 in
Interpupillary Distances: 56-72 mm
Power: 10X
Objective Diameter: 42 mm
Exit Pupil: 4.2 mm
Field of View: 299 ft @ 1000 yds
Twilight Factor: 20.4
Eye Relief: 17.4 mm
Waterproof: Yes
Fogproof: Yes
25-Year Limited Warranty
Features: The new Nikon Monarch 3 uses fully multi-coated Nikon Eco-Glass lenses and phase-corrected, silver-alloy multilayer prism coatings with multi-click, turn-and-slide rubber eyecups, long eye relief, and a new lightweight fully rubber-armored ATB ("all terrain binocular") body. Includes flip-down lens covers.
Estimated "Real World" Price: **$249.95**

MONARCH ATB 12X56 MM

(also in 8x36 mm, 10x36 mm, 8.5x56 mm, and 10x56 mm)
Weight: 41.6 oz
Length: 7 ⁴/₅ in
Width: 5 ⁷/₁₀ in
Power: 12X
Objective Diameter: 56 mm
Exit Pupil: 4.7 mm
Field of View: 288 ft @ 1000 yards
Twilight Factor: 25.92
Eye Relief: 16.3 mm
Waterproof: Yes
Fogproof: Yes
25-Year Limited Warranty
Features: The 56 mm Monarch ATB ("All Terrain Binocular") features fully-multi-coated lenses, phase-correction-coated high-index roof prisms, black rubber armor, lead- and arsenic-free "Eco-Glass," center-focus knob, and multi-setting click-stop eyecups. The 12x56 mm includes a tripod adapter, and the binocular is also available in mid-sized 36 mm configurations.
Manufacturer's Suggested Retail Price: **$638.95**
Estimated "Real World" Price: **$479.95**

Nikon Monarch 3 10x42 MM

Nikon Monarch ATB 12x56 MM

MONARCH X 8.5X45 MM

(also in 10.5x45 mm)
Weight: 25.4 oz
Length: 6 ¹/₁₀ in
Width: 5 ½ in
Power: 8.5X
Objective Diameter: 45 mm
Exit Pupil: 5.3 mm
Field of View: 330 ft @ 1000 yards
Twilight Factor: 19.55
Eye Relief: 20.6 mm
Waterproof: Yes
Fogproof: Yes
25-Year Limited Warranty
Features: The Nikon Monarch X 8.5x45 mm features dielectric multi-layered high-reflective phase-coated roof prisms, fully-multi-coated optics, enlarged center-focus knob, rubber armoring with soft-grip tactile surface. Includes flip-down objective-lens covers.
Manufacturer's Suggested Retail Price:. **$836.95**
Estimated "Real World" Price:. **$579.95**

Nikon Monarch X 8.5x45 MM

PREMIER 8X20 MM

(also in 10x26 mm)
Weight: 9.5 oz
Length: 3 ⁷/₁₀ in
Width: 4 ³/₁₀ in
Power: 8X
Objective Diameter: 20 mm
Exit Pupil: 2.5 mm
Field of View: 356 ft @ 1000 yards
Twilight Factor: 12.64
Eye Relief: 15 mm
Waterproof: Yes
Fogproof: Yes
25-Year Limited Warranty
Features: The smallest version of Nikon's Premier line is double-hinged with multi-coated lenses and phase-corrected silver-coated roof-prisms. Includes center focus and turn-and-slide rubber click-stop eyecups.
Manufacturer's Suggested Retail Price:. **$758.95**

PROSTAFF 7 ATB 8X42 MM

(also in 10x42 mm and in RealTree APG)
Weight: 23.5 oz
Length: 6 ⁹/₁₀ in
Width: 5 ¹/₁₀ in
Power: 8X

Nikon Premier 8x20 MM

Objective Diameter: 42 mm
Exit Pupil: 5.3 mm
Field of View: 330 ft @ 1000 yards
Twilight Factor: 18.33
Eye Relief: 19.5 mm
Waterproof: Yes
Fogproof: Yes
25-Year Limited Warranty
Features: Nikon's "All Terrain Binocular" rubber-armored ProStaff 7 has fully-multi-coated lenses, aluminum high-reflective multi-layer roof-prism coating, multi-click turn-and-slide eyecups, and is tripod adaptable.
Manufacturer's Suggested Retail Price: **$268.95**
Estimated "Real World" Price:. **$189.95**

Nikon ProStaff 7 ATB 8x42 MM

BINOCULARS

Nikon Sport Optics
www.nikonhunting.com/products/binoculars

Nikon ProStaff Waterproof ATB 8x25 MM

Nikon StabilEyes VR 14x40 MM

Nikon SHE Adventure 8x36 MM

PROSTAFF WATERPROOF ATB 8X25 MM

(also in 10x25mm and 12x25 mm)
Weight: 12.5 oz
Length: 3 ⁹/₁₀ in
Width: 4 ½ in
Power: 8X
Objective Diameter: 25 mm
Exit Pupil: 3.1 mm
Field of View: 330 ft @ 1000 yards
Twilight Factor: 14.14
Eye Relief: 15.5 mm
Waterproof: Yes
Fogproof: Yes
25-Year Limited Warranty
Features: The compact "All Terrain Binocular" Nikon ProStaff Waterproof is rubber-armored, waterproof, fog-proof, and features BaK-4 glass Porro-prisms, multi-coated aspherical ocular lenses, and a center-focus knob.
Manufacturer's Suggested Retail Price: **$180.95**
Estimated "Real World" Price: **$128.95**

SHE ADVENTURE 8X36 MM ALL TERRAIN

(also in 10x36 mm)
Weight: 20.1 oz
Length: 4 ⁹/₁₀ in
Width: 5 ¹/₁₀ in
Power: 8X
Objective Diameter: 36 mm
Exit Pupil: 4.5 mm
Field of View: 367 ft @ 1000 yards
Twilight Factor: 16.97
Eye Relief: 17 mm
Waterproof: Yes
Fogproof: Yes
25-Year Limited Warranty
Features: The Nikon SHE Adventure 8x36 mm ATB (All Terrain Binocular) in plum comes with an embossed leather binocular strap and a shoulder bag with multi-function pockets and

built-in optics case. The arsenic- and lead-free "Eco-Glass" lenses are fully-multi-coated and the roof prism have phase-correction coating. The body is rubber armored with a center-focus knob and multi-click-stop eyecups.
Estimated "Real World" Price: **$129.95**

STABILEYES VR 14X40 MM

(also in 12x32 mm and 16x32 mm)
Weight: 47.3 oz
Length: 7 ³/₁₀ in
Width: 5 ⁴/₅ in
Power: 14X
Objective Diameter: 40 mm
Exit Pupil: 2.9 mm
Field of View: 210 ft @ 1000 yards
Twilight Factor: 23.66
Eye Relief: 13 mm
Waterproof: Yes
Fogproof: Yes
25-Year Limited Warranty
Features: The waterproof-fogproof Nikon StabilEyes VR 14x40 mm stabi-lizes its high-magnification image with a servo-control system powered by included AA batteries. The optics are fully multi-coated. The eyecups are twist-out click-stop.
Manufacturer's Suggested Retail Price: **$2080.95**
Estimated "Real World" Price: **$1299.95**

BINOCULARS

TRAILBLAZER ATB 10X42 MM

(also in 8x42 mm and 10x50 mm)
Weight: 22.4 oz
Length: 5 ⁹/₁₀ in
Width: 5 ¹/₅ in
Power: 10 X
Objective Diameter: 42 mm
Exit Pupil: 4.2 mm
Field of View: 293 ft @ 1000 yards
Twilight Factor: 20.49
Eye Relief: 15.4 mm
Waterproof: Yes
Fogproof: Yes
25-Year Limited Warranty
Features: The Nikon All Terrain Binocular (ATB) is a full-sized roof-prism binocular with turn-and-slide rubber eyecups.
Manufacturer's Suggested Retail Price: $226.95
Estimated "Real World" Price: $149.95

Nikon Trailblazer ATB MM

Nikon Trailblazer Waterproof ATB 8x25 MM

Nikon Travelite 8x25 MM

TRAILBLAZER WATERPROOF ATB 8X25 MM

(also in 10x25 mm)
Weight: 9.9 oz
Length: 4 ¹/₁₀ in
Width: 4 ¹/₂ in
Power: 8X
Objective Diameter: 25 mm
Exit Pupil: 3.1 mm
Field of View: 429 ft @ 1000 yards
Twilight Factor: 14.14
Eye Relief: 10 mm
Waterproof: Yes
Fogproof: Yes
25-Year Limited Warranty
Features: The compact waterproof and fogproof Trailblazer All Terrain binocular uses lead- and arsenic-free "Eco-Glass" multi-coated optics with Bak-4 high-index-glass roof prisms. Has a center-focus knob.
Manufacturer's Suggested Retail Price: $120.95
Estimated "Real World" Price: $84.95

TRAVELITE 8X25 MM

(also in 10x25 mm, 12x25 mm, and 8-24x25 Zoom)
Weight: 9.3 oz
Length: 4 ¹/₂ in
Width: 4 ³/₅ in
Power: 8X
Objective Diameter: 25 mm
Exit Pupil: 3.1 mm
Field of View: 293 ft @ 1000 yards
Twilight Factor: 14.14
Eye Relief: 14.0 mm
Waterproof: No
Fogproof: No
25-Year Limited Warranty
Features: The Nikon Travelite binocular features redesigned fixed-power models with enhanced ergonomics and maximized durability. Aspherical ocular lenses allow for a flat viewing field with edge-to-edge clarity.
Manufacturer's Suggested Retail Price: $140.95
Estimated "Real World" Price: $99.95

Pentax

www.pentaxsportoptics.com

9X32 MM DCF BC
Weight: 17.6 oz
Length: 5 ²/₅ in
Width: 5 in
Power: 9X
Objective Diameter: 32 mm
Exit Pupil: 3.6 mm
Field of View: 351 ft @ 1000 yards
Twilight Factor: 16.9
Eye Relief: 16 mm
Waterproof: Yes
Fogproof: Yes
Limited Lifetime Warranty
Features: The binocular has fully multi-coated glass lens elements and phase-coated roof prisms. The housing is fiber-reinforced polycarbonate and rubber-armored with an open-bridge design, locking diopter ring with click stops, and click-stop helicoid eyepiece rings.
Manufacturer's Suggested Retail Price: **$299**
Estimated "Real World" Price: **$299**

9X32 MM DCF BC
Weight: 23.5 oz
Length: 5 ⁴/₅ in
Width: 5 in
Power: 9X
Objective Diameter: 42 mm
Exit Pupil: 4.7 mm
Field of View: 321 ft @ 1000 yards
Twilight Factor: 19.4
Eye Relief: 18 mm
Waterproof: Yes
Fogproof: Yes
Limited Lifetime Warranty
Features: Features fully multi-coated glass lens elements and phase-coated roof prisms. Has a fiber-reinforced, polycarbonate, rubber-armored body and open-bridge design with helicoid eyepiece rings with click stops.
Manufacturer's Suggested Retail Price: **$349**
Estimated "Real World" Price: **$349**

8X42 MM DCF CS
(also in 10x42 mm)
Weight: 22.6 oz
Length: 5 ⁴/₅ in
Width: 5 ³/₁₀ in
Power: 8X
Objective Diameter: 42 mm

Exit Pupil: 5.2 mm
Field of View: 393 ft @ 1000 yards
Twilight Factor: 18.3
Eye Relief: 21 mm
Waterproof: Yes
Fogproof: Yes
Limited Lifetime Warranty
Features: This full-sized binocular has fully multi-coated glass lens elements and phase-coated, silver-deposited roof prisms. The housing is fiber-reinforced polycarbonate, fully rubber-armored. With a locking diopter ring with click stops and click-stop helicoid eyepiece rings.
Manufacturer's Suggested Retail Price: **$279**
Estimated "Real World" Price: **$279**

Pentax 9x32 MM DCF BC

Pentax 9x42 MM DCF BR

Pentax 8x42 MM DCF CS

8X32 MM DCF ED

(also in 8x43 mm, 10x43 mm, and 10x50 mm)
Weight: 23.5 oz
Length: 5 in
Width: 5 in
Power: 8X
Objective Diameter: 32 mm
Exit Pupil: 4 mm
Field of View: 393 ft @ 1000 yards
Twilight Factor: 16
Eye Relief: 17 mm
Waterproof: Yes
Fogproof: Yes
Limited Lifetime Warranty
Features: This binocular uses ED ("extra-low dispersion"), hybrid-aspherical, fully multi-coated glass lens elements, with phase-coated, silver-deposited roof prisms in a magnesium-alloy, rubber-armored body. Has a locking diopter ring with click stops.
Manufacturer's Suggested Retail Price: **$899**
Estimated "Real World" Price: **$899**

Pentax 8x32 MM DCF ED   Pentax 8x36 MM DCF NV

9X28 MM DCF LV

Weight: 12.9 oz
Length: 4 ³/₅ in
Width: 4 ½ in
Power: 9X
Objective Diameter: 28 mm
Exit Pupil: 3.1 mm
Field of View: 294 ft @ 1000 yards
Twilight Factor: 15.9
Eye Relief: 18 mm
Waterproof: Yes
Fogproof: Yes
Limited Lifetime Warranty
Features: Compact binocular with fully multi-coated glass lens elements and phase-coated roof prisms. The housing is fully rubber-armored with diopter ring and helicoid eyepiece rings, both with click-stops.
Manufacturer's Suggested Retail Price: **$249**
Estimated "Real World" Price: **$249**

Pentax 9x28 MM DCF LV

8X36 MM DCF NV

(also in 10x36 mm)
Weight: 22.6 oz
Length: 6 ¹/₁₀ in
Width: 5 ¹/₁₀ in
Power: 8X
Objective Diameter: 36 mm
Exit Pupil: 4.5 mm
Field of View: 342 ft @ 1000 yards
Twilight Factor: 17
Eye Relief: 16 mm
Waterproof: Yes

Fogproof: Yes
Limited Lifetime Warranty
Features: Has fully multi-coated glass lens elements, phase-coated prisms, fully rubber armored fiber-reinforced polycarbonate housing, large diopter ring with click stops, and click-stop helicoid eyepiece rings.
Manufacturer's Suggested Retail Price: **$219**
Estimated "Real World" Price: **$219**

BINOCULARS

Pentax

www.pentaxsportoptics.com

Pentax 8x32 MM DCF SP

Pentax 8x40 MM PCF WP II

Pentax 8x25 MM UCF WP

8X32 MM DCF SP

(also in 8x43 mm, 10x43 mm, and 10x50 mm)
Weight: 23.2 oz
Length: 5 in
Width: 5 in
Power: 8X
Objective Diameter: 32 mm
Exit Pupil: 4 mm
Field of View: 393 ft @ 1000 yards
Twilight Factor: 16
Eye Relief: 17 mm
Waterproof: Yes
Fogproof: Yes
Limited Lifetime Warranty
Features: This binocular uses hybrid-aspherical, fully multi-coated glass lens elements and phase-coated roof prisms. With a magnesium-alloy, rubber-armored body, scratch-resistant external lens coatings, a locking click-stop diopter, and helicoid eyepiece rings with 4 click stops.
Manufacturer's Suggested Retail Price:. **$549**
Estimated "Real World" Price:. **$549**

8X40 MM PCF WP II

(also in 10x50 mm, 12x50 mm, and 20x60 mm)

Weight: 28.2 oz
Length: 5 ½ in
Width: 7 in
Power: 8X
Objective Diameter: 40 mm
Exit Pupil: 5 mm
Field of View: 330 ft @ 1000 yards
Twilight Factor: 17.9
Eye Relief: 20 mm
Waterproof: Yes
Fogproof: Yes
Limited Lifetime Warranty
Features: The binocular features fully multi-coated optical elements and BaK4 glass prisms in a die-cast aluminum body with full-rubber armoring. With click-stop diopter ring and 4-click-stop helicoid eyepiece rings.

Manufacturer's Suggested Retail Price:. **$159**
Estimated "Real World" Price:. **$159**

8X25 MM DCF UCF WP

(also in 10x25 mm)
Weight: 12.3 oz
Length: 4 ³⁄₁₀ in
Width: 4 ³⁄₅ in
Power: 8X
Objective Diameter: 25 mm
Exit Pupil: 3.1 mm
Field of View: 324 ft @ 1000 yards
Twilight Factor: 14.1
Eye Relief: 15 mm
Waterproof: Yes
Fogproof: Yes
Limited Lifetime Warranty
Features: This compact binocular uses an inverted porro-prism design with BaK4 glass. Fully multi-coated optics with a dual-axis, single body housing with synchronized eyepiece adjustment with a central diopter adjustment and slide-style eyepiece rings.
Manufacturer's Suggested Retail Price:. **$124**
Estimated "Real World" Price:. **$124**

BINOCULARS

Pentax

www.pentaxsportoptics.com

16X50 MM XCF

(also in 10x50 mm and 12x50 mm)
Weight: 31.7 oz
Length: 6 ½ in
Width: 7 ⅘ in
Power: 16X
Objective Diameter: 50 mm
Exit Pupil: 3.1 mm
Field of View: 183 ft @ 1000 yards
Twilight Factor: 28.2
Eye Relief: 13 mm
Waterproof: Yes
Fogproof: Yes
Limited Lifetime Warranty
Features: The XCF has multi-coated optical elements and BaK4 glass prisms. Rubber armored with a large center focusing knob.
Manufacturer's Suggested Retail Price: **$119.95**
Estimated "Real World" Price: **$119.95**

Pentax 16x50 MM XCF

Redfield

www.redfield.com

Redfield Rebel 8x32 MM

REBEL 8X32 MM

(also in 10x42 mm; other Redfield binoculars include the Renegade Porroprism in 7x50 mm and 10x50 mm)
Weight: 17.1 oz
Length: 5 in
Interpupillary Distances: 58-73 mm
Power: 8X
Objective aperture: 32 mm
Exit Pupil: 4 mm
Field of View: 394 ft @ 1000 yds
Twilight Factor: 16
Eye Relief: 15.8 mm
Weatherproof: Yes
Fogproof: Yes
Limited Lifetime Warranty
Features: The ergonomic, center-focus, roof-prism Rebel 8x32 mm binocular's features include fully multi-coated lenses and premium BaK-4 prisms. The aluminum body is fully armored. Includes twist-up-and-down eyecups and neoprene neck strap, lens caps, tripod-adaptable mount, and soft case. Able to close focus down to 3.8 feet.
Manufacturer's Suggested Retail Price: **$129.99**

BINOCULARS

Shepherd Enterprises

www.shepherdscopes.com

8X42 MM
(also in 10x42 mm and 12x50 mm)
Weight: 22.5 oz
Length: 6 in
Width: 4 ½ in
Power: 8X
Objective Diameter: 42 mm
Exit Pupil: 5.25 mm
Twilight Factor: 18.33
Resolution: 4.4 seconds of angle
Eye Relief: 19.4 mm
Waterproof: Yes

Fogproof: Yes
Lifetime Warranty
Features: The Shepherd binocular uses Multi Mag-Phase©™ coating and A.E.F.©™ ("anti-eye-fatigue") high resolution. The binocular has an armor-coated, aircraft-aluminum body. Resolution is stated to be ⅘ in at 1000 yards under ideal conditions.
Manufacturer's Suggested Retail Price: **$661.50**

Shepherd 8x42 MM

Simmons

www.simmonsoptics.com

PROSPORT 10X42 MM CAMO
(also in 8x42 mm, 10x50 mm, 12x50mm, 8x 21mm, and 10x25mm, and in black)
Weight: 23.8 oz
Length: 6 in
Width: 5 in
Interpupillary Distance: 59-75 mm
Power: 10X
Objective Diameter: 42 mm
Exit Pupil: 4.2 mm
Field of View: 303 ft @ 1000 yds

Twilight Factor: 20.5
Eye Relief: 16
Waterproof: Yes
Fogproof: Yes
Limited Lifetime Warranty
Features: The Simmons ProSport 10x 42mm Camo binocular features multi-coated optics and BaK-4 prisms. Equipped with rubber armor coating, and is fully waterproof and fogproof.
Manufacturer's Suggested Retail Price: **$152.95**

Simmons ProSport 10x42 MM

Steiner Optik

www.steiner-binoculars.com

PREDATOR PRO 12X40 MM
(also in 8x30 mm)
Weight: 24.7 oz
Length: 7 in
Width: 7 in
Interpupillary Distances: 56-74 mm
Power: 12X
Objective Diameter: 40 mm
Exit Pupil: 3.3 mm
Field of View: 264 ft @ 1000 yds
Twilight Factor: 21.9
Eye Relief: 15.6 mm
Waterproof: No
Fogproof: No
Ten-Year Limited Warranty
Features: The high-power 12x40 mm Predator Pro Porro-prism binocular uses high-contrast lens coating (called

CAT or "Color Adjusted Transmission," to enhance brown and red colors) to aid in picking up objects against green backgrounds. The 12x40 Predator Pro has Steiner's "Sports Auto-Focus" system that, once set for the user's eyes, fixes the focus at distances from approximately 30 yards to infinity. The Predator Pro uses NBR rubber armoring that also reduces sound during handling. The new rubber offers a firm grip and is more tactile in wet weather. Forest-green in color with 18.5 mm eye relief and soft, fold-down eyecups.
Manufacturer's Suggested Retail Price: **$489.00**
Estimated "Real World" Price: **$349.99**

Steiner Predator Pro 12x40 MM

BINOCULARS

MERLIN 10X50 MM

(also in 8x32 mm, 8x42 mm, and 10x42 mm)

Weight: 28.2 oz
Length: 7 ½ in
Width: 5 ⅕ in
Interpupillary Distances: 57-73 mm
Power: 10X
Objective Diameter: 50 mm
Exit Pupil: 5 mm
Field of View: 288 ft @ 1000 yds
Twilight Factor: 18
Eye Relief: 22.4 mm
Waterproof: Yes
Fogproof: Yes
10 Year Limited Warranty
Features: The center-focus Steiner Merlin 10x50 mm has phase-corrected roof prisms and fully-multi-coated lenses. Comes with a weatherproof travel case, a neoprene non-slip strap, rain guard and objective lens caps.
Manufacturer's Suggested Retail Price:................. **$998.00**
Estimated "Real World" Price:................. **$639.99**

MILITARY 10X50 MM LRF

Weight: 45.9 oz
Length: 6 ⅕ in
Width: 8 in
Interpupillary Distances: 56-74 mm
Power: 10X
Objective Diameter: 50 mm
Exit Pupil: 5 mm
Field of View: 318 ft @ 1000 yds
Twilight Factor: 22.4
Eye Relief: 15.8 mm
Waterproof: Yes
Fogproof: Yes
Two-Year Warranty
Features: The Steiner 10x50 Military LRF's built-in laser rangefinder-binocular utilizes an eye FDA Class 1 laser in the left half of the unit. The digital display is superimposed over the image seen in the unit's right half. By centering the target display on the subject while touching and releasing the "RANGING" button located on top of the right half, the digital display will provide a distance value. Holding the ranging button for more than three seconds activates the unit's scan mode for measuring small or moving targets.

Scan mode switches off automatically after 20 seconds to conserve battery life. The LRF ranges from 20 to 1600 yards. With sunshine and good visibility, the unit's accuracy is within one yard at ranges up to 380 yards, within two yards to 763 yards, and within approximately one-half of one percent to 1600 yards. The Military LRF can also be set up to provide metric measurements. A 3-volt CR123A battery provides and estimated 5000 individual measurements at 68 degrees F. The LRF is a Porro-prism design, and user focus is set by individual ocular adjustments. The chassis is made from Makrolon, a impact-resistant fiber-reinforced polycarbonate; alloy components that are anodized; external metal parts finished in enamel to prevent corrosion; and the body is armored in Nitrile Butadiene Rubber (NBR).
Manufacturer's Suggested Retail Price:................. **$3979.00**
Estimated "Real World" Price:................. **$2859.99**

MILITARY MARINE 10X50 MM

(also in 8x30 mm)

Weight: 35.3 oz
Length: 5 ⅕ in
Width: 8 ⅕ in
Interpupillary Distances: 56-74 mm
Power: 10X
Objective Diameter: 50 mm
Exit Pupil: 5 mm
Field of View: 300 ft @ 1000 yds
Twilight Factor: 22.4
Eye Relief: 17 mm
Waterproof: Yes
Fogproof: Yes
Ten-Year Limited Warranty
Features: The high depth-of-field Porro-prism Steiner Military Marine is built for military service. Rubber armored with long eye relief. The oculars are adjustable and then the focus is fixed from 20 yards to infinity. Good configuration for low light.
Manufacturer's Suggested Retail Price:................. **$827.00**
Estimated "Real World" Price:................. **$549.99**

Steiner Merlin 10x50 MM

Steiner Military 10x50 MM LRF

Steiner Military Marine 10x50 MM

Steiner Optik

www.steiner-binoculars.com

Steiner Nighthunter XP 8x56 MM

Steiner Peregrine XP 10x44 MM

NIGHTHUNTER XP 8X56 MM

(also in 8x42 mm, 10x42 mm, and 10x56 mm)
Weight: 40.2 oz
Length: 8 ⅓ in
Width: 5 ⅔ in
Power: 8X
Objective Diameter: 56 mm
Exit Pupil: 7 mm
Field of View: 400 ft @ 1000 yds
Twilight Factor: 21.2
Eye Relief: 16.3 mm
Waterproof: Yes
Fogproof: Yes
30-Year Limited Warranty
Features: Advertised as being built to military specifications for durability, the Nighthunter XP claims to deliver light transmission broadly across the human-eye color spectrum for better detail in low light. The roof-prism Nighthunter XP uses high-definition (HD) glass and "Nano-Protection" on the outer ocular and objective lenses to prevent adhesion of water and moisture to the lens surfaces.
Manufacturer's Suggested Retail Price:................ **$1447.00**
Estimated "Real World" Price:.................. **$999.99**

PEREGRINE XP 10X44 MM

(also in 8x44 mm)
Weight: 30.1 oz
Length: 7 ⅖ in
Width: 5 in

Steiner Predator Xtreme 8x42 MM

Interpupillary Distances: 56-74 mm
Power: 10X
Objective Diameter: 44 mm
Exit Pupil: 4.4 mm
Field of View: 328 ft @ 1000 yds
Twilight Factor: 21
Eye Relief: 20 mm
Waterproof: Yes
Fogproof: Yes
30-Year Limited Warranty
Features: Steiner's top-priced Peregrine XP uses high-definition optics, consisting of refractive-index-matched glass coated with rare-earth formulations such as titanium, fluorite, and other mineral substrates. The dielectric-mirror roof-prisms are phase-correction coated. The 30 mm ocular (eyepiece) lenses provide for reduced peripheral interference and longer eye relief. Has a magnesium-alloy housing, and includes "Nano-Protection" water-repellent lens coating, twist-up eye-cups, smooth rubber armoring, gel-pad thumb grips, and center focus

down to 6 ½ feet. Comes with a fitted neoprene rain hood.
Manufacturer's Suggested Retail Price:................ **$2556.00**
Estimated "Real World" Price:................ **$1629.99**

PREDATOR XTREME 8X42MM

(also in 8x22 mm, 10x26 mm, and 10x42 mm)
Weight: 26.5 oz
Length: 7 in
Width: 5 in
Power: 8X
Objective Diameter: 42 mm
Exit Pupil: 5.25 mm
Field of View: 369 ft @ 1000 yds
Twilight Factor: 18.3
Eye Relief: 18.5 mm
Waterproof: Yes
Fogproof: Yes
Ten-Year Limited Warranty
Features: The polycarbonate-housing Predator Xtreme 8x42 mm binocular uses high-contrast lens coating to enchance reds and browns to make game stand out against green backgrounds. Has an ergonomic rubber armoring and is purged with nitrogen and argon gas. Comes with a padded travel case, a neoprene rain-guard on the oculars and attached objective lens caps. A padded neck strap included with the 42mm models.
Manufacturer's Suggested Retail Price:................ **$535.00**
Estimated "Real World" Price:................ **$399.99**

BINOCULARS

Steiner Optik

www.steiner-binoculars.com

Steiner Safari Pro 8x30 MM

SAFARI PRO 8X30 MM

(also in 8x22 mm and 10x26 mm)
Weight: 18 oz
Length: 4 ¾ in
Width: 6 ¾ in
Interpupillary Distances: 56-74 mm
Power: 8X
Objective Diameter: 30 mm
Exit Pupil: 3.8 mm
Field of View: 360 ft @ 1000 yds
Twilight Factor: 15.5
Eye Relief: 15 mm
Waterproof: No
Fogproof: No

Ten-Year Limited Warranty
Features: The 8x30 mm Porro-prism Safari Pro's UV coating blocks almost all UV-A and UV-B rays to reduce glare. The housing holding the bronze-colored lenses is armor-coated impact-resistant fiber-reinforced polycarbonate, and the prisms are made from BaK-4 glass. Includes wrap-around eyecups.
Manufacturer's Suggested Retail Price:. $286.00
Estimated "Real World" Price:. $199.99

Swarovski Optik North America LTD

www.Swarovskioptik.com

CL COMPANION 8X30

(also in 10x30 mm and in tan, black, and green)
Weight: 17.6 oz
Length: 4 ⁷/₁₀ in
Width: 4 ½ in
Interpupillary Distance: 56-74 mm
Power: 8X
Objective Diameter: 30 mm
Exit Pupil: 3.8
Field of View. 372 ft @ 1000 yards
Twilight Factor: 15.5
Eye Relief: 15 mm
Waterproof: Yes
Fogproof: Yes
Limited Lifetime Warranty
Features: The CL Companion is among the smallest 30mm binoculars on the market. It has a polycarbonate housing that is rubber armored in tan, black, and green, with Swarobright, Swarotop, and Swarodur Swarovski lens coatings.
Manufacturer's Suggested Retail Price:. $1032.22
Estimated "Real World" Price:. $929

EL 8.5X42 SWAROVISION

(also in 10x42 mm)
Weight: 29.5 oz
Length: 6 ³/₁₀ in
Width: 4 ⁴/₅ in
Power: 8.5X
Objective Diameter: 42 mm

Exit Pupil: 4.9 mm
Field of View: 7.6 degrees/399 ft @ 1000 yards
Twilight Factor: 18.9
Eye Relief: 20 mm
Waterproof: Yes
Fogproof: Yes
Limited Lifetime Warranty
Features: A medium-sized binocular that combines field-flattener lenses and HD optics for image resolution over the entire field of view. Eyeglass-wearers have a full wide-angle field of view due to the large eye relief distance. Close focus of 4.9 feet.
Manufacturer's Suggested Retail Price:. $2610
Estimated "Real World" Price:. $2349

Swarovski CL 8x30 MM

Swarovski EL 8.5x42 MM
Swarovision

BINOCULARS

Swarovski Optik North America LTD

www.Swarovskioptik.com

EL 10X32 MM

(also in 8x32 mm)
Weight: 21.2 oz
Length: 5 ³/₁₀ in
Width: 4 ½ in
Power: 10X
Objective Diameter: 32 mm
Exit Pupil: 3.2 mm
Field of View: 6.9 degrees/360 ft @ 1000 yards
Twilight Factor: 18
Eye Relief: 15 mm
Waterproof: Yes
Fogproof: Yes
Limited Lifetime Warranty
Features: Lightweight and compact. Close focus of 6 feet. Large field of view. Swarobright, Swarodur and Swarotop coatings, optimized roof prism system. Torsion free twin bridge construction. Integrated diopter adjustment in pull out focus wheel. Available with green or tan (Traveler Model) armoring.
Manufacturer's Suggested Retail Price: $2221.11
Estimated "Real World" Price: $1999

Swarovski EL 10x32 MM

Swarovski EL Swarovision 12x50 MM

Swarovski SLC 15x56 MM

Swarovski SLC 10x42 MM HD

EL 10X50 MM SWAROVISION

(also in 12x50 mm)
Weight: 35.2 oz
Length: 6 ⁴/₅ in
Width: 5 ³/₁₀ in
Power: 10X
Objective Diameter: 50 mm
Exit Pupil: 5
Field of View: 345 ft @ 1000 yards
Twilight Factor: 22.4
Eye Relief: 20 mm
Waterproof: Yes
Fogproof: Yes
Limited Lifetime Warranty
Features: The 50 mm objective lens provides brighter images than the 42 mm. Features HD and field-flattener lenses. Magnesium housing with EL wrap around grip and new large focus mechanism. Product video available at http://el50.swaroski.com.
Manufacturer's Suggested Retail Price: $2887.78
Estimated "Real World" Price: $2599

SLC 10X42 HD BINOCULAR

(also in 8x42 HD)
Weight: 28 oz
Length: 5 ⁷/₁₀ in
Width: 4 ⁷/₁₀ in
Power: 10X
Objective Diameter: 42 mm
Exit Pupil: 4.2 mm
Field of View: 330 ft @ 1000 yards
Twilight Factor: 20.5
Eye Relief: 16 mm
Waterproof: Yes
Fogproof: Yes
Limited Lifetime Warranty
Features: The fluoride-containing HD lenses ensure bright, high contrast images with maximum color fidelity. Enhanced special coatings support this effect. The new SLC HD also provides a wide field of view for eyeglass wearers.
Manufacturer's Suggested Retail Price: $2376.67
Estimated "Real World" Price: $2139

SLC 15X56 MM

(also in 8x56 mm)
Weight: 45.5 oz
Length: 8 ½ in
Width: 5 in
Power: 15X
Objective Diameter: 56 mm
Exit Pupil: 3.7 mm
Field of View: 231 ft @ 1000 yards
Twilight Factor: 29
Eye Relief: 13 mm
Waterproof: Yes
Fogproof: Yes
Limited Lifetime Warranty
Features: Large hunting binocular suitable for long-range glassing under daylight conditions. Can be used on a tripod with optional adapter. For dawn and dusk the 8x56 will give higher performance. Housing is made of metal and armored in green rubber.
Manufacturer's Suggested Retail Price: $2554.44
Estimated "Real World" Price: $2299

BINOCULARS

Swarovski Optik North America LTD

www.Swarovskioptik.com

POCKET 8X20 MM

(also in 10x25)
Weight: 7.6 oz
Length: 3 7/10 in
Width: 2 3/10 in
Power: 8X
Objective Diameter: 20 mm
Interpupillary Distance: 56-72 mm
Exit Pupil: 2.5 mm
Field of View: 6.6 degrees/345 ft @ 1000 yards
Twilight Factor: 12.6
Eye Relief: 13 mm
Waterproof: Yes
Fogproof: Yes
Limited Lifetime Warranty
Features: The pocket fits into any jacket pocket. Offers bright, high-contrast images in high resolution. Uses the same Swarovski proprietary lens coatings as full-sized binoculars. Leather covering in Tyrol model, available also in black, green, and grayish-brown armor coatings.
Manufacturer's Suggested Retail Price: $965.56
Estimated "Real World" Price: $869

Swarovski Pocket Tyrol 8x20 MM

Vortex Optics

www.vortexoptics.com

DIAMONDBACK 10X42 MM

(also in 8x28 mm, 10x28 mm, 7x36 mm, 9x36 mm, 8x42 mm, 8.5x50 mm, 10x50 mm, and 12x50 mm)
Weight: 24.4 oz
Length: 6 in
Width: 5 2/3 in
Interpupillary Distance: 57-73 mm
Power: 10X
Objective Diameter: 42 mm
Exit Pupil: 4.2
Field of View: 345 ft @1000 yds
Twilight Factor: 20.49
Eye Relief: 16 mm
Waterproof: Yes
Fogproof: Yes
Unconditional Lifetime Warranty
Features: The Vortex Diamondback binocular features fully multi-coated lenses with multiple anti-reflective coatings on all air-to-glass surfaces. Optics are sealed with O-rings and argon-gas purged. The housing is rubber armor and provides a non-slip grip and external protection. Multi-position eyecups twist up and down. The binocular has a center focus wheel, right eye diopter, and is tripod adaptable.
Manufacturer's Suggested Retail Price: $279.00
Estimated "Real World" Price: $229.99

TALON 10X42 MM

(also in 8x42 mm)
Weight: 26.5 oz
Length: 6 3/4 in
Width: 5 in
Interpupillary Distance: 56-73 mm
Power: 10X
Objective Diameter: 42 mm
Exit Pupil: 4.2 mm
Field of View: 348 ft @1000 yds
Twilight Factor: 20.49
Eye Relief: 16 mm
Waterproof: Yes
Fogproof: Yes
Unconditional Lifetime Warranty
Features: The Vortex Talon binocular features high-density extra-low-dispersion glass and Vortex proprietary XR anti-reflective coatings. The optics are fully multi-coated on all air-to-glass lens surfaces. The binocular is O-ring-sealed and argon-gas purged. The body is rubber-armored, creating a non-slip grip and providing external protection. Includes ultra-hard, scratch-resistant coating that also protects exterior lens from dirt and oil. Eyecups twist up and down. There is a right-eye diopter, and the binocular is tripod adaptable.
Manufacturer's Suggested Retail Price: $549.00
Estimated "Real World" Price: $449.99

Vortex Diamondback 10x42 MM

Vortex Talon 10x42 MM

BINOCULARS

Vortex Optics
www.vortexoptics.com

VIPER HD 10X42 MM

(also in 6x32 mm, 8x32 mm, 8x42 mm, 10x50 mm, and 15x50 mm)
Weight: 24.6 oz
Length: 5 ⁴/₅ in
Width: 5 ¹/₃ in
Interpupillary Distance: 59-75 mm
Power: 10X
Objective Diameter: 42 mm
Exit Pupil: 4.2 mm
Field of View: 331 ft @1000 yds
Twilight Factor: 20.49
Eye Relief: 16.5 mm
Waterproof: Yes
Fogproof: Yes
Unconditional Lifetime Warranty
Features: The Vortex Viper HD full-size binocular uses high-density extra-low-dispersion glass and Vortex proprietary XR anti-reflective coatings (used on roof prism models only). The optics are fully multi-coated on all air-to-glass lens surfaces. The binocular is O-ring-sealed and argon-gas purged. The body is rubber-armored, creating a non-slip grip and providing external protection. Includes ultra-hard, scratch-resistant coating that also protects exterior lenses from dirt and oil. Eyecups twist up and down. There is a locking right-eye diopter, and the binocular is tripod adaptable.
Manufacturer's Suggested Retail Price: $699
Estimated "Real World" Price: $599

Vortex Viper HD 10x42 MM

Weaver
www.weaveroptics.com

BUCK COMMANDER SERIES 8X42 MM

(also in 8x25 mm and 10x25 mm compact, and in 10x42 mm standard)
Weight: 24.9 oz
Length: 5 ³/₄ in
Width: 5 in
Power: 8X
Objective Diameter: 42 mm
Exit Pupil: 5.3 mm
Field of View: 330 ft @ 1000 yards
Twilight Factor: 18.3
Eye Relief: 19.5 mm
Waterproof: Yes
Fogproof: Yes
Limited Lifetime Warranty
Features: Weaver's Buck Commander series of phase-coated roof-prism binoculars includes compact and standard models. Lenses are fully-multi-coated and the exteriors are scratch-resistant. Eyecups are extendable and the rubber-armored finish has molded gripping surfaces.
Manufacturer's Suggested Retail Price: $493.49
Estimated "Real World" Price: $489.99

Weaver Buck Commander Series 8x42 MM

CLASSIC SERIES 8X42 MM

(also in 8x32 mm, 8x36 mm, and 10x42 mm)
Weight: 27.5 oz
Length: 7 in
Width: 5 in
Power: 8X
Objective Diameter: 42 mm
Exit Pupil: 5.3 mm
Field of View: 330 ft @ 1000 yards
Twilight Factor: 18.3
Eye Relief: 19.5 mm
Waterproof: Yes
Fogproof: Yes
Limited Lifetime Warranty
Features: Weaver's lowest-priced series

Weaver Classic Series 8x42 MM

of binocular, the roof-prism Classic comes in mid- and standard-sized. Includes fully-multi-coated lenses and extendable eyecups and is waterproof and fogproof.
Manufacturer's Suggested Retail Price: $313.49
Estimated "Real World" Price: $299.99

Weaver

GRAND SLAM 8X32 MM

(also in 12x50 mm and 8-16x42 mm)
Weight: 18.7 oz
Length: 4 ⁴/₅ in
Width: 5 in
Power: 8X
Objective Diameter: 32 mm
Exit Pupil: 4 mm
Field of View: 393 ft @ 1000 yards
Twilight Factor: 16
Eye Relief: 15.5 mm
Waterproof: Yes
Fogproof: Yes
Limited Lifetime Warranty
Features: The closed-bridge mid-sized roof-prism 8x32 mm Weaver Grand Slam binocular has fully-multi-coated lenses, armored housing, and extendable eyecups. Along with the large 12x50 mm for tripod viewing, the Grand Slam also has a 42 mm-objective three-position zoom that can be set at 8-, 12-, and 16X.
Manufacturer's Suggested Retail Price: $389.95
Estimated "Real World" Price: $374.99

Weaver Grand Slam 8x32 MM

Weaver Super Slam 10.5x45 MM

SUPER SLAM 10.5X45 MM

(also in 8.5x45 mm)
Weight: 31.6 oz
Length: 6 ¹/₃ in
Width: 5 ²/₃ in
Power: 10.5X
Objective Diameter: 45 mm
Exit Pupil: 4.3 mm
Field of View: 325 ft @ 1000 yards
Twilight Factor: 21.7
Eye Relief: 15 mm
Waterproof: Yes
Fogproof: Yes

Limited Lifetime Warranty
Features: The open-bridge Super Slam binocular has a rubber-armored cover on a magnesium housing. Lenses are ED glass with SHR metallic coating, and the prisms are made from BaK-4 glass and the higher quality SK glass. Includes focus lock for adjustments and extendable eyecups.
Manufacturer's Suggested Retail Price: $1114.49
Estimated "Real World" Price: $1099.99

Carl Zeiss Sports Optics

CONQUEST 8X50 MM T*

(also in 10x50)
Weight: 31.92 oz
Length: 7 ²/₅ in
Width: 5 ¼ in
Power: 8X
Objective Diameter: 50 mm
Exit Pupil: 6.25 mm
Field of View: 330 ft @ 1000 yards
Twilight Factor: 20
Eye Relief: 16 mm
Waterproof: Yes
Fogproof: Yes

Transferable Limited Lifetime Warranty
Features: The 50mm Conquest binocular, good for low-light conditions, has ZEISS T* multi-coating on the lenses and P* phase coating on the Abbe-Konig prisms. Rubber armored with twist-up eyecups for eyeglass or non-eyeglass wearers.
Manufacturer's Suggested Retail Price: $1349.99
Estimated "Real World" Price: $1349.99

Zeiss Conquest 8x50 MM

BINOCULARS

Carl Zeiss Sports Optics

www.zeiss.com/sports

CONQUEST 8X30 MM T*

(also in 10x30 mm)
Weight: 17.46 oz
Length: 5 ⅕ in
Width: 4 ½ in
Power: 8X
Objective Diameter: 30 mm
Exit Pupil: 3.75 mm
Field of View: 360 ft @ 1000 yards
Twilight Factor: 19.0
Eye Relief: 14.6 mm
Waterproof: Yes
Fogproof: Yes
Transferable Limited Lifetime Warranty
Features: The lightweight Conquest 30 mm binocular has ZEISS T* multi-coating on the lenses and P* phase coating on the Abbe-Konig prisms. Rubber armored with twist-up eyecups for eyeglass or non-eyeglass wearers.
Manufacturer's Suggested Retail Price: $649.99
Estimated "Real World" Price: $649.99

Zeiss Conquest 8x30 MM

Zeiss Conquest 10x40 MM

CONQUEST 10X40 MM T*

(also in 8x40)
Weight: 28.92 oz
Length: 6 in
Width: 5 in
Power: 10X
Objective Diameter: 40 mm
Exit Pupil: 4 mm
Field of View: 315 ft @ 1000 yards
Twilight Factor: 20.0
Eye Relief: 16 mm
Waterproof: Yes
Fogproof: Yes
Transferable Limited Lifetime Warranty
Features: The mid-sized Conquest binocular has ZEISS T* multi-coating on the lenses and P* phase coating on the Abbe-Konig prisms. Rubber armored with twist-up eyecups for eyeglass or non-eyeglass wearers.
Manufacturer's Suggested Retail Price: $999.99
Estimated "Real World" Price: $999.99

CONQUEST 10X56 MM T*

(also in 8x56)
Weight: 33.5 oz
Length: 7 ¼ in
Width: 5 ½ in

Ziess Conquest 10x56 MM

Power: 10X
Objective Diameter: 56 mm
Exit Pupil: 5.6 mm
Field of View: 315 ft @ 1000 yards
Twilight Factor: 23.7
Eye Relief: 16 mm
Waterproof: Yes
Fogproof: Yes
Transferable Limited Lifetime Warranty
Features: The largest of the Conquest binoculars, though only slight heavier than the 50 mm, for extreme low-light conditions, the 56 mm has ZEISS T* multi-coating on the lenses and P* phase coating on the Abbe-Konig prisms. Rubber armored with twist-up eyecups for eyeglass or non-eyeglass wearers.
Manufacturer's Suggested Retail Price: $1499.99
Estimated "Real World" Price: $1499.99

CONQUEST 15X45 MM T*

(also in 12x45)

Zeiss Conquest 15x45 MM T*

Weight: 21.87 oz
Length: 6 ⅖ in
Width: 4 ⁷⁄₁₀ in
Power: 15X
Objective Diameter: 45 mm
Exit Pupil: 3.0 mm
Field of View: 192 ft @ 1000 yards
Twilight Factor: 26.0
Eye Relief: 14.6 mm
Waterproof: Yes
Fogproof: Yes
Transferable Limited Lifetime Warranty
Features: The Conquest binocular has ZEISS T* multi-coating on the lenses and P* phase coating on the Abbe-Konig prisms, and at 15x can work as a spotting scope for long-range glassing. Rubber armored with twist-up eyecups for eyeglass or non-eyeglass wearers.
Manufacturer's Suggested Retail Price: $1099.99
Estimated "Real World" Price: $1099.99

BINOCULARS

Carl Zeiss Sports Optics

www.zeiss.com/sports

CONQUEST 10X25 MM T*

(also in 8x20)
Weight: 7.05 oz
Length: 4 ⅓ in
Width: 3 ⅘ in
Power: 10X
Objective Diameter: 25 mm
Exit Pupil: 2.5 mm
Field of View: 264 ft @ 1000 yards
Twilight Factor: 15.8
Eye Relief: 15 mm
Waterproof: Sealed Against Spray Water.
Fogproof: No
Transferable Limited Lifetime Warranty
Features: The compact Conquest binocular has ZEISS T* multi-coating on the lenses and P* phase coating on the prisms. With fold-down rubber eyecups for eyeglass or non-eyeglass wearers.
Manufacturer's Suggested Retail Price: **$499.99**
Estimated "Real World" Price: **$499.99**

CONQUEST HD 8X42 MM

(also in 10x42 mm)
Weight: 24.7 oz
Length: 6 ½ in
Width: 4 ¾ in
Power: 8X
Objective Diameter: 42 mm
Exit Pupil: 5.25 mm
Field of View: 384 ft @ 1000 yards
Twilight Factor: 18.3
Eye Relief: 18 mm
Waterproof: Yes (to 400 mbar)
Fogproof: Yes
Warranty: Limited Lifetime Transferable
Features: Conquest HD Porro-prism binocular in 8x42 mm employs Zeiss T* multi-coating, dielectric coatings on mirrors, and LotuTec water protection on the lenses and promises an extra-wide field of view. The aluminum housings are armored with an ergonomically designed gripping area, and the binocular features a large focus wheel and close focus down to eight feet.
Manufacturer's Suggested Retail Price: **$1055.54**

Zeiss Conquest Compacts 10x25 MM T*

Zeiss Conquest HD 8x42 MM

Zeiss Victory 8x32 MM T* FL

Estimated "Real World" Price: **$949.99**

VICTORY 8X32 MM T* FL

(also in 10x32)
Weight: 19.75 oz
Length: 4 ⅗ in
Width: 4 ½ in
Power: 8X
Objective Diameter: 32 mm
Exit Pupil: 4 mm
Field of View: 420 ft @ 1000 yards
Twilight Factor: 16
Eye Relief: 15.5 mm

Waterproof: Yes
Fogproof: Yes
Transferable Limited Lifetime Warranty
Features: The lightweight 32 mm Victory T* FL binocular uses ZEISS T* multi-coating on the lenses and P* phase coating on the prisms along with ZEISS FL glass and LotuTec® lens coating. With four-position twist-up locking eyecups for eyeglass or non-eyeglass wearers.
Manufacturer's Suggested Retail Price: **$1849.99**
Estimated "Real World" Price: **$1849.99**

BINOCULARS

Carl Zeiss Sports Optics

www.zeiss.com/sports

VICTORY 10X56 \MM T* FL

(also in 8x56)
Weight: 44.09 oz
Length: 7 ⅖ in
Width: 5 ⁷⁄₁₀ in
Power: 10X
Objective Diameter: 56 mm
Exit Pupil: 5.6 mm
Field of View: 330 ft @ 1000 yards
Twilight Factor: 20.5
Eye Relief: 16 mm
Waterproof: Yes
Fogproof: Yes
Transferable Limited Lifetime Warranty
Features: The 56 mm Victory T* FL binocular, made for extreme low-light conditions, uses ZEISS T* multi-coating on the lenses and P* phase coating on the prisms along with ZEISS FL glass and LotuTec® lens coating. With four-position twist-up locking eyecups for eyeglass or non-eyeglass wearers.
Manufacturer's Suggested Retail Price: **$2299.99**
Estimated "Real World" Price: **$2299.99**

Zeiss Victory 10x56 MM T*

Zeiss Victory 10x42 MM T* FL

VICTORY 10X42 MM T* FL

(also in 7x42 and 8x42)
Weight: 26.98 oz
Length: 6 ⅓ in
Width: 5 in
Power: 10X
Objective Diameter: 42 mm
Exit Pupil: 4.2 mm
Field of View: 330 ft @ 1000 yards
Twilight Factor: 20.5
Eye Relief: 16 mm
Waterproof: Yes
Fogproof: Yes
Transferable Limited Lifetime Warranty
Features: The mid-sized 42 mm Victory T* FL binocular uses ZEISS T* multi-coating on the lenses and P* phase coating on the prisms along with ZEISS FL glass and LotuTec® lens coating. With four-position twist-up locking eyecups for eyeglass or non-eyeglass wearers.
Manufacturer's Suggested Retail Price: **$1999.99**
Estimated "Real World" Price: **$1999.99**

Zeiss Victory Compacts 10x25 MM T*

VICTORY 10X25 MM T*

(also in 8x20)
Weight: 8.82 oz
Length: 4 ⅓ in
Width: 3 ⅘ in
Power: 10X
Objective Diameter: 25 mm
Exit Pupil: 2.5 mm
Field of View: 285 ft @ 1000 yards
Twilight Factor: 15.8
Eye Relief: 13.5 mm
Waterproof: Yes

Fogproof: Yes
Transferable Limited Lifetime Warranty
Features: The shirt-pocket-sized Victory T* FL binocular uses ZEISS T* multi-coating on the lenses and P* phase coating on the. With twist-up locking eyecups for eyeglass or non-eyeglass wearers.
Manufacturer's Suggested Retail Price: **$699.99**
Estimated "Real World" Price: **$699.99**

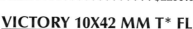

BINOCULARS

IRON SIGHTS

lass lenses are not required to make an optical device, which simply means a device that assists sight. The earliest optical devices may have been as simple as sticks that ancient navigators used for sighting the stars, which later were refined into the quadrant and the sextant. Piles of rocks were used to mark the position of the solstice, leading to massive structures such as Stonehenge and the Egyptian and Mayan pyramids that were in fact instruments for observing astronomical alignments.

On a human scale Arabs developed the *alidade*, made of metal, wood, or sometimes ivory, which used a front and rear sight to line up a distant object with a reference point to determine an angle on a horizontal or vertical plane. The concept of the alidade could be found in the first gunsight which was probably similar to the front bead on a shotgun, with the shooter's eye serving as the rear sight, giving us a term like "drawing a fine bead," meaning to hold the bead partially covered by the barrel for a longer range shot. When firearms became capable of greater accuracy, the need for more precise sights grew. A fixed front blade

and rear notch or V could be adjusted for elevation by filing and for windage by "drifting"–tapping on a sight in a sliding dovetail joint on the barrel to move it left or right. Advancements included notched elevators on the rear sight, like those often seen on Winchester lever-action rifles. Further refinements included tang and ladder sights that could be screwed up and down for elevation, and sometimes also for windage, and aperture sights for precision shooting, on the theory that a peep or aperture sight causes the eye to see a target in sharper detail.

Iron or open sights vary in design with application. Some sights, like the "express" found on double rifles, are for fast pointing in dangerous situations rather than for extreme accuracy. Rifles for combat will often have a "back up" iron sight as added insurance to go along with a telescopic or reflex sight. And aperture sights are still favored by many hunters and are used in different kinds of target-shooting competitions, producing often startling precision: In Olympic 10-meter air-rifle competition the "10 ring" is actually a 0.5 mm dot, so the sight has to be capable of nearly microscopic accuracy.

C. Sharps Arms

www.csharpsarms.com

DELUXE LONG RANGE TANG WITH WINDAGE

(also available in Mid Range)

Length: 6 in
Width: ⁵/₈ in
Weight: 5 oz
Elevation and Windage Adjustment
Range: 24 MOA windage, elevation to approximately 1100 meters
Features: C. Sharps's Deluxe Long Range tang sight is calibrated for windage by a screw adjustment on the top of the elevator body. The sight includes an elevation lock screw on the left side, a large 1 ¹/₈-in eyecup, and a knurled take-down screw for installation and removal of the sight staff. Elevation range varies according to the rifle's caliber, barrel length, and height of the front sight.
Manufacturer's Suggested Retail Price: $290

NEW IDEAL SPORTING TANG

Length: 2 in
Width: ½ in
Weight: 4 oz
Elevation and Windage Adjustment
Range: 12 MOA windage and elevation to approximately 300 to 400 yds
Features: The C. Sharps Arms New Ideal Sporting Tang is a hunting and sporting sight featuring screw-type windage and elevation adjustments. The sight can be folded down along the tang without interfering with the use of optional barrel sights. The elevation range depends on caliber, barrel length, and the height of the front sight.
Manufacturer's Suggested Retail Price: $120

SOULE STYLE LONG RANGE TANG

(also available in Mid Range)

Length: 6 in
Width: ⁵/₈ in
Weight: 6 oz
Elevation and Windage Adjustment
Range: 24 MOA windage, elevation to approximately 1500 meters
Features: The C. Sharps Soule sight (Soule is pronounced "Sool" or more properly "SOO-lay" and varies from other vernier—defined as a short scale made to slide along the divisions of a

C. Sharps Deluxe Long Range Tang with Windage

C. Sharps Soule Style Long Range Tang

graduated instrument for indicating parts of divisions—sights by having its windage adjustment done by a rotating drum on the sight base) is screw adjustable for 24 MOA of windage from left or right of center and can be adjusted for elevations out to 1500 meters, depending on a rifle's caliber, barrel length, and height of the front sight—for proper sight picture with the Soule an elevated front sight, like the C. Sharps's Arms Globe sight, is required. Includes a large 1 ¹/₈-in eyecup (providing positive locking elevation) and is available with different bases for mounting on either Sharps or Winchester rifles.
Manufacturer's Suggested Retail Price: $440

C. Sharps New Ideal Sporting Tang

C. Sharps Sporting Buckhorn Rear Barrel Sight

SPORTING BUCKHORN REAR BARREL SIGHT

Length: 2 in
Width: ½ in
Weight: 2 oz
Elevation and Windage Adjustment
Range: Driftable windage and ladder elevation out to approximately 300 to 400 yds
Features: C. Sharps's Sporting Buckhorn sight is 2 ¹/₁₀-in long and provides a fixed buckhorn sight as well as an adjustable flip-up elevator body. Windage is driftable and is available for Sharps (⁷/₁₆-in dovetail) and Winchester (³/₈-in dovetail) rifles.
Manufacturer's Suggested Retail Price: $95

IRON SIGHTS

C. Sharps Arms

www.csharpsarms.com

GLOBE SIGHT WITH WIND GAUGE AND SPIRIT LEVEL

Length: 1 in
Width: ¾ in
Weight: 1 oz
Elevation Adjustment Range: 24 MOA from center
Features: The C. Sharps Globe Sight has a fine adjustment for windage and a spirit level to prevent canting of the rifle. The sight also comes with a set of ten different styles of aperture inserts.

Manufacturer's Suggested Retail Price: $295

C. Sharps Globe Sight with Wind Gauge and Spirit Level

Davide Pedersoli & C.

www.davide-pedersoli.com

U.S. MODEL 1879 SPRINGFIELD TRAPDOOR REAR SIGHT, MODEL USA 473

Features: Sometimes referred to as "Buckhorn" style. Used on Trapdoor rifles from 1874 until superseded by Buffington style in 1884. Side ramps are graduated to 500 yards and the ladder to 1500 yards. Slide has windage adjustment.

Manufacturer's Suggested Retail Price: $147

"SOULE TYPE" MIDDLE RANGE SET, MODEL USA 170

Elevation Adjustment: 3 inches
Features: Wooden-box set including Soule XL Middle Range Sight; Tunnel Front Sight with a micrometric screw for windage adjustment, spirit level, and fifteen interchangeable inserts; Professional "Hadley Style" Eyepiece with eight varying diameter viewing holes, depending on available light, on a rotating disk which can be selected without disassembling or loosening the eyepiece, and a rubber ring on the eyepiece; six interchangeable glass bubbles (spirit level) with different colors for varying light conditions.

Manufacturer's Suggested Retail Prices: $848

IRON SIGHTS

Davide Pedersoli USA 473

Davide Pedersoli USA 170

Davide Pedersoli & C.

www.davide-pedersoli.com

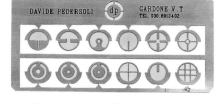

Davide Pedersoli USA 425

Davide Pedersoli-USA 409

SPIRIT LEVEL TUNNEL SIGHT ADJUSTABLE WITH 12 INSERTS SET, MODEL USA 425

Features: Spirit level tunnel sight with micrometer adjustment for windage, equipped with twelve interchangeable inserts.

Manufacturer's Suggested Retail Price: $229

FIBER OPTIC FRONT AND REAR SIGHT, MODEL USA 409

Features: Front sight and rear sight set for muzzleloading rifles (Model 410 for breechloaders). Front sight with dovetail base; rear sight with base for octagonal barrel.

Manufacturer's Suggested Retail Prices: $127

ENGLISH REAR SIGHT, MODEL USA 428

Features: Rear sight with convex base, with two adjustable and folding leaves.

Manufacturer's Suggested Retail Prices: $142

Davide Pedersoli-USA 428

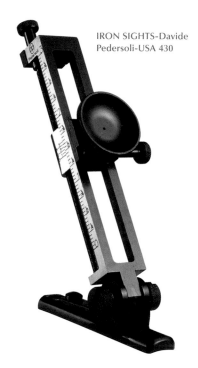

IRON SIGHTS-Davide Pedersoli-USA 430

UNIVERSAL CREEDMOOR SIGHT, MIDDLE AND LONG RANGE, MODELS USA 465 AND 430

Distance between the two mounting holes: 2 ³/₁₆ up to 2 ⁵/₁₆ inches
Elevation Adjustments: 2 and 3 inches

Features: Tang sight with elevation and windage adjustment in the eye piece. For long-distance target shooting both with muzzle-loading and breech-loading rifles.

Manufacturer's Suggested Retail Prices: . . . . $244 and $248

Kelley Sights

www.kelleysights.com

LONG RANGE SOULE SIGHT

(also in mid-range Soule, Schuetzen Soule, custom staff heights, and globe front sights)
Length: 5 in
Width: ⁵/₈ in
Elevation and Windage Adjustment Range: 27 ½-MOA on both sides of zero; 300 MOA of elevation.
Features: The elevation adjustment on

the Kelley Long Range Soule Sight uses a silicon bronze bearing. Base, mainframe, eyecup, and carrier are color case hardened. Silicon bronze knobs, windage bearings, and elevation bearings. Extra interchangeable bases available. Elevation calibrations are in one MOA. Windage is in ½ MOA.

Manufacturers Suggested Retail Price: $490

Kelley Long Range Soule Sight

Lee Shaver

www.leeshavergunsmithing.com

17 SERIES FRONT SIGHT (IN THREE HEIGHTS AND SEVERAL DOVETAIL SIZES)

Length: 1 5/16 in, front to rear

Height: Three heights available measured to center of aperture—1/2 in, 5/8 in, and .85 in

Width: 1 5/16 in across the level; 9/16 in across sight body

Features: The Lee Shaver 17 Series front sights feature a removable level (set inside the tunnel of the sight for shade and protection) to eliminate canting of the rifle. Each front sight is finished in a dull-matte non-reflective finish and comes with a set of ten interchangeable inserts that may be stacked within the sight for custom sight pictures.

Manufacturer's Suggested Retail Price: $85

ECONOMY SOULE-TYPE TANG SIGHT

(also in Long Range, Mid Range, and Muzzle Loader versions)

Weight: 4 oz

Length: Long Range 5 1/4 in; Mid Range 4 in

Width: 1 3/4 in across the windage knobs.

Elevation and Windage Adjustment Range: Windage movement is 1/4 in either way from center. The actual MOA movement is dependent on the sight radius of the rifle. Elevation adjustment is 2 3/4 in of vertical travel on the long range, and 1 1/4 in of travel on the mid range. The long range is suitable for up to 1200 yards on most rifles, and the mid range is suitable for up to 600 yards or more.

Features: The Lee Shaver Economy Soule-type tang sight features the micrometer movements of the "Soule" type windage adjuster, graduated in .0025 in increments. This equates to a 1/4 MOA movement on most rifles. It also features a standard 1 1/16 in-diameter eye cup. This sight is available with the proper bases for nearly all original and reproduction black-powder-cartridge rifles, and an assortment of bases for muzzle loaders as well. Advertises itself as not just a stripped down version of Lee Shaver's Supergrade sight, but as being

designed to provide a quality sight to those on a budget.

Manufacturer's Suggested Retail Price: $225

PH SERIES FRONT SIGHT

(available in several dovetail sizes)

Weight: 1 oz

Length: 1 1/4 in, front to rear

Height: 9/10 in to top of sight; from bottom of dovetail to center of aperture is .55 in

Width: 1 1/16 in across the level; 3/4 in across sight body.

Product Description: The Lee Shaver PH Series front sight is designed for those who desire a slightly larger and longer front sight. It features a removable level to eliminate canting of the rifle; the level is set inside the tunnel of the sight for shade and protection. Each front sight is finished in a dull-matte non-reflective finish and includes a set of ten interchangeable inserts that may be stacked within the sight for custom sight pictures.

Manufacturer's Suggested Retail Price: $100

Lee Shaver 17 Series Front Sight

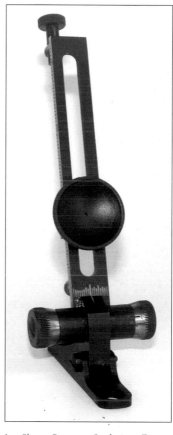

Lee Shaver Economy Soule-type Tang

Lee Shaver PH Series Front Sight

IRON SIGHTS

Lee Shaver

www.leeshavergunsmithing.com

SUPERGRADE SOULE-TYPE TANG SIGHT

(also in Long Range, Mid Range, and Muzzle Loader versions)

Weight: 5 oz

Length: Long Range 5 ¾ in; Midrange 4 ¼ in

Width: 1 ¾ in across the windage knobs.

Elevation and Windage Adjustment Range: Windage movement is ¼ in either way from center. The actual MOA movement is dependent on the sight radius of the rifle. Elevation adjustment is 2 ¾ in of vertical travel on the long range, and 1 ¼ in of travel on the mid range. The long range is suitable for up to 1200 yards on most rifles, and the mid range is suitable for up to 600 yards or more.

Features: The Lee Shaver Supergrade Soule type tang sight features the micrometer movements of the "Soule" type windage adjuster, graduated in .0025 in increments. This equates to a 1/4 MOA movement on most rifles. It also features a 1 ¼ inch-diameter eye cup with nine different size peep holes that rotate into place for various light conditions. Includes an adjustable detent spring that allows the staff to be adjusted to suit the shooter. This sight is available with the proper bases for nearly all original and reproduction black-powder-cartridge rifles, and an assortment of bases for muzzle loaders as well.

Manufacturer's Suggested Retail Price: $385

WINDAGE ADJUSTABLE FRONT SIGHT

Weight: 2 oz

Length: 1⁵/₁₆ in, front to rear

Height: Available in four heights from 1 in to 1 ⅓ in, measured from bottom of dovetail to center of aperture

Width: 1⁵/₁₆ in across the level; 1 ²/₅ in across windage knobs

Windage Adjustment Range: Windage adjustment of ⅛ in, in either direction from center.

Features: The Lee Shaver Windage Adjustable Series front sight features our 17 Series sight on an 1880's style windage adjuster that is graduated with a vernier scale to ¹/₁₀₀ in. It features a removable level to eliminate canting of the rifle, set inside the tunnel of the sight for shade and protection. Each front sight is finished in a dull-matte non-reflective finish, and comes with a set of ten interchangeable inserts that may be stacked within the sight for custom sight pictures.

Manufacturer's Suggested Retail Price: $165

HADLEY STYLE EYE CUPS

Weight: 1 oz

Length: ⁷/₁₆ in, front to rear of body of eye cup

Diameter: 1 ¼ in

Features: The Lee Shaver Hadley Style eye cups feature nine holes of various sizes from diameters of .03 in to .09 in, on a wheel that allows them to rotate and lock into place for varying light conditions, and sight pictures. They also feature a rubber-padded ring in the rim of the eye cup to protect shooting glasses from damage. These eye cups are available for most makes of tang sights.

Manufacturer's Suggested Retail Price: . . . . $75-$100

Lee Shaver Supergrade Soule-type Tang

Lee Shaver Hadley Style Eye Cups

Lee Shaver Windage Adjustable Front Sight

Lee Shaver

www.leeshavergunsmithing.com

SIGHT INSERT SETS

Length: Steel inserts of .010 in-thick spring steel.

Diameter: Variable according to sight they fit

Features: The Lee Shaver Sight Inserts are manufactured from .010 in spring steel to fit Shaver own sights and also current and obsolete sights made by Lyman, Redfield, Anschutz, Parker Hale, and others. They are offered in styles ranging from an assortment set, to a set of round apertures, to an unusual set made to fit around the silhouette animals for black-powder-rifle cartridge (BPCR) use.

Manufacturer's Suggested Retail price: $20

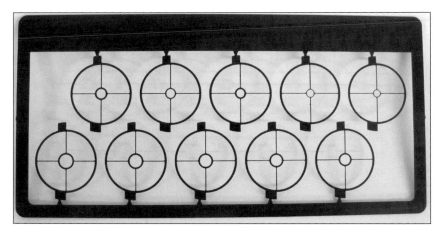

Lee Shaver Sight Insert Sets

Lyman Products Corp.

www.lymanproducts.com

57 RECEIVER SIGHT

Elevation and Windage Adjustment Range: Approximately ³⁄₈ in

Features: The Lyman 57 Receiver Sight is designed to fit bolt-action rifles with round receivers, such as the Remington 700 and Winchester Model 70. They feature ¼-minute audible click adjustments for windage and elevation, quick-release slide, coin-slotted "stayset" knobs, and two interchangeable aperture discs (large opening for hunting and small opening for target).

Manufacturer's Suggested Retail Price: $94.95

Estimated "Real World" Price: 80

66 RECEIVER SIGHT

Elevation and Windage Adjustment Range: Approximately ³⁄₈ in

Features: The Lyman 66 Receiver Sight is designed to fit rifles with flat receivers, such as the Marlin 336 and Winchester 94. They feature ¼-minute audible click adjustments for windage and elevation, quick release slide, coin slotted "stayset" knobs, and two interchangeable aperture discs (large opening for hunting and small opening for target).

Manufacturer's Suggested Retail Price: $94.95

Estimated "Real World" Price: $80

Lyman 57 Receiver Sight

Lyman 66 Receiver Sight

Lyman Products Corp.

www.lymanproducts.com

90 MJT RECEIVER SIGHT

Elevation and Windage Adjustment Range: Approximately ⅜ in
Product Description: The Lyman 90 MJT Receiver Sight is designed to fit most .22 rimfire rifles with round receivers. They feature ¼-minute audible click adjustments for windage and elevation, quick-release slide, large knurled target knobs, and a large ⅞-in diameter non-glare aperture disc with a .040-in opening.

Manufacturer's Suggested Retail Price: **$94.95**
Estimated "Real World" Price: **$80**

#2 TANG SIGHT

Elevation Adjustment Range: .800-in maximum adjustment
Features: The Lyman #2 Tang Sight is designed to fit lever action rifles such

Lyman 90 MJT Receiver

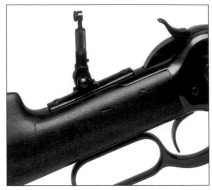

Lyman #2 Tang

as the Winchester 94 and the Marlin 336. They feature all-steel construction and are supplied with two aperture discs. One has a .093-in opening for fast target acquisition for hunting and one with a .040-in opening for target use. The sight is adjustable for eleva-

tion and the elevation post can be locked into position using the two knurled adjustment sleeves.

Manufacturer's Suggested Retail Price: **$89.95**
Estimated "Real World" Price: **$75**

Weaver

www.weaveroptics.com

AR-15/M16 FIXED BACK-UP

Features: The Weaver AR-15/M16 Back-Up switches from precision to CQB aperture. The main body is constructed of Type III hard-coat anodized 6061 T6 aluminum with manganese phosphate-coated steel components. The sight is fully compatible with Mil-Spec front sights and the ½ MOA clicks are calibrated for carbine length sight radius. Has a large clamp for stable attachment.

Manufacturer's Suggested Retail Prices: **$80.49**

Weaver AR15-M16 Fixed Back-up

NIGHT VISION

*A*n exemplary tale: One summer night at around the ages of eight and ten, my younger brother and I resolved to camp out in the backyard. In the dark we struck out into the erstwhile orange grove behind our house with our kapok sleeping bags and ribbed-aluminum flashlights. Halfway from the house the playing beams picked up the terrifying glare of eyes, two disks of demonic green fire. In a moment we were both in panicked flight to the back door. Inside the house we described the horror to our father in anxiety-ridden gasps, and he calmly explained that it was only the cat's eyes we'd seen. In fact, what we'd actually seen was one of nature's oldest night-vision devices.

Behind or within the retina of the eye of dark-stalking animals like house cats lies a layer of tissue called the *tapetum lucidum* (the "bright tapestry") that reflects light back through the retina, increasing the illumination available to the rods and cones, enhancing night vision. So when we shine light on such eyes we see glowing orbs, what is called "eyeshine."

Being able to "see in the dark" like cats is an advantage humans have long sought in military and shooting situations. And efforts to create artificial "tapeta lucida" date back three-quarters of a century.

Development of "active" optical night-vision devices began in the 1930s in the US, based on projected infrared light. By the end of World War II the German military was deploying the Zielgerät 1229 "Vampir" infrared night-vision system on the Sturmgewehr 44 assault rifle carried by Nachtjäger snipers; the Vampir utilized a large sight and required a 30-pound battery pack to power an infrared spotlight.

The Vietnam War saw the first "passive" night-vision optics that operated by enhancing ambient light. One example was the "Starlight" scope that functioned best on moonlit nights. Later "generations" of night-vision scopes use improved image-intensifying electronics which can boost the ambient light up to 50,000 times.

The other type of night-vision device employs thermal imaging. These "read" thermal radiation, such as body heat. Thermal-imaging devices can be extremely sensitive to variations in temperature and can detect them on the darkest nights and through rain or fog.

The tactical and law-enforcement applications of night-vision devices ought to be obvious. But more and more recreational shooters are finding legitimate uses for night-vision optics in the hunting of varmints and increasingly in the control of the country's exploding population of feral hogs. With devices even better than glowing cat's eyes available, even non-shooters are using them to see things that go bump in the night.

Bushnell

www.bushnell.com

EQUINOX 6X50 MM

(also in 4x40 mm and Generation 1 2x28 mm)
Weight: 20 oz.
Size: 7 ⁴/₅ in x 4 in x 2 ½ in
Power: 6X
Objective Diameter: 50 mm
Exit Pupil: 8.3 mm
Field of View: 23 ft @ 100 yds
Waterproof: Water-resistant
Fogproof: No
Two-Year Warranty
Features: The digital Bushnell Equinox 6x50 mm offers two night-vision options—the traditional green view for use in the darkest conditions and white imaging when ambient light is available. Uses a CCD ("charge-coupled device," like the image sensor found in astronomical telescopes to turn a charge into a digital value) rather than an image-intensifier tube and can view images out to ranges of almost 1000 feet. Has a water-resistant housing, long battery life, and includes a video out cable.
Manufacturer's Suggested Retail Price: **$649.95**
Estimated "Real World" Price: **$379.99**

STEALTHVIEW

Weight: 20.2 oz
Size: 6 ½ in x 4 in x 2 ⅓ in
Power: 5X
Objective Diameter: 42 mm
Exit Pupil: 8.4 mm
Field of View: 30 ft @ 100 yds
Waterproof: Weather-resistant
Fogproof: No
Two-Year Warranty
Features: The Bushnell StealthView has built-in infrared spotlight illuminators and advanced light-gathering technology. Effective in complete darkness up to 600 feet. Other notable features are the CMOS (CMOS is referred to as "complementary-symmetry metal-oxide-semiconductor"; in CMOS devices power is drawn only when the transistors switch from on to off, producing less waste heat) versus Generation 1 image-intensifier tube, in-view black-and-white micro display, weather-resistant housing, video output, and 2 to 8 hours of continuous run time (based on mode).
Manufacturer's Suggested Retail Price: **$683.95**
Estimated "Real World" Price: **$374.99**

STEALTHVIEW II

Weight: 13.4 oz.
Size: 6 in x 3 ⅖ in x 2 in
Power: 3X
Objective Diameter: 32 mm
Field of View: 70 ft @ 100 yds
Waterproof: Weather-resistant
Fogproof: No
Two-Year Warranty
Features: Bushnell's StealthView II features an LCD Color Night Vision, rather than the traditional green, and digital resolution and clarity; automatic infrared spotlight, and claims to be comparable to "Gen 2+" night vision. Includes 3X magnification, weather-resistant, rugged housing, viewing range of more than 300 feet, and a wide field of view.
Manufacturer's Suggested Retail Price: **$449.95**
Estimated "Real World" Price: **$239.99**

Bushnell StealthView II 3x32 MM

Bushnell Equinox 6x50 MM

Bushnell StealthView 5x42 MM

NIGHT VISION

Night Optics USA, Inc

www.nightoptics.com

D-740 4X NIGHT VISION WEAPON SCOPE, GEN 3 GATED

(also D-760 6X)

Product URL: http://www.nightoptics.com/no/product/NO-NS-740-3AG.htm
Weight: 38 oz
Dimensions: 9 in x 3 ½ x 4 in
Power: 4X
Lens System: 100 mm, f/1.5
Elevation and Windage Adjustments: ¼ MOA per click
Field of View: 525 ft @ 1000 yds
Image Intensifier: Generation 3 Autogated–Thin Film
Waterproof: Yes
Fog proof: Resistant
2-Year Limited Warranty
Features: The 4X Night Optics D-740 night-vision weapon scope features a waterproof, purge-capable housing; Mil-Dot illuminated red-on-green or amber-on-green reticle; high-grade multi-coated optics; manual gain control; and a quick-release, throw-lever mount. Zero retention is guaranteed on medium-caliber weapons (including .308 caliber). Also includes a hard case, two AA batteries, and the operating manual.
Manufacturer's Suggested Retail Price: **$4199.99**
Real World Price: **$3999.99**

PVS-14 GEN 3 GATED NIGHT VISION MONOCULAR

Product URL: http://www.nightoptics.com/no/product/NO-NM-P14-3AG.htm
Weight: 13.8 oz
Dimensions: 4 ½ in x 2 ¼ in x 2 in
Power: 1X (3X, 4X, or 5X optional)
Objective Diameter: 26 mm, f/1.2
Field of View: 2100 ft @ 1000 yds
Image Intensifier: Generation 3 Autogated
Waterproof: Yes
Fog proof: Resistant
2-Year Limited Warranty
Features: Currently in use by US Armed Forces, the Night Optics PVS-14 night-vision monocular can be used as a hand-held or hands-free single-eye goggle, or as a night vision weapon system when coupled to a daytime close-quarters battle sight. Each system ships with a fully adjustable Headmount Assembly and adaptor to allow right or left eye use. User controls include a 3-position switch (OFF/ON/Momentary and constant IR). The system's Generation 3 or Generation 2 (NO-6015 variant) image tube features automatic brightness control and has fully-automated sensors that shut off the unit if accidentally exposed to bright light. Electronics turn off the NO/PVS-14 when removed from the head or helmet mount or when shifted into to the "UP" position. Includes mil-spec optics, internal low-battery and IR indicators, sacrificial filter, de-mist shield, AA battery, lens tissues, operating manual, and hard case. Operates between minus-60 to 125 degree F. There is also an optional proprietary day-night adaptor (product URL: http://www.nightoptics.com/no/product/NO-NA-DN2.htm) available, allowing the night-vision device to swing to an alternate locked position on the side of the weapon. Recommended for use with medium height scope rings.
Manufacturer's Suggested Retail Price: **$3499.99**
Real World Price: **$3299.99**

Night Optics D-740 4X Night Vision Weapon Scope, Gen 3 Gated

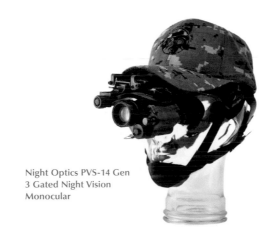

Night Optics PVS-14 Gen 3 Gated Night Vision Monocular

NIGHT VISION

Night Optics USA, Inc

www.nightoptics.com

LRB-7 GEN 3 GATED 10X LONG-RANGE NIGHT-VISION BINOCULAR

(also available in 6X,)

Product URL: http://www.nightoptics.com/no/product/NO-NB-LR10-3AG.htm

Weight: 6.6 lbs

Dimensions: 18 in x 5 ⅓ in x 6 in

Power: 10X

Lens System: 250 mm, f/2

Field of View: 262 ft @ 1000 yds

Image Intensifier: Generation 3 Autogated–Thin Film

Waterproof: Yes

Fog proof: Resistant

2-Year Limited Warranty

Features: The LRB-7 long-range night-observation device can acquire targets in excess of 3000 yards. Has AN/PVS-7 user controls and fully automated image tube protection. Minimum range of focus is 33 feet. Includes +4 to -4 diopter adjustment and IR illuminator. Powered by two AA batteries with 60 hours of life. Operates down to minus-40 degrees F up to 122 degrees F.

Manufacturer's Suggested Retail Price: **$5949.99**

Real World Price: **$5699.99**

TS-640 640X480 THERMAL WEAPON SCOPE

(also in 3X and in TS-320 320x240, 1X and 3X,)

Product URL: https://www.nightoptics.com/no/product/NO-TS-640-1.htm

Weight: 25 oz

Dimensions: 8 in x 2 ⅔ in x 2 ⅘ in

Power: 1X

Lens System: 640x480 pixels, f/1.2

Field of View: 735 ft @ 1000 yds

Image Intensifier: Uncooled Amorphous Silicon Core

Eye Relief: 27 mm

Waterproof: Yes

Fog proof: Resistant

2-Year Warranty

Features: The medium- to long-range Night Optics TS-640 640x480 Thermal Weapon Sight has a quick-release 1913 mount. The TS-640 combines a 640x480-pixel uncooled amorphous-silicon-micro bolometer detector with real-time image processing. The electronics are sealed in a lightweight, waterproof housing. Sensitive to less than 50 mK, the uncooled detector has a 7-14 μm spectral response. The TS-640 includes four instantly recalled user settings with reticles custom tailored for individual weapons with corresponding zero, color, brightness and contrast. Additional integrated features include a proximity sensor-triggered, power-conserving standby mode; shortcut key for quick access to "Favorites" settings; focus, brightness and contrast adjustments; white-hot/black-hot polarity, and digital zoom controls; and NTSC or PAL video-out capability. Powered by internal batteries or a 12v external power source, the TS-640 converts to a hand-held monocular with optional hand strap.

Manufacturer's Suggested Retail Price: **$14,999.99**

Real World Price: **$14,599.99**

Night Optics TS-640 640x480 Thermal Weapon Scope

Night Optics LRB-7 Gen 3 Gated 10X Long-Range Night-Vision Binoculars

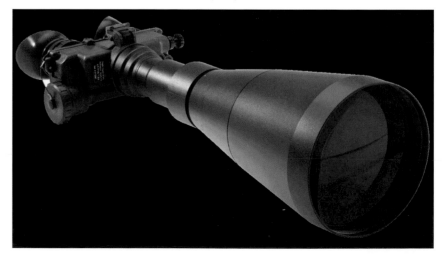

Night Optics USA, Inc

D-930 GEN 3AG AUTOGATED CLIP-ON NIGHT VISION SCOPE

Product URL: http://www.nightoptics.com/no/product/NO-NS-930-3AG.htm
Weight: 22 oz
Length: 7 ²/₅ in x 2 ¾ in x 2 ⁴/₅ in
Power: 1X
Lens: f/1.5
Field of View: 462 ft @ 1000 yds
Image Intensifier: Generation 3 Autogated–Thin Film
Waterproof: Yes
Fog proof: Resistant
Warranty: 2 Years
Features: The Night Optics D-930 night vision weapon sight converts a variety of 1 to 20X daytime riflescopes to full night-vision capability by mounting directly to the front of the scope or to a rail with an optional adaptor (D-930 throw-lever adaptor, for 40 or 50 mm objectives, product URL: http://www.nightoptics.com/no/product/NO-NA-TLA.htm), using the

Night Optics D-930 Gen 3AG Autogated Clip-On Night Vision Scope

aiming point of the daytime scope without the need for additional bore-sighting. The D-930 kit provides a custom-sized adaptor for quick-attachment to the objective lens of the daytime riflescope. A built-in 1913 Weaver rail provides a platform for a choice of optional IR illuminators or other accessories. Includes manual gain control, one 3-volt CR-123 battery, lens tissues, and operating manual. Operates down to -40 degrees F.

Manufacturer's Suggested Retail Price: $5249.99
Real World Price: $4999.99

Nitehog Systems, LLC

SNORT

Weight: 2.2 lbs with batteries
Length: 9 ⁹/₁₀ in with eyecup
Main Tube Body Diameter: 3 ²/₅ x 2 ⁴/₅ in
Power: 3X
Objective Diameter: 57 mm
Elevation and Windage Adjustments: ¼ MOA per click
Exit Pupil: 6 mm
Field of View: 13.6 degrees
Image Intensifier: Gen II, II+, or Gen III
Eye Relief: 2 ¹/₁₀ in
Waterproof: Yes
Fogproof: Yes
One-Year Warranty
Features: The SNORT is a true night-vision weapon scope with military-grade image-intensifier technology. It has multiple night-vision options (Gen II, Gen II+, or US-manufactured Gen III). The illuminated reticle is glass-etched in the first focal plane. Magnification is 3X with coated optics. Has a daylight filter that enables day-night capability. Comes with a quick-detachable mount for use on MIL-STD-1913 Picatinny weapon rail and a Picatinny mounting rail (MIL STD-1913) on the scope for lasers, lights, and other accessories.

Metal construction that is waterproof, dustproof, and shockproof and with protected reticle turrets with true elevation and windage adjustments. Compatible with a variety of calibers, including 5.56, 7.62, .300 WinMag, .338 Lapua Magnum, and others.

Manufacturer's Suggested Retail Price: . . . . $4800-$5300

Nitehog Snort

Nitehog Systems, LLC

www.nitehog.com

TUSKIR384

Weight: 2.9 lbs
Length: 7 ²/₅ in
Main Tube Body Diameter: 3 x 5 in
Power: 3X optical (6X and 12X with digital zoom)
Objective Diameter: 60 mm
Elevation and Windage Adjustments: 1 MOA per click
Field of View: 9.2 degrees horizontal x 6.9 degrees vertical
Sensor Material: VoX Microbolometer
Resolution—Pixel Count: 384 x 288
Eye Relief: 2 ³/₅ in
Waterproof: Yes
Fogproof: Yes
One-Year Warranty
Features: The Nitehog TUSKIR384 is a 384x288 Pixel Resolution Enhanced Thermal System with VoX Microbolometer 25µm detector technology. Alloy body shock-rated for most common MIL/LE rifle platforms. Will detect human beings beyond 1100 meters and has a human recognition range of 360 meters. Has four hours of continuous battery life with rechargeable LiOn battery. Includes quick-detach mounting system for MIL-STD-1913 Picatinny rails. Has video output to enable remote viewing, recording, or training. Can be used as handheld or tripod-mounted device with rail adapter.
Manufacturer's Suggested Retail Price: $15,000

WARTHOG

Weight: 1.90 lbs without batteries
Length: 7 ³/₅ in
Width: 2 ⁷/₁₀ in
Power: 1X
Objective Diameter: 50 mm
Sight Type: Unites with day optics used
Sight Size: Aligned to ½ MOA or better
Field of View: 13 degrees
Image Intensifier: Gen III
Waterproof: Yes

Fogproof: Yes
One-Year Warranty
Features: The Nitehog WARTHOG works in conjunction with existing daylight optics, providing night-vision capability only when need. Operator maintains consistent eye relief and shooting position. The body is metal and is shock-rated for most common MIL/LE Platforms. Comes with a quick-detachable mounting system for MIL-STD-1913 Picatinny rails. Can be used, as well, as a handheld or tripod-mounted device with a rail adapter. The Gen III night vision comes with image-intensifier-tube options.
Manufacturer's Suggested Retail Price: $5000

Nitehog TUSKIR384

Nitehog Warthog

RANGEFINDERS

The concept of the rangefinder is an old one, necessitated by warfare. Artillerymen needed to know the distances to their targets, which for reasons that need no explanation could not be stepped off, so the science of trigonometry was called upon. By triangulation, the angles and distances to a particular point could be arrived at. To determine these angles, measuring devices were employed, the most famous one and the one used from the late sixteenth century into the nineteenth century being the graphometer. The graphometer consisted of a brass graduated semicircle with two alidades–the flat strips, described in the ironsights section, with sights that revolve around the radius of the semicircle, the name meaning "sighting rods" from the Arab word al-'idāda.

The graphometer was not what is assumed to be an optical instrument only to the degree to which it did not have lenses, unless the lens covering the compass that was usually a part of the device counts. Optical rangefinders, known as coincidence rangefinders (or CRF), came into use in the early nineteenth century. In a CRF two images of the same target, seen at different angles, would be brought together by the viewer until they overlapped in the field of view, and the distance recorded by the device could then be read. The two image viewers on these CRFs could be anywhere from three to dozens of feet apart, depending on how accurate the measurements had to be.

Credit for the very first "short-base" CRF goes to a pair of English professors who entered a competition held in 1888 by the British War Office to design a CRF that an infantryman could carry; but when the Army rejected it, the Royal Navy adopted a modified version which at the outbreak of World War I was carried on every British battleship and battlecruiser. Soon all navies had such rangefinders on board.

CRFs were state-of-rangefinding-art until the development of the laser. Einstein is credited with laying the theoretical foundations for the laser in his work of almost a century ago. The working laser was developed in the mid-1950s and by the mid-1960s it was being used in rangefinders which projected a narrow beam of laser light and then measured the time it took for the light to reflect off the target and return to the device, giving the distance to the target. The ultimate, so far, refinement of the laser for shooters and hunters is the rangefinding binocular that combines the optical advantages of a binocular with a rangefinder in a single device. See it, range it, all in one.

Bushnell

www.bushnell.com

BOWHUNTER CHUCK ADAMS EDITION

(also in RealTree AP camouflage)
Size: 1 ⁴/₅ in x 3 ⁴/₅ in x 3 in
Weight: 5.3 oz
Power: 4X
Range: 5-850 yds
Objective Diameter: 20mm
Exit Pupil: 5 mm
Eye Relief: 17 mm
Field of View: 430 ft @ 1000 yds
Twilight Factor: 9
Waterproof: Rainproof
Fogproof: No
Two-Year Warranty
Features: The light and compact Bowhunter Chuck Adams Edition laser rangefinder includes Angle Range Compensation (ARC). This unit simultaneously displays line-of-sight, angle and true horizontal distance from 5-99 yards at inclinations and declinations of 90 degrees to within 1 degree of angle and 1 yard of distance. Able to read deer-sized game out to 200 yards. Multi-coated optics.
Manufacturer's Suggested Retail Price: $334.95
Estimated "Real World" Price: $199.99

ELITE 1600 ARC

Size: 1 ¾ in x 5 in x 3 ¾ in
Weight: 12.1 oz
Power: 7X
Range: 5-1600 yds
Objective Diameter: 26mm
Exit Pupil: 3.7 mm
Twilight Factor: 13.5
Waterproof: Yes
Fogproof: Yes
Two-Year Warranty
Features: The Bushnell Elite 1600 ARC comes with both a bow mode that reads "shoots-like" horizontal distance from 5 to 99 yards and a rifle mode that calculates bullet drop and holdover, customizable to the zeroed range of a rifle using Variable Sight-In distance technology. Angle-reading range is from +90 degrees to -90 degrees to a stated accuracy of within 1 degree. The rangefinder has three selective targeting modes—Standard Scan, BullsEye, and Brush— and reads reflective surfaces to 1600 yards, trees to 1000, and deer-sized animals to

500 yards within 1 yard. Has fully multi-coated optics and Vivid Display Technology, along with twist-up eyepiece and diopter adjustment.
Manufacturer's Suggested Retail Price: $843.95
Estimated "Real World" Price: $459.99

LEGEND 1200 ARC

Size: 1.7" x 4.3" x 2.9"
Weight: 7.4 oz.
Power: 6x
Range: 5-1200 yds.
Objective Diameter: 24mm
Waterproof: Yes
Fogproof: Yes
Two-Year Warranty
Features: In ranging distance and ballistic capability, no unit in the market packs this much power in a format this handy. The Bushnell Legend 1200 ARC has built-in ARC Bow and Rifle modes, combining features typically offered in separate units. In Bow Mode, the Legend provides true horizontal distance from 5-99 yards. In Rifle Mode, it provides bullet-drop and holdover information. Weather is never an issue, thanks to its fully waterproof construction and RainGuard HD anti-fog technology. The Legend is available in either RealTree AP camouflage or black.
Manufacturer's Suggested Retail Price: $587.95
Estimated "Real World" Price: $349.99

Bushnell Bowhunter Chuck Adams

Bushnell Elite 1600 ARC

Bushnell Legend 1000 ARC

SCOUT 1000 ARC (ALSO IN REALTREE AP CAMOUFLAGE)

Size: 1 ²/₃ in x 2 ⁴/₅ in x 4 ¹/₃ in
Weight: 6.6 oz.
Power: 5X
Range: 5-1000 yds
Objective Diameter: 24mm
Exit Pupil: 4.8 mm
Field of View: 367 ft @ 1000 yds
Twilight Factor: 11
Waterproof: Rainproof
Fogproof: Yes
Two-Year Warranty
Features: The Bushnell Scout 1000 ARC has selectable rifle and bow modes with the Angle Range Compensation (ARC). Gives true horizontal distance for bow from 5 to 99 yards, and for rifle it provides bullet drop and holdover in inches. Has Bullseye, Brush, and Scan modes and reads reflective surfaces to 1000 yards, trees to 650 yards, and deer-sized game to 325 yards to a stated accuracy of within 1 yard.
Manufacturer's Suggested Retail Price: $501.95
Estimated "Real World" Price: $299.99

Bushnell Scout 1000 ARC

Bushnell Sport 450

SPORT 450

(also in RealTree AP camouflage)
Size: 1 ³/₄ in x 4 in x 3 in
Weight: 7.4 oz
Power: 4X
Range: 5-999 yds
Objective Diameter: 20mm
Exit Pupil: 5 mm
Field of View: 320 ft @ 1000 yds
Twilight Factor: 9
Waterproof: Rainproof
Fogproof: No
Two-Year Warranty
Features: The Bushnell Sport 450 offers ranging on reflective objects to 999 yards, on trees to 450, and deer-sized animals to 200 yards with a stated accuracy of within 1 yard.
Manufacturer's Suggested Retail Price: $273.95
Estimated "Real World" Price: $154.99

SPORT 850

Size: 1 ²/₅ in x 3 ⁴/₅ in x 3 in
Weight: 6 oz

Bushnell Sport 850

Power: 4X
Range: 5-850 yds
Objective Diameter: 20mm
Exit Pupil: 5 mm
Field of View: 430 ft @ 1000 yds
Twilight Factor: 9
Waterproof: Rainproof
Fogproof: No
Two-Year Warranty
Features: Pocket sized, the Sport 850 has a single-button operation, ranging targets from 5 to 850 yards. Ranges are within 1 yard, and the 850 will measure reflective objects to 850 yards, trees to 600 yards, and deer-sized animals to 200 yards. Rainproof with anti-slip, sure-grip finish.
Manufacturer's Suggested Retail Price: $307.95
Estimated "Real World" Price: $189.99

RANGE FINDERS

Leica Sport Optics

www.leica-sportoptics.com

RANGEMASTER CRF 1600

(also in CRF 1000)
Weight: 8
Length: 4 ²⁄₅ in
Width: 1 ¹⁄₃ in
Power: 7X
Objective Diameter: 24 mm
Display: LED, red
Speed of Reading: <0.3 sec
Exit Pupil: 3.4 mm
Field of View: 347 ft @ 1000 yds
Twilight Factor: 13
Eye Relief: 20 mm
Waterproof: Yes
Fogproof: Yes
Two-Year Warranty
Features: For long-range shooting the CRF 1600 provides the temperature, angle, and atmospheric pressure at the site of the shot. It also has 12 ballistics curves that will match most cartridge trajectories.
Estimated "Real World" Price:..................$799.99

Leica Rangemaster CRF 1600

Leupold & Stevens, Inc.

www.leupold.com

RX-1000I TBR WITH DIGITALLY ENHANCED ACCURACY (DNA)

(also in RX-1000i TBR with DNA Mossy Oak Break-Up, RX-1000i with DNA, RX-750 TBR, RX-600, RX-IV, and RX-IV Boone and Crockett Edition)
Weight: 7.8 oz
Length: 3 ⁴⁄₅ in
Width: 2 ⁴⁄₅ in
Objective Diameter: 22 mm
Power: 6X
Display: Illuminated red OLED
Exit Pupil: 3.6 mm
Field of View: 320 ft @ 1000 yds
Twilight Factor: 11.5
Eye Relief: 14 mm
Weatherproof
2-Year Electronics Warranty
Features: The compact Leupold RX-1000i TBR with DNA features digitally enhanced ranging with a stated accuracy to ¹⁄₁₀ of a yard against all background colors and textures. Maximum range is 1000 yards on reflective targets to a minimum of 10 yards (700 yards for trees and 600 yards for wildlife). With the True Ballistic Range (TBR) feature, the RX-1000i can calculate the shot angle and provide the true ballistic range rather than the straight-line distance to the target.
Manufacturer's Suggested Retail Price:..................$399.99

Leupold RX-1000i TBR

Leupold & Stevens, Inc.

www.leupold.com

VENDETTA

Weight: 10 oz
Length: 3 ²/₅ in
Width: 1 ¹/₃ in
Display: Illuminated red LED
Weatherproof
1-Year Electronics Warranty
Features: The new Leupold Vendetta is a bow-mounted rangefinder activated by squeezing a pressure pad on the bow's grip, enabling a hunter to range a target with the bow at full draw, minimizing movement. Leupold's True Ballistic Range® feature calculates the shot angle and provides the incline-adjusted distance to the target, rather than the straight-line distance. Vendetta has a maximum range of 75 yards and a one-touch scan mode that allows a hunter to range an animal as it approaches. Minimum range is ten yards.
Manufacturer's Suggested Retail Price:. **$299.99**

Leupold Vendetta

Nikon Sport Optics.

www.nikonhunting.com/products/rangefinders

ARCHER'S CHOICE LASER

Weight: 6.3 oz
Length: 5 ¹/₁₀ in
Width: 1 ¹/₂ in
Power: 6X
Objective Diameter: 21 mm
Exit Pupil: 3.5 mm
Field of View: 315 feet @ 1000 yards.
Twilight Factor: 11.22
Eye Relief: 18.2 mm
Waterproof: Yes
Fogproof: Yes
25-Year Limited Warranty
Features: Nikon's Archer's Choice bowhunting rangefinder reads distances from five to 100 yards, depending on the target object's shape, surface texture and nature, and/or weather conditions, in .5 yard increments (.2 yards in Incline-Decline mode). The LCD display reads in meters or yards. Includes fitted neoprene case in RealTree APG.
Manufacturer's Suggested Retail Price:. **$400.95**
Estimated "Real World" Price:. **$259.95**

Nikon Archer's Choice

RANGE FINDERS

Nikon Sport Optics.
www.nikonhunting.com/products/rangefinders

ARCHER'S CHOICE MAX LASER

Weight: 6.9 oz
Length: 4 3/5 in
Width: 1 3/5 in
Power: 6X
Objective Diameter: 21 mm
Exit Pupil: 3.5 mm
Field of View: 393.75 feet @ 1000 yards
Twilight Factor: 11.22
Eye Relief: 18.3 mm
Waterproof: Yes
Fogproof: Yes
25-Year Limited Warranty
Features: The green Nikon Archer's Choice MAX's Active Brightness Control Viewfinder uses both traditional LCD (liquid-crystal display) and an orange LED (light-emitting diode) display. The rangefinder will apply automatically switched and controlled LED illumination to the LC (liquid crystal) characters by detecting the brightness within this viewing field as necessary for increased visibility. Nikon ID (Incline-Decline) technology compensates for various up or down shooting angles to plus-or-minus 89 degrees. Displays in .1 yard-meter increments, .2 out to 100 yards in ID mode. Has a priority mode for brush and grass. Single operation button, multi-coated optics, and powered by a CR2 lithium battery; battery chamber not waterproof. Comes with a neoprene case.
Manufacturer's Suggested Retail Price: $510.95
Estimated "Real World" Price: $329.95

MONARCH GOLD LASER1200 LONG RANGE 7X25 WATERPROOF/ FOGPROOF – TEAM REALTREE HARDWOODS GREEN

(also in black)
Weight: 9.8 oz
Length: 5 7/10 in
Width: 1 4/5 in
Power: 7X
Objective Diameter: 25 mm

Exit Pupil: 3.6 mm
Field of View: 262.5 feet @ 1000 yards
Twilight Factor: 13.22
Eye Relief: 18.6 mm
Waterproof: Yes
Fogproof: Yes
25-Year Limited Warranty
Features: Nikon's Monarch Gold Laser1200 will measure distances out to 1200 yards, depending on target object's size, shape, and surface texture and on weather conditions. Features a LCD display, continuous ranging feature, 7-power multi-coated optics with focusing diopter, Nikon Tru-Target Ranging System, and 34 mm laser-pulse receiver. Powered by one CR2 lithium battery; battery compartment not waterproof. Tripod adaptable.
Manufacturer's Suggested Retail Price: $684.95
Estimated "Real World" Price: $479.95

PROSTAFF 550 LASER

(also in Team RealTree APG HD camo)
Weight: 6.3 oz
Length: 5 1/10 in
Width: 1 1/2 in
Power: 6X
Objective Diameter: 21 mm
Exit Pupil: 3.5 mm
Field of View: 315 feet @ 1000 yards
Twilight Factor: 11.22
Eye Relief: 18.2 mm
Waterproof: Yes
Fogproof: Yes
25-Year Limited Warranty
Features: The green-rubber-armored lithium-battery-powered Nikon ProStaff 550 measures in yards and meters, out to 550 yards, depending on the reflective surface being beamed. Battery compartment is not waterproof.
Manufacturer's Suggested Retail Price: $312.95
Estimated "Real World" Price: $199.95

Nikon Archer's Choice MAX

Nikon Monarch Gold Laser1200

Nikon ProStaff 550

RANGE FINDERS

RIFLEHUNTER 550 LASER

(also in RealTree MAX-1 HD camo)
Weight: 6.3 oz
Length: 5 ¹⁄₁₀ in
Width: 1 ½ in
Power: 6X
Objective Diameter: 21 mm
Exit Pupil: 3.5 mm
Field of View: 315 feet @ 1000 yards
Twilight Factor: 11.22
Eye Relief: 18.2 mm
Waterproof: Yes
Fogproof: Yes
25-Year Limited Warranty
Features: The RifleHunter 550 incorporates Nikon's ID (Incline-Decline) Technology to indicate true yardage to compensate for bullet drop at varying shooting angles. Measures in meters or yards to ranges from 11 to 550 yards, depending on the reflectivity of the target. Reads in .2 yard-meter increments in ID and .5 yard in standard mode. LCD display. Battery compartment not waterproof.
Manufacturer's Suggested Retail Price: **$420.95**
Estimated "Real World" Price: **$289.95**

Nikon RifleHunter 550

Nikon RifleHunter 1000 LR

RIFLEHUNTER 1000 LASER

Weight: 6.9 oz
Length: 4 ³⁄₅ in
Width: 1 ³⁄₅ in
Power: 6X
Objective Diameter: 21 mm
Exit Pupil: 3.5 mm
Field of View: 393.75 ft @ 1000 yards
Twilight Factor: 11.2
Eye Relief: 18.3 mm
Waterproof: Yes
Fogproof: Yes
25-Year Limited Warranty
Features: The Nikon RifleHunter 1000 has a 1000-yard range in increments of .1 yard. It features Nikon Tru-Target Technology for ranging through grass

and brush. The Active Brightness Control Viewfinder offers both traditional LCD and an LED display, with automatic brightness control for LED illumination. The rangefinder will apply automatically switched and controlled LED illumination to the LC (liquid crystal) characters by detecting the brightness within this viewing field as necessary for increased visibility. Powered by a single CR2 lithium battery.
Manufacturer's Suggested Retail Price: **$530.95**
Estimated "Real World" Price: **$349.95**

Redfield

www.redfield.com

RAIDER 550

(also in Mossy Oak Break-Up Infinity camo)
Weight: 5 oz
Length: 3 ¾ in
Power: 6X
Objective Aperture: 23 mm
Exit Pupil: 3.3 mm
Field of View: 325 ft @ 1000 yds
Twilight Factor: 11
Eye Relief: 12 mm
Waterproof: Weatherproof
Redfield Electronics Warranty (Limited 1 Year)
Features: The monocular Raider 550

rangefinder provides straight-line distance measurements out to 550 yards on reflective targets. Other features include a fully multi-coated lens system and a scan mode that allows searching at a distance for a moving object, then following it. Powered by a CR-2 lithium camera battery. Has a 3-channel design, one-touch scan mode and is stated as accurate to 1 yard. Includes a belt case.
Manufacturer's Suggested Retail Price: **$169.99**

Redfield Raider 550

Swarovski Optik North

www.Swarovskioptik.com

LASER GUIDE 8X30 MM

Weight: 13.2 oz
Length: 4 7/10 in
Width: 3 9/10 in
Power: 8X
Objective Diameter: 30 mm
Exit Pupil: 3.8 mm
Field of View: 408 ft @ 1000 yards
Twilight Factor: 16
Eye Relief: 15 mm
Waterproof: Yes
Fogproof: Yes
Limited Lifetime Warranty
Features: Class 1 laser (eye safe), maximum range of 1600 yards, scan mode, adjustable eyecup, monocular.
Manufacturer's Suggested Retail Price: **$1110**
Estimated "Real World" Price: **$999**

Swarovski Laser Guide 8x30 MM

Carl Zeiss Sports Optics

www.zeiss.com/sports

Zeiss Victory 8x26 T* PRF

VICTORY 8X26 T* PRF RANGEFINDER

Weight: 10.93 oz
Length: 5 1/2 in
Width: 3 9/10 in
Power: 8X
Objective Diameter: 26 mm
Exit Pupil: 3.25 mm
Field of View: 330ft @ 1000 yards
Twilight Factor: 14.4
Eye Relief: 17.5 mm
Waterproof: Yes
Fogproof: No
Transferable Limited Lifetime Warranty on Mechanics, 2 Year

Warranty on Electronics
Features: The Victory 8x26 T* PRF monocular rangefinder has ZEISS T* multi-coating on the lenses as well as water-repelling LotuTec® lens coating. Twist-up locking eyecup for eyeglass or non-eyeglass wearers. One-touch rangefinder rated to 1300 yards. Beam divergence of 1 yard at 1000 yards. ZEISS BIS™ (Ballistic Information System) for holdover correction, and automatic rain-snow mode.
Manufacturer's Suggested Retail Price: **$699.99**
Estimated "Real World" Price: **$699.99**

VICTORY 8X45 T* RF BINOCULAR

(also in 10x45 mm)
Weight: 35 oz
Length: 6 ³/₅ in
Width: 5 ³/₁₀ in
Power: 8X
Objective Diameter: 45 mm
Exit Pupil: 5.6 mm
Field of View: 375ft @ 1000 yards
Twilight Factor: 19
Eye Relief: 16 mm
Waterproof: Yes
Fogproof: Yes
Transferable Limited Lifetime Warranty on Mechanics, 5 Year Warranty on Electronics
Features: Victory T* RF binocular rangefinder uses ZEISS T* multi-coating on the lenses and P* phase coating on the prisms, along with water-shedding exterior LotuTec® lens coating. Four position twist-up locking eyecups for eyeglass or non-eyeglass wearers. One-touch operation with the laser rated to 1300 yards and a beam divergence of 1 yard at 1000 yards. Includes ZEISS BIS™ (Ballistic Information System) for holdover correction and automatic rain-snow mode.
Manufacturer's Suggested Retail Price: $2899.99
Estimated "Real World" Price: $2899.99

VICTORY 10X56 T* RF BINOCULAR

(also in 8x56 mm)
Weight: 40.59 oz
Length: 7 ½ in
Width: 5 ½ in
Power: 10X
Objective Diameter: 56 mm
Exit Pupil: 5.6 mm
Field of View: 330ft @ 1000 yards
Twilight Factor: 23.7
Eye Relief: 16 mm
Waterproof: Yes
Fogproof: Yes
Transferable Limited Lifetime Warranty on Mechanics, 5 Year Warranty on Electronics
Features: This Victory T* RF binocular rangefinder is built for low light with a 56 mm objective. Has ZEISS T* multi-coating on the lenses and P* phase coating on the prisms, along with LotuTec® lens coating. With four position twist-up locking eyecups. The one-t0uch laser is rated to 1300 yards with a beam divergence of 1 yard at 1,000 yards, and comes with the ZEISS BIS™ (Ballistic Information System) for holdover correction and automatic rain-snow mode.
Manufacturer's Suggested Retail Price: $3399.99
Estimated "Real World" Price: $3399.99

Zeiss Victory 8x45 MM RF

Zeiss Victory 10x56 MM RF

RANGE FINDERS

REFLEX SIGHTS

The reflex or reflector sight grew out of the desire to have the wide field of view of iron sights, restricted only to the limit of the shooter's peripheral vision, without the retarding factor of having to align the front and rear sight before firing. "Witnessing" iron sights–lining up marks on the front and back sights or fitting the blade on the muzzle of a firearm into the notch or V on the back–takes time and requires precise head position, which can be a great disadvantage in certain types of shooting.

In an article in a scientific journal in 1902, the problems were expressed this way, "The object aimed at, the fore-sight, and the back-sight, are brought into line by the eye of the marksman, always with this defect, viz., that the eye is out of focus with respect to two of the points mentioned when focussed on the third." As early as the turn of the 20th century, according to the article, the problem was being "attacked by several leading experimentalists," culminating in 1900 in Irish optics-designer Sir Howard Grubb's patent for a "Collimating-telescope Gun-sight" [sic], described again in the article, as being "free from imperfections inherent in the old form of telescope-sights used on rifles."

Grubb's optical sight used reflecting surfaces to project a sighting reticle onto the shooter's eye, which was then superimposed "virtually" onto the target and could be adjusted to align it with the rifle's bore. This allowed the shooter to keep both eyes open and not have to worry about parallax. The military applications became clear in World War I when German fighter pilots used reflex sights on their Fokker airplanes's dual Spandau machine guns, leading to the "head-up" sighting displays employed on fighter planes to this day.

The point-and-shoot benefits of the 1X reflex sight soon became clear for both combat situations and even for shotgun shooters who would not have to be as conscious of keeping their heads down when they shot. Reflex sights were first illuminated by ambient light; and some very fine reflex sights, such as those made by Trijicon, still are with the technological advancement of fiber optics. It is Malmo, Sweden's, Aimpoint AB company that is credited with introducing the first commercial electronic light-emitting-diode (LED) "red dot" reflex sight in 1975. Curiously–or perhaps it's just the way the military bureaucracy has of doing things–despite red dots having the ideal characteristics for close-quarters combat, it took a generation before the US Army mounted them on combat rifles.

The red dot is in wide use, today, by tactical shooters in both the military and law enforcement, competitive combat shooters on their handguns and rifles, by trap and skeet shooters, muzzleloader hunters, pistol hunters, turkey hunters, big-game hunters who expect to be in fast-shooting close-range situations such as in deep woods, and even bowhunters.

Aimpoint

www.aimpoint.com and www.aimpointdealer.com

9000 SERIES (9000L and 9000SC)

Weight: 7.4 oz (9000SC) and 8.1 oz (9000L)
Length: 6 ³/₁₀ in (9000SC) and 7 ⁹/₁₀ in (9000L)
Main Tube Body Diameter: 30 mm
Power: 1X
Objective Diameter: 38 mm
Sight Type: Red dot
Sight Size: 2 MOA and 4 MOA
Exit Pupil: 38 mm
Twilight Factor: 6.2
Eye Relief: Unlimited
Waterproof: Yes
Fogproof: Yes
10-Year Warranty
Features: The Aimpoint 9000 Series includes a 10-position rotary intensity switch. The 9000L is primarily designed for bolt-action rifles with short, standard, or magnum-length actions, while the 9000SC is designed for use on semi-automatic shotguns and rifles. Both are built to withstand heavy recoil.
Manufacturer's Suggested Retail Price: **$442**
Estimated "Real World" Price: **$400**

COMP C3

Weight: 7.1 oz
Length: 4 ⁷/₁₀ in
Main Tube Body Diameter: 30 mm
Power: 1X
Objective Diameter: 38 mm
Sight Type: Red dot
Sight Size: 2 MOA
Twilight Factor: 6.2
Eye Relief: Unlimited
Waterproof: Yes
Fogproof: Yes
10-Year Warranty
Features: The Aimpoint CompC3 reflex sight is the lightest in its class. It mounts using a single ring on a single mount base, and provides 50,000 hours of operation on a single battery.
Manufacturer's Suggested Retail Price: **$476**
Estimated "Real World" Price: **$425**

HUNTER H34L

(other models include H34S, H30S, and H30L)

Weight: 9.2 oz
Length: 9 in
Main Tube Body Diameter: 34 mm
Power: 1X
Objective Diameter: 47 mm
Sight Type: Red dot
Sight Size: 2 MOA
Twilight Factor: 6.2
Eye Relief: Unlimited
Waterproof: Yes
Fogproof: Yes
10-Year Warranty
Features: The 34 mm-tube Aimpoint Hunter H34L is built for long-action rifles; two 34 mm Weaver-style rings are supplied with the sight. ACET diode technology allows for turning the sight on and leaving it on for up to 5 years on a single CR-2032 battery. The objective lens is multi-coated. Has a 12-position push-button intensity adjustment. Elevation and windage adjustments can be made with the turret caps without other tools.
Manufacturer's Suggested Retail Price: **$862**
Estimated "Real World" Price: **$800**

Aimpoint 9000

Aimpoint Hunter H34L

Aimpoint Comp C3

Aimpoint

MICRO H-1

Weight: 3.7 oz
Length: 2 ²/₅ in
Width: 1 ³/₅ in
Objective Diameter: 20 mm
Power: 1X
Sight Type: Red dot
Sight Size: 4 MOA
Eye Relief: Unlimited eye relief
Waterproof: Yes
Fogproof: Yes
10 Year Warranty
Features: The compact Micro H-1 has a non-reflective bead-blast finis and can be used interchangeably on rifles, shotguns, handguns, and bows by changing the mount. A single battery provides over 5 years of use.
Manufacturer's Suggested Retail Price: **$640**
Estimated "Real World" Price: **$600**

Aimpoint Micro H-1

Browning

REFLEX SIGHTS

BUCK MARK

Power: 1X
Field of View: 47 ft @ 100 yards
Eye Relief: Unlimited
Product Description: The Buck Mark has an aluminum housing, four red reticle patterns, a seven-position brightness rheostat powered by a lithium battery, and mounts on a standard Weaver-style base.
Manufacturer's Suggested Retail Price: **$49.99**

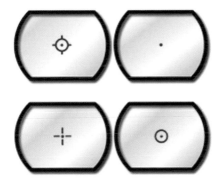

Browning Buck Mark Reticle Patterns

Browning Buck Mark

BSA OPTICS

www.bsaoptics.com

TACTICAL WEAPONS RED DOT TWRD30L 1X30 MM

(also available with 140-lumen flashlight)

Weight: 22 oz
Length: 8 ¾ in
Mount: ⅝ in Weaver style
Elevation and Windage Adjustments: ¼ MOA per click
Power: 1X
Objective Diameter: 30 mm
Exit Pupil: 30 mm
Field of View: 19.30 ft @ 100 yds
Twilight Factor: 5.5
Eye Relief: 2 in
Waterproof: Yes
Fogproof: Yes
Lifetime Limited Warranty
Features: Engineered for tactical-style firearms, the BSA Tactical Weapons Red Dot TWRD30L 1x30 mm features fully multi-coated optics. It has an output power of 5 milliwatts and has an integrated 650-nanometer wavelength red-dot laser sight. Includes a one-piece mount and rubber eye guard. Some models feature detachable AR carry handle mounts and rings.

Manufacturer's Suggested Retail Price: **$99.95**
Estimated "Real World" Price: **$79.95**

BSA Tactical Weapons
Red Dot 1x30 MM

Burris

www.burrisoptics.com

AR-332 PRISM

Weight: 14.2 oz
Length: 5 ¼ in
Power: 3X
Objective Diameter: 32 mm
Sight Type: Ballistic-CQ Red Dot
Exit Pupil: 10 mm
Field of View: 32 ft @ 100 yards
Twilight Factor: 8
Eye Relief: 2 ½ in
Waterproof: Yes
Fogproof: Yes
Warranty: 1 year
Features: The reticle on the AR-332 can be used for both "close-quarters" combat and as a ballistic compensator for various 5.56 mm and 7.62 mm bullets and loads for ranges out to 500 yards. Ships with integrated lens covers, multi-coated lens, a 1 ½ inch sunshade, and a Picatinny-rail mounting bracket. The sight can also be mounted on an AR carrying handle.

Manufacturer's Suggested Retail Price: **$481**
Estimated "Real World" Price: **$319**

Burris AR-332 Prism

FASTFIRE II RED DOT WITH PICATINNY MOUNT

(also available in no-mount style)
Weight: 2 oz
Power: 2X
Sight Type: 4 MOA Red Dot
Waterproof: Yes
Fogproof: Yes
Warranty: 1 year
Features: The FastFire II is made for shotguns, long guns and handguns. The sight is fully windage and elevation adjustable and lockable. It features both an on-off switch and a light sensor that adjusts the dot's brightness to the ambient light. Includes a plastic hood that covers the light sensor and puts the unit into sleep mode when the sight is switched to "on." Sight is powered by a CR2032 battery. Special bases are available for most firearms.
Manufacturer's Suggested Retail Price: **$327**
Estimated "Real World" Price: **$209**

Burris Burris FastFire II Red Dot

Burris SpeedDot 135

SPEEDDOT 135 RED DOT

Weight: 5 oz
Length: 5 in
Power: 1X
Objective Diameter: 35 mm
Sight Type: 3 MOA Red Dot
Twilight Factor: 5.9
Waterproof: Yes
Fogproof: Yes
Warranty: 1 year
Features: The rheostat on the SpeedDot 135 has from 0-to-11 brightness intensity. The sight is powered by a CR2032 3-volt lithium battery with 200 hours of life. The sight comes with Weaver-style rings.
Manufacturer's Suggested Retail Price: **$315**
Estimated "Real World" Price: **$199**

XTS-135 XTREME TACTICAL SPEEDDOT

Weight: 6.2 oz
Length: 4 ¾ in
Main Tube Diameter: 30 mm
Power: 1X
Objective Diameter: 35 mm
Sight Type: 5 MOA Red Dot
Field of View: 66 ft @ 100 yards

Burris XTS-135 Xtreme Tactical SpeedDot

Twilight Factor: 5.9
Waterproof: Yes
Fogproof: Yes
Warranty: 1 year
Features: The XTS-135 is advertised as being built to withstand the "repeated recoil of automatic weapons." It has a 0-to-11 brightness rheostat and can be mounted as low as a ¼ inch with 6-screw Picatinny-style Burris Xtreme Tactical Rings, or high enough to clear iron sights. Powered by a 3-volt lithium CR2032 battery. The XTS-135 has ⅓ MOA per click windage and elevation adjustment values. Available with AR-Tripler and AR-Pivot Ring.
Manufacturer's Suggested Retail Price: **$383**
Estimated "Real World" Price: **$249**

Burris

www.burrisoptics.com

Burris SpeedBead Red Dot Sight

SPEEDBEAD RED DOT

(available for Benelli Super Black Eagle 12 gauge, Super Black Eagle II, M2 12 gauge, Montefeltro Ultra Light, M1 12 gauge, Legacy, Sport II, Super Sport, Cordoba, Super Nova, R1, and ARGO; Beretta Xtrema-2, 391, 391 Light, and Urika-2; Browning Gold 12 gauge; Franchi I-12; Remington 1100, 11-87, and 870; Stoeger 2000, P-350, and 3500; and Winchester XS3)
Weight: 1.6 oz

Power: 1X
Sight Type: 4 MOA Red Dot
Eye Relief: 3 ½-4 ½ in
Waterproof: Yes
Fogproof: Yes
Warranty: 1 year
Features: This reflex sight is specifically built for shotguns and long guns. It mounts between the receiver and the rear stock, aligning the red dot just above the bore and eliminating the need for perfect head position for an accurate shot. Powered by CR2032 battery and available with ⅛- and ¼-inch risers for rising targets.
Manufacturer's Suggested Retail Price: **$383**
Estimated "Real World" Price: **$249**

Konus USA

www.konuspro.com

Konus Sight Pro QR

SIGHT PRO ATOMIC QR WITH LOCKING QUICK RELEASE TACTICAL MOUNT

(also available without mount)
Weight: 4.6 oz with mount
Length: 2 ¾ in
Main Tube Body Diameter: 20 mm
Power: 1X
Objective Diameter: 20 mm
Sight Type: Dual red-and-green illuminated dot Sight Size: 4MOA
Field of View: 76 ft @ 100 yds
Eye Relief: Unlimited

Waterproof: Water Resistant
Fogproof: Yes
Warranty: Lifetime Replacement
Product Description: The lightweight Konus Sight Pro Atomic QR bills itself as the smallest traditional electronic dot on the market and built to withstand heavy recoil. It can be mounted on pistols, shotguns, or rifles. The new locking quick-release mount is suitable for AR platforms and tactical shooting.
Manufacturer's Suggested Retail Price: **$229.99**
Estimated "Real World" Price: **$179.99**

Kruger Optical, Inc.

www.krugeroptical.com

Kruger 1-8x40 MM DTS

1-8X40 MM DTS ("DUAL TACTICAL SIGHT") GEN II

Weight: 30 oz
Length: 10 ½ in
Power: 1X reflex and 2-8X Mil-Dot zoom
Dimensions of Sight Window: 38 mm x 50.8 mm (1 ½ in x 2 in)
Objective Diameter: 40 mm
Reticles: 4 MOA red-dot in reflex mode and standard Mil-Dot in zoom mode
Illumination Brightness Levels: 6
Eye Relief: Unlimited in reflex mode and in zoom mode 3 in
Field of View: 126 ft @ 1000 yds in reflex mode and 53-13 ft @ 1000 yds in zoom mode

Exit Pupil: Unlimited in red-dot reflex mode and 12-4 mm zoom mode (according to manufacturer)
Waterproof: Yes
Fogproof: Yes
Limited Lifetime Warranty
Warranty: Lifetime against defects in materials & workmanship.
Features: The Kruger Dual Tactical sight is designed for complex combat situations with a high-resolution 1 Mil-Dot reflex sight that switches with the use of a lever from the close-quarter red-dot reflex sight to a 2-8x40 mm zoom standard Mil-dot sight. Includes independently adjustable windage and elevation for each system with more than 100 MOA of up adjustment from optical center for long-range shooting and with "Rapid Target Technology" (RTT) eye box. Manufactured from a carbon-fiber outer body with built-in Picatinny accessory rail attachment system.
Manufacturer's Suggested Retail Price: **$1763.53**

REFLEX SIGHTS

Leupold & Stevens, Inc.

www.leupold.com

DELTAPOINT

Weight: 0.6 oz
Length: 1 ²/₃ in
Width: 1 in
Height: 1 ²/₅ in
Sight Size: 3.5 MOA Dot, 7.5 MOA Delta
Waterproof: Yes
Fogproof: Yes
Limited Lifetime Warranty with Electronics Warranted Against Defect for Two Years
Features: Leupold's DeltaPoint Reflex Sight can be used on handguns, shotguns, and AR-style rifles. It comes in a kit that includes numerous mounting options. Includes an aspheric lens, motion activation, auto-brightness sensor, locking elevation and windage adjustment system, and a magnesium housing. Two reticle options are available: 7.5 MOA Delta and 3.5 MOA Dot.

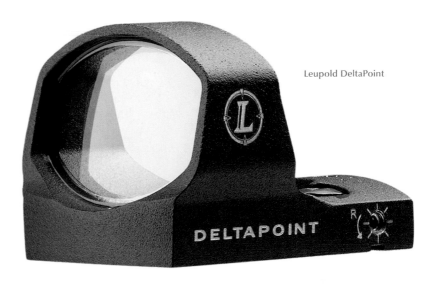

Leupold DeltaPoint

Manufacturer's Suggested Retail Price: $399.99
(cross-slot mount), ... $449.99
(all mounts)

Lucid

www.mylucidgear.com

HD7 RED DOT

Weight: 13 oz
Length: 5½ in
Width: 2¾ in
Power: 1X
Objective Diameter: 34mm
Field of View: 44 ft @ 100 yards with a 4 inches of eye relief
Eye Relief: Unlimited
Waterproof: Yes
Fogproof: Yes
Limited Lifetime Warranty
Features: The HD7 comes with an integral Picatinny rail and reversible mounting pins for bullpup-style firearms. It is shockproof and has two modes of operation (manual & "Auto-Brightness") with 12 brightness settings in the reticle control, four operator-selectable reticles based on a 2 MOA dot (2 MOA dot, 25 MOA circle-crosshair, 25 MOA crosshair, and 25 MOA circle with 2 MOA dot) with ½ MOA click adjustments. Parallax free, it is powered by one AAA battery, providing over 1000 hours of life in high and nearly 5000 hours when the Auto-Brightness mode is employed and has a two-hour auto shutoff. The frame is cast aluminum armored in chemical rubber and is available with a 2X screw-in eyepiece.

Manufacturer's Suggested Retail Price: $249
Estimated "Real World" Price: $229

Lucid HD7

Nikon Sport Optics

www.nikonhunting.com/products/riflescopes/dot_sights

MONARCH VSD 1X30 MM

Weight: 7.8 oz (without batteries)
Length: 3 ⁴/₅ in
Power: 1X
Objective Diameter: 30 mm
Exit Pupil: 30 mm
Twilight Factor: 5.5
Eye Relief: Unlimited
Waterproof: Yes
Fogproof: Yes
Limited Lifetime Warranty
Features: The Monarch Dot Sight VSD's (Variable Sized Dot) offers selections of 1, 4, 6, 8, or 10 MOA dot size. Includes 11-position rheostat and integral mounting system attachable to any Weaver-style base. Waterproof, fogproof, and shockproof (except battery chamber). Objective and ocular lenses are 30mm and are multi-coated.
Estimated "Real World" Price:.................$274.95

Nikon Monarch VSD 1x30 MM

Pentax Imaging Co.

www.pentaxsportoptics.com

GAMESEEKER HS-20

Weight: 3.4 oz
Length: 3 ⁹/₁₀ in
Width: 2 in
Power: 1X
Halo Size: 33x22 mm
Dot Size: 5 MOA
Field of View: 55-50 ft @ 100 yards
Waterproof: Yes
Fogproof: Yes
Limited Lifetime Warranty
Features: Has 5 MOA dot with 11 brightness settings and 72 hours of continuous battery use. Uses continuous, non-click adjustments. With Weaver-style mounting system.
Manufacturer's Suggested Retail Price:......................$59
Estimated "Real World" Price:......................$59

Pentax Gameseeker HS20

Pentax Imaging Co.

www.pentaxsportoptics.com

GAMESEEKER RD-10

Weight: 7.07 oz
Length: 3 ⁴/₅ in
Tube Diameter: 39 mm
Power: 1X
Objective Diameter: 30 mm
Dot Size: 4 MOA
Field of View: 54 ft @ 100 yards
Waterproof: Yes
Fogproof: Yes
Limited Lifetime Warranty
Features: A reflex sight with a 4 MOA dot, 11 brightness settings, 72 hours continuous battery life, and continuous windage and elevation adjustments. With Weaver-style mounting system.
Manufacturer's Suggested Retail Price: **$69**
Estimated "Real World" Price: **$69**

Pentax Gameseeker RD10

Trijicon Inc.

www.trijicon.com

RMR™ ADJUSTABLE LED RM06

(also in Dual-Illuminated RMR with 13.0 MOA dot, 7.0 MOA dot, 9.0 MOA dot, and triangle-reticle RMR LED with 3.25 MOA dot and 8.0 MOA dot)
Weight: 1.2 oz
Length: 45 mm
Power: 1X
Dot Size: 3.25 MOA
Waterproof: Yes
Fogproof: Yes
Limited Lifetime Warranty
Features: Electronic reflex sight with a military-grade investment-cast aircraft-aluminum-alloy and hard-coat anodized-finish housing. With eight brightness levels powered by a long-life lithium battery.
Manufacturer's Suggested Retail Price: **$675**
Estimated "Real World" Price: **$599**

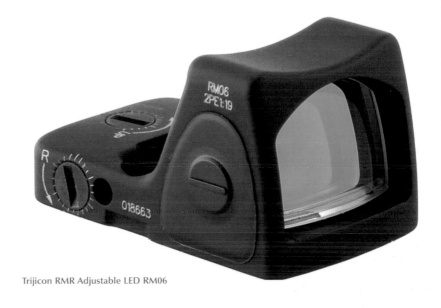

Trijicon RMR Adjustable LED RM06

Vortex Optics

www.vortexoptics.com

REFLEX SIGHTS

SPARC RED DOT

Weight: 5.2 oz
Length: 3 in
Power: 1X
Objective Diameter: 22 mm
Twilight Factor: 4.7
Elevation and Windage Adjustments: 1 MOA per click
Eye Relief: Unlimited
Waterproof: Yes
Fogproof: Yes
Unconditional Lifetime Warranty
Features: The Vortex SPARC red dot features fully multi-coated lenses with multiple anti-reflective coatings on all air-to-glass surfaces. Optics are sealed with O-rings and nitrogen-gas purged. Rated for high-recoil firearms with non-critical eye relief for rapid target acquisition for shooting with both eyes open. Rated from -40 to 140 degrees F. Includes ten variable illumination settings. Night vision mode for use in conjunction with night vision optics. Screw-in doubler provides extra magnification for longer distance shooting. Six-hour auto-shutdown for battery life. Typical battery life in normal mode of operation: 120 hours (maximum brightness), 3400 hours (minimum brightness). Typical battery life in night vision mode: 4200 hours (maximum brightness), 4600 hours (minimum brightness).
Manufacturer's Suggested Retail Price: **$289**
Estimated "Real World" Price: **$199.99**

Vortex Sparc

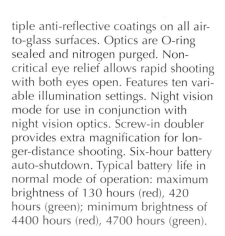

Vortex StrikeFire

STRIKEFIRE RED DOT

Weight: 7.2 oz
Length: 6 in
Main Body Tube Diameter: 30 mm
Power: 1X
Objective Diameter: 30 mm
Elevation and Windage Adjustments: ½ MOA per click
Twilight Factor: 5.5
Eye Relief: Unlimited
Waterproof: Yes
Fogproof: Yes
Unconditional Lifetime Warranty
Features: The Vortex StrikeForce was recoil tested with 1000 rounds of .375 H&H Magnum. Manufactured from a 30 mm aluminum-alloy tube. The lenses are fully multi-coated with mul-

tiple anti-reflective coatings on all air-to-glass surfaces. Optics are O-ring sealed and nitrogen purged. Non-critical eye relief allows rapid shooting with both eyes open. Features ten variable illumination settings. Night vision mode for use in conjunction with night vision optics. Screw-in doubler provides extra magnification for longer-distance shooting. Six-hour battery auto-shutdown. Typical battery life in normal mode of operation: maximum brightness of 130 hours (red), 420 hours (green); minimum brightness of 4400 hours (red), 4700 hours (green).

Typical battery life in night vision mode: maximum brightness of 7200 hours (red), 7200 hours (green); minimum brightness of 7600 hours (red), 8000 hours (green). Rated to -40 degrees F. The included extra-high 30mm ring puts the scope's bore center 37 mm above the base height. Commonly used for mounting with a flat-top AR15, providing absolute co-witness with iron sights.
Manufacturer's Suggested Retail Price: **$179**
Estimated "Real World" Price: **$149.99**

RED/GREEN DOT SIGHT

Weight: 8 oz
Length: 5 in
Main Body Tube Diameter: 30 mm
Power: 1X
Objective Diameter: 30 mm
Sight Type: micro dot, dot, circle, and circle with micro dot
Sight Size: 3-6 MOA dot and 25 MOA circle
Exit Pupil: 30 mm
Field of View: 50 ft @ 100 yards
Twilight Factor: 5.5
Waterproof: Yes
Fogproof: Yes
Limited Lifetime Warranty
Features: The Weaver Red/Green dot sight can be used for turkey, deer, and other big game and mounts on AR platforms with Weaver-style bases. Made from a one-piece 30 mm tube with 10 brightness settings (five red and five green) and four different selectable aim-point styles: 6 MOA

Weaver Red Dot - Green Dot

dot, 3 MOA micro dot, 25 MOA-diameter circle, and 3 MOA dot in 25 MOA circle.

Manufacturer's Suggested Retail Price: $316.95
Estimated "Real World" Price: $299.99

Carl Zeiss Sports Optics
www.zeiss.com/sports

COMPACT POINT

Weight: 2.64 oz
Length: 2 ¼ in
Width: 1 in
Power: 1.05X
Halo Size: 23x16 mm
Waterproof: Yes
Fogproof: Yes
Transferable Limited Lifetime Warranty on Mechanics, 5 Year Warranty on Electronics
Features: Approximately 25 percent larger than the average reflex sight, the Compact Point uses an illuminated red dot for target acquisition and LotuTec moisture-resistant coating on the lens. Available for Picatinny or Weaver-style mounts and suitable for hunting rifles, AR-style weapons, shotguns, and handguns.
Manufacturer's Suggested Retail Price: $499.99
Estimated "Real World" Price: $499.99

Zeiss Compact Point

REFLEX SIGHTS

Carl Zeiss Sports Optics

www.zeiss.com/sports

Z-POINT (RED DOT REFLEX SIGHT)

Weight: 5.65 oz
Length: 2 ½ in
Width: 1 ²/₅ in
Power: 1X
Waterproof: Yes
Fogproof: Yes
Transferable Limited Lifetime Warranty on Mechanics, 5 Year Warranty on Electronics
Features: This acquisition sight for shotguns, rifles, and handguns and uses a dual-source illuminated: a solar cell for daylight hours and battery power for dark, extending the overall the life of the battery. The red dot automatically adapts to the brightness of the surroundings and can also be regulated manually. Available for Weaver or Picatinny mounts.
Manufacturer's Suggested Retail Price: $574.99
Estimated "Real World" Price: $574.99

Zeiss Z-Point

RIFLESCOPES

he logic of the telescopic sight is inescapable.

Experimentation in telescopic firearms scopes, to enhance the range and accuracy of the human eye when employed in shooting, apparently dates back to at least the 17th century, and there is even a legend that Sir Isaac Newton tried putting one of his reflecting-mirror telescopes on a gun. The first reportedly verifiable instance of a firearm with a telescopic sight was a handgun in 1834.

By the end of the eighteenth century, American gunsmiths were building long, full-stocked target rifles with double set triggers. These rifles also had "tube sights," which consisted of a crosshair mounted inside a tube without lenses to shade the crosshairs from glare so that they remained clear to the shooter. Even greater firearm accuracy became possible in the 1820s with the introduction of the percussion cap which eliminated the delayed lock time (not to mention blinding flash and frizzen-pan smoke) of the flintlock. Rifles could now arguably shoot well beyond the capabilities of their non-telescopic aiming systems, at least to the abilities of most shooters.

The invention of the optical-lens riflescope is thought to have taken place in the United States sometime between 1835 and 1840. The principles of these early riflescopes were set out in 1844 by a British civil engineer, John Ratcliffe Chapman, author of *Instructions to Young Marksmen, in All that Relates to the General Construction, Practical Manipulation, Causes and Liability to Error in Making Accurate Rifle Performances, and the Theoretic Principles upon Which Such Accurate Performances Are Founded, as Exhibited in the Improved American Rifle.* In that book, not much longer than its title, Chapman disparages the "shorter" riflescopes that had "been in use for some time" and states that "so far as sighting is concerned, [the] telescope [sight], properly made and properly fixed, is nearer perfection than any other method of sighting known." Chapman's description of a riflescope "which will perform perfect at all times" is of a "3 feet 1 inch long" tube fashioned from either "good and stiff" sheet iron or the preferred sheet steel, "⅝ of an inch diameter outside, and 1/20th of an inch thick, weighing about 10 ounces."

In 1855 in Syracuse, New York, William Malcolm became the first mass producer of riflescopes. He included achromatic lenses and highly refined external adjustments, and his riflescopes could achieve magnifications of 20X and higher.

Malcolm's scopes, and those of another maker, L. M. Amidon of Vermont, became standard among Union sharpshooters during the Civil War. To join the ranks of Union Colonel Hiram Berdan's sharpshooters, a soldier had to place ten consecutive shots into a 10-inch bull at 200 yards. While the record of the riflescope's use in the Civil War is well-documented, its later employment in hunting, especially on the Great Plains by the hunters of the buffalo, is less so. Perhaps those long-tubed scopes did not stand up to the harsh handling they had to endure when hundreds of heavy caliber rounds might be fired through a rifle in a single day, day in and day out.

Refinements and improvements of the riflescope, many coming from Europe—including the work done in 1880 by the Austrian August Fiedler, forestry commissioner to Bohemian Prince Reuss IV, which 18 years later led to what is considered the first commercially produced internally adjustable riflescope, the "Telorar," manufactured by Karl Robert Kahles in his "Vienna Optical Manufactury," and the extended-eye-relief scopes that arose out of the close-quarters combat needs of the Wehrmacht in World War II—have been steady and continuous. Such advancements have been state-of-the-art lens coatings, waterproofing and fog-proofing through the use of seals and purging with inert gases, developments in metallurgy, parallax adjustments, tactical turrets, and a cornucopia of specialized reticles including illuminated, mil-dot, and ballistic compensating, until today the range of scopes for every type of shooting discipline, range, style, target, and game animal is virtually, if not visually, unlimited.

Alpen Optics

www.alpenoptics.com

APEX XP EXTREME PERFORMANCE RADICAL HUNTER SERIES 2-10X44 MM WITH MOSSY OAK CAMO

(also in matte black in 3-9x40 mm, 2-10x44 mm, and 4-16x44 mm)

Weight: 17 oz
Length: 14 in
Power: 2x-10X
Objective Diameter: 44 mm
Main Tube Diameter: 1 in
Exit Pupil: 15 mm-4.4 mm
Field of View: 40 ft-9 ft @ 100 yds
Twilight Factor: 9.4-21
Eye Relief: 3 ⁴/₅ inches
Waterproof: Yes
Fogproof: Yes
Lifetime No-Fault Warranty
Features: The Alpen Apex XP riflescope series features fully multi-coated optical design, one-piece-tube construction, and zero reset windage and elevation dials with ¼ MOA click adjustments (⅛ MOA in the 4-16x44). A fast-focus eye piece is standard, and all come with side-focus parallax adjustments. Reticles include the BDC, WBDC-A, and WBDC-B. Also comes with a 4 inch detachable sun shade.
Manufacturer's Suggested Retail Price: $500
Estimated "Real World" Price: $330

APEX XP EXTREME PERFORMANCE 6-24X50 MM, MATTE BLACK

(also in 1.5-6x42 mm, and in red-dot illuminated-reticle 1.5-6x42 mm, 2.5-10x50 mm, and 4-16x56 mm)

Weight: 24 oz
Length: 15 ½ in
Width: 2 ½ in
Power: 6x-24x
Objective Diameter: 50 mm
Main Tube Diameter: 30 mm
Exit Pupil: 8 mm-2 mm
Field of View: 16 ft-4 ft @ 100 yds
Twilight Factor: 17.3-34.6
Eye Relief: 3 ½ inches
Waterproof: Yes
Fogproof: Yes
Lifetime No-Fault Warranty
Features: Similar features to those on the 1 inch tube model XP. The 6-24x50 and the 4-16x56 have ⅛

Alpen Apex XP 2-10x44 MM

Alpen Apex XP 6-24x50 MM

Alpen Kodiak 3.5-10x50 MM

MOA adjustment increments, while the others have ¼ MOA.
Manufacturer's Suggested Retail Price: $530
Estimated "Real World" Price: $360

KODIAK 3.5-10X50, MATTE BLACK

(also in 1.5-4x32 mm, 3-9x32 mm, 4x32 mm, 3-9x40 mm, 4-12x40 mm, and 6-24x50 mm)

Weight: 21 oz
Length: 13 ⅕ in
Width: 2 in
Power: 3.5x-10x
Objective Diameter: 50 mm
Main Tube Diameter: 1 in
Exit Pupil: 13.5 mm-4.9 mm

Field of View: 35 ft-12 ft @ 100 yds
Twilight Factor: 13.2-22.4
Eye Relief: 3 in
Waterproof: Yes
Fogproof: Yes
Limited Lifetime Warranty
Features: The Alpen Kodiak riflescope series features multi-coated optical design. It has oversized zero-reset windage and elevation dials adjustable in ¼ MOA (⅛ MOA in the 6-24x50) clicks and comes with the AccuPlex Tapered duplex-style reticle. A fast-focus eye piece is standard.
Manufacturer's Suggested Retail Price: $195
Estimated "Real World" Price: $135

ETERNA MIL-DOT RETICLE 6-24X40 MM

Weight: 20 oz
Length: 17 in
Main Body Tube Diameter: 1 in
Power: 6-24X
Objective Diameter: 40 mm
Elevation and Windage Adjustments: ⅛ MOA per click
Exit Pupil: 6.66-1.66 mm
Field of View: 171-79 ft @ 100 yds
Twilight Factor: 15.49-30.98
Eye Relief: 3 in
Waterproof: Yes
Fogproof: Yes
Unconditional "HALO" Warranty
Features: The Eterna riflescope's optics are fully multi-coated. The scope's equipped with a fast-focus eyepiece and Eterna Mil-Dot glass-etched reticle.
Manufacturer's Suggested Retail Price: **$870**

ETERNA BDC RETICLE 4.5-14X50 MM

(also in 3-9x40 mm and 6.5-20x50 mm)
Weight: 22 oz
Length: 14 in
Main Body Tube Diameter: 1 in
Power: 4.5-14X
Objective Diameter: 50 mm
Elevation and Windage Adjustments: ¼ MOA per click
Exit Pupil: 11.11-3.57 mm
Field of View: 211-54 ft @ 100 yds
Twilight Factor: 15-26.45
Eye Relief: 3 ¼ in
Waterproof: Yes
Fogproof: Yes
Unconditional "HALO" Warranty
Features: The Eterna riflescope has fully multi-coated optics and a fast-focus eyepiece. The glass-etched BDC reticle allows for bullet-drop compensation.
Manufacturer's Suggested Retail Price: **$965**

ETERNA DUPLEX RETICLE 1.5-5X20 MM

Weight: 10 oz
Length: 9 ½ in
Main Body Tube Diameter: 1 in
Power: 1.5-5X
Objective Diameter: 20 mm

Elevation and Windage Adjustments: ¼ MOA per click
Exit Pupil: 13.33-4 mm
Field of View: 598-209 ft @ 100 yds
Twilight Factor: 5.47-10
Eye Relief: 10-33 mm
Waterproof: Yes
Fogproof: Yes

Unconditional "HALO" Warranty
Features: The Eterna duplex reticle has heavy glass-etched crosshairs, stepping down to fine. Includes fully multi-coated optics and fast-focus eyepiece.
Manufacturer's Suggested Retail Price: **$425**

Brunton Eterna Mil-Dot Reticle 6-24x40 MM

Brunton Eterna BDC Reticle

Brunton Eterna Duplex Reticle 1.5-5x20 MM

BSA Optics

www.bsaoptics.com

BP39X40 BLACK POWDER 3-9X40 MM

Weight: 13.29 oz
Length: 11 ⁹/₁₀ in
Width: 2 ¹/₅ in
Main Tube Body Diameter: 1 in
Power: 3-9X
Objective Diameter: 40 mm
Exit Pupil: 13.3-4.4 mm
Field of View: 42-14 ft @ 100 yds
Twilight Factor: 10.95-18.97
Eye Relief: 3 ½ in
Waterproof: Yes
Fogproof: Yes
Lifetime Limited Warranty
Features: The BSA BP39X40 Black Powder 3-9x40 mm is designed to withstand the heavy recoil of black-powder guns. The lenses are fully multi-coated and include BSA "Xtreme Climate Protection" coatings.
Manufacturer's Suggested Retail Price: **$79.95**
Estimated "Real World" Price: **$71.95**

BSA Optics BP39X40 Black Powder 3-9x40 MM

BOSS BO1545X32 1.5-4.5X32 MM

(also available with turkey reticle)
Weight: 14.70 oz
Length: 11 in
Main Tube Body Diameter: 1 in
Power: 1.5-4.5X
Objective Diameter: 32 mm
Exit Pupil: 15.3-6.7 mm
Field of View: 60.7-18.2 ft @ 100 yards
Twilight Factor: 6.93-12.0
Eye Relief: 4 in
Waterproof: Yes
Fogproof: Yes
Lifetime Limited Warranty
Features: The BSA Boss BO1545X32 1.5-4.5x32 mm riflescope, designed and patented by BSA engineers in the USA, is equipped with a ranging reticle designed to estimate the ranges to objects of known size, the size of objects at known distances, and to compensate for bullet drop and wind drift. Comes with a black-matte finish, fully multi-coated optics, push-pull locking turrets, and erector-tube coil spring.
Manufacturer's Suggested Retail Price: **$104.95**
Estimated "Real World" Price: **$94.45**

BSA Optics Boss 1.5-4.5x32 MM

BSA Optics Catseye CAT312X44SP 3-12x44 MM

CATSEYE CAT312X44SP 3-12X44 MM

(also in 4-16x44 mm and 3.5-10x50 mm and with RGB–red-green-blue– illuminated reticle)
Weight: 18.69 oz
Length: 12 ½ in
Main Body Tube Diameter: 1 in
Elevation and Windage Adjustments: ¼ MOA per click
Power: 3-12X
Objective Diameter: 44 mm
Exit Pupil: 14.6-3.7 mm
Field of View: 32.4-9.7 ft @ 100 yds
Twilight Factor: 11.5-23
Eye Relief: 4 in
Waterproof: Yes
Fogproof: Yes
Lifetime Limited Warranty
Features: BSA Catseye CAT312X44SP 3-12x44 mm, designed and patented by BSA engineers in the USA, features fully multi-coated optics, ball-and-coil-spring erector tube retention, fast focus, nitrogen purging, integrated sunshade, push-pull zero-reset turrets, and in some models RGB illuminated glass-etched reticles and adjustable side parallax.
Manufacturer's Suggested Retail Price: **$119.95**
Estimated "Real World" Price: **$107.45**

RIFLESCOPES

CONTENDER COMD416X40SP 4-16X40 MM

(also in 3-12x40 mm and 6-24x40 mm, and available with RGB–"red-green-blue"–illuminated reticle)
Weight: 17.79 oz
Length: 12 ½ in
Main Body Tube Diameter: 1 in
Power: 4-16X
Objective Diameter: 40 mm
Elevation and Windage Adjustment: ⅛ MOA per click
Exit Pupil: 10-2.5 mm
Field of View: 30-27 ft @ 100 yds
Twilight Factor: 12.64-25.29
Eye Relief: 4 in
Waterproof: Yes
Fogproof: Yes
Lifetime Limited Warranty
Features: The BSA Contender COMD416X40SP 4-16x40 mm was designed and patented by BSA engineers in the USA. It features fully multi-coated lenses, push-pull turrets with zero reset, ball-and-coil-spring erector tube retention, fast focus, and nitrogen purged.
Manufacturer's Suggested Retail Price: **$169.95**
Estimated "Real World" Price: **$152.95**

CB4X30CP CROSSBOW

(1X 5-MOA red-dot archery scopes also available for compounds and crossbows)
Weight: 15 oz
Length: 7 ⁴/₅ in
Width: 2 in
Power: 4X
Objective Diameter: 30 mm
Exit Pupil: 7.5 mm
Field of View: 21 ft @ 100 yds
Twilight Factor: 11
Eye Relief: 4 in
Waterproof: Yes
Fogproof: Yes
Lifetime Limited Warranty
Features: The BSA CB4X30CP Crossbow scope has a reticle especially designed for crossbow shooting. Fixed 4X magnification with fully multi-coated optics. Great all around sights for your crossbow and bow equipment. These sights are for use on both compound and standard bows or crossbows. Each version has a specific reticle to help maintain precision on target accuracy.
Manufacturer's Suggested Retail Price: **$59.95**
Estimated "Real World" Price: **$53.95**

DEER HUNTER DHML39X40 3-9X40 MM

(also in 4-16x44 mm and 3-9x50 mm)
Weight: 14.8 oz
Length: 12 ½ in
Main Body Tube Diameter: 1 in
Elevation and Windage Adjustments: ¼ MOA per click
Power: 3-9X
Objective Diameter: 40 mm
Exit Pupil: 13.0-4.4 mm
Field of View: 31.9-10.9 ft @ 100 yds
Twilight Factor: 10.95-18.97
Eye Relief: 4 in
Waterproof: Yes
Fogproof: Yes
Lifetime Limited Warranty
Features: The BSA Deer Hunter DHML39X40 3-9x40 mm muzzle-loader scope is one-piece-tube construction with fully multi-coated optics (on DHML models) and a black-matte finish.
Manufacturer's Suggested Retail Price: **$119.95**
Estimated "Real World" Price: **$107.95**

BSA Optics Contender (COMD416X40SP)

BSA Optics CB4X30CP Crossbow

RIFLESCOPES

BSA Optics

www.bsaoptics.com

EDGE PS27X28 2-7X28 MM

(also in 2x20 mm and 2-7x32 mm)
Weight: 9.9 oz
Length: 9 in
Main Body Tube Diameter: 1 in
Elevation and Windage Adjustments:
¼ MOA per click
Power: 2-7X
Objective Diameter: 28 mm
Exit Pupil: 14-4 mm
Field of View: 60-16 ft @ 100 yds
Twilight Factor: 7.48-14.0
Eye Relief: 12-20 in
Waterproof: Yes
Fogproof: Yes
Lifetime Limited Warranty
Features: The BSA Edge PS27X28
2-7x28 mm extended eye-relief pistol
scope includes a duplex reticle, fully
multi-coated optics, one-piece tube
construction, and standard focus eye
piece design.
**Manufacturer's Suggested Retail
Price:** $119.95
**Estimated "Real World"
Price:** $107.95

ESSENTIAL AR4X32 4X32 MM

*(also in 2-7x32 mm, 3-9x40 mm AO,
and 3-12x44 mm)*

Weight: 14 oz
Length: 11 in
Main Body Tube Diameter: 1 in
Elevation and Windage Adjustments:
¼ MOA per click
Power: 4X
Objective Diameter: 32 mm
Exit Pupil: 8.4 mm
Field of View: 17.8 @ 100 yards
Twilight Factor: 11.31
Eye Relief: 3 ½ in
Waterproof: Yes
Fogproof: Yes
Lifetime Limited Warranty
Features: The BSA Essential AR4X32
4x32 mm is built for the reverse recoil
of magnum-spring-powered air rifles.
They are equipped with parallax
adjustable down to 10 yards or less
(7.5 yards in the case of the 4x32
mm). All AR Models have target-style
turrets with finger adjustable ¼ MOA
clicks for windage and elevation, fully
coated optics, and rubber-inlaid paral-
lax and power adjustments (on variable models).
**Manufacturer's Suggested Retail
Price:** $89.95
**Estimated "Real World"
Price:** $80.95

GOLD STAR GS212X44 2-12X44 MM

*(also in 1-6x20 mm, and 3-18x50 mm
and 4-25x50 mm with side parallax
adjustment)*
Weight: 18 oz
Length: 13 in
Main Body Tube Diameter: 1 in
Elevation and Windage Adjustments:
¼ MOA per click
Power: 2-12X
Objective Diameter: 44 mm
Exit Pupil: 22-3.7 mm
Field of View: 60-10 ft @ 100 yds
Twilight Factor: 9.38-22.97
Eye Relief: 4 in
Waterproof: Yes
Fogproof: Yes
CEO Signature Lifetime Full Warranty
Features: The 6X-zoom-range BSA
Gold Star GS212X44 2-12x44 mm
riflescope features the "EZ Hunter" ret-
icle, fully multi-coated optics, and
fast-focus eyepiece.
**Manufacturer's Suggested Retail
Price:** $269.95
**Estimated "Real World"
Price:** $242.96

BSA Optics Edge PS27X28 2-7x28 MM

BSA Optics Essential AR4X32 MM

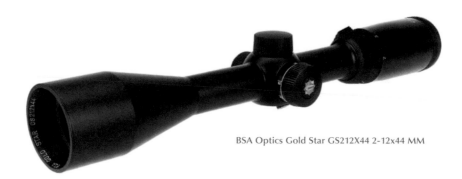

BSA Optics Gold Star GS212X44 2-12x44 MM

BP39X40 BLACK POWDER 3-9X40 MM

Weight: 13.29 oz
Length: 11 ⁹/₁₀ in
Width: 2 ¹/₅ in
Main Tube Body Diameter: 1 in
Power: 3-9X
Objective Diameter: 40 mm
Exit Pupil: 13.3-4.4 mm
Field of View: 42-14 ft @ 100 yds
Twilight Factor: 10.95-18.97
Eye Relief: 3 ½ in
Waterproof: Yes
Fogproof: Yes
Lifetime Limited Warranty
Features: The BSA BP39X40 Black Powder 3-9x40 mm is designed to withstand the heavy recoil of black-powder guns. The lenses are fully multi-coated and include BSA "Xtreme Climate Protection" coatings.
Manufacturer's Suggested Retail Price: $79.95
Estimated "Real World" Price: $71.95

PLATINUM PT624X44TS 6-24X44 MM

(also in 8-32x44 mm and with Mil-Dot and illuminated Mil-Dot reticles)
Weight: 24.3 oz
Length: 15 ⁴/₅ in
Main Tube Body Diameter: 1 in
Elevation and Windage Adjustments: ⅛ MOA per click
Power: 6-24X
Objective Diameter: 44 mm
Exit Pupil: 7.3-1.8 mm
Field of View: 20-5 ft @ 100 yds
Twilight Factor: 16.25-32.5
Eye Relief: 3 ½ in
Waterproof: Yes
Fogproof: Yes
Lifetime Limited Warranty
Features: The BSA Platinum target and hunting scope features multi-coated optics, target turrets, fine-crosshair ⅛ MOA dot reticle, and parallax setting of 25 yards to infinity. Clicks on the windage and elevation turrets are consistently precise.
Manufacturer's Suggested Retail Price: $159.95
Estimated "Real World" Price: $143.95

SWEET S17-312X40SP 3-12X40 MM

(also in 2-7x32 mm, 3-9x40 mm, 3-12x40 mm RGB, and 6-18x40 mm, and calibrated for .17 HMR or .22 LR bullets)
Weight: 17.1 oz
Length: 13 ²/₅ in
Main Body Tube Diameter: 1 in
Elevation and Windage Adjustments: ¼ MOA per click
Power: 3-12X
Objective Diameter: 40 mm
Exit Pupil: 13.3-3.3 mm
Field of View: 31.4-8.3 ft @ 100 yds
Twilight Factor: 10.95-21.9
Eye Relief: 4 in
Waterproof: Yes
Fogproof: Yes
Lifetime Limited Warranty
Features: The BSA Sweet S17-312X40SP 3-12x40 mm is trajectory compensated for the .17HMR bullet, from 100 to 300 yards. Features multi-grain turrets with zero reset, adjustable with an Allen-head screw. Has fully multi-coated optics, with adjustable parallax and includes a 3-inch sunshade.
Manufacturer's Suggested Retail Price: $159.95
Estimated "Real World" Price: $139.95

BSA Optics BP39X40 Black Powder 3-9x40

BSA Optics Platinum PT6-24x44 MM TS

BSA Optics Sweet S17-312X40SP 3-12x40 MM

RIFLESCOPES

Burris

www.burrisoptics.com

TIMBERLINE 3-9X32 MM WITH BALLISTIC PLEX RETICLE

(also in 4.5-14x32 mm)
Weight: 13 oz
Length: 10 ⅓ in
Main Body Tube Diameter: 1 in
Power: 3-9X
Objective Diameter: 32 mm
Exit Pupil: 11-3.6 mm
Field of View: 25-9 ft @ 100 yards
Twilight Factor: 9.8-16.9
Eye Relief: 3 ¾-5 in
Waterproof: Yes
Fogproof: Yes
Limited Lifetime Warranty
Features: A fully multi-coated-lens scope. Offers a low mount for short-action rifles. With a maximum eye relief of 5 inches it is suitable for use on muzzleloaders and slug guns.
Manufacturer's Suggested Retail Price: $302
Estimated "Real World" Price: $199

BLACK DIAMOND 8-32X50 MM WITH BALLISTIC MIL-DOT

(also in 3-12x50 mm illuminated, 4-16x50 mm, and 6-24 x50 mm, and with Ballistic Plex and Ballistic Plex E1).
Weight: 21 oz
Length: 17 in
Main Body Tube Diameter: 30 mm
Power: 8-32X
Objective Diameter: 50 mm
Exit Pupil: 6.2-1.6 mm
Field of View: 14-4 ft @ 100 yards
Twilight Factor: 20-40
Eye Relief: 3-3 ½ in
Waterproof: Yes
Fogproof: Yes
Limited Lifetime Warranty
Features: The Black Diamond has fully multi-coated lenses, side-focus parallax adjustment, and finger-adjustable turrets with ⅛ MOA-click windage and elevation adjustments (¼ MOA on 3-12X and 4-16X) and resettable to zero.
Manufacturer's Suggested Retail Price: $1353
Estimated "Real World" Price: $849

ELIMINATOR LASERSCOPE 4-12X42 MM

Weight: 26 oz
Length: 13 in
Power: 4-12X
Objective Diameter: 42 mm
Display: LED, red
Exit Pupil: 10.5-3.5 mm
Field of View: 295-9 ft @ 100 yards
Twilight Factor: 12.9-22.4
Eye Relief: 3-3 ½ in
Waterproof: Yes
Fogproof: Yes
Warranty: 3 years

Features: The Eliminator combines optics with rangefinding and trajectory compensation. It calculates distance to target, angle of shot, trajectory, and illuminates holdover. Ranges reflective surfaces to 800 yards, and animals to 550, to a stated accuracy of within 1 yard. Windage and elevation adjustable in ¼ MOA clicks.
Manufacturer's Suggested Retail Price: $1375
Estimated "Real World" Price: $899

Burris Timberline 3-9X 32 MM

Burris BD 8-32X 50 MM

Burris Eliminator LaserScope 4-12x42 MM

FULLFIELD 30 EUROPEAN 3.5-10X50 MM ILLUMINATED WITH 3P#4 LRS

(also in 3-9x40 mm and 3-9x40 mm illuminated, and with Ballistic Plex reticle and 3P#4 non-illuminated)
Weight: 16.6 oz
Length: 13 in
Main Body Tube Diameter: 30 mm
Power: 3.5-10X
Objective Diameter: 50 mm
Exit Pupil: 14-5 mm
Field of View: 28-11 ft @ 100 yards
Twilight Factor: 13.2-22.3
Eye Relief: 3-3 ⁴/₅ in
Waterproof: Yes
Fogproof: Yes
Limited Lifetime Warranty
Features: The 50 mm objective gives extra light-gathering ability. Made with fully multi-coated lenses and checkered-steel power-adjustment ring. Windage and elevation adjustments are in ¼ MOa-clicks.
Manufacturer's Suggested Retail Price: $835
Estimated "Real World" Price: $539

FULLFIELD E1 2-7X35 MM WITH BALLISTIC PLEX E1 RETICLE

(also in 3-9x40 mm, 3-9x50 mm, and 4.5-14x42 mm)
Weight: 12 oz
Length: 11 ²/₅ in
Main Body Tube Diameter: 1 in
Power: 2-7X
Objective Diameter: 35 mm
Exit Pupil: 17-5 mm

Field of View: 45-13 ft @ 100 yards
Twilight Factor: 8.3-15.6
Eye Relief: 3-4 in
Waterproof: Yes
Fogproof: Yes
Limited Lifetime Warranty
Features: The Fullfield E1 is based on Burris's 1-inch Fullfield II scopes—with a lower profile, ergonomic windage-and-elevation knobs, and Ballistic Plex E1 etched reticle. The Ballistic Plex E1 is wind compensating with ¼ MOA dots to the left and right of the crosshair, each dot representing the bullet drift from a 10 mph crosswind for most hunting cartridges. Lenses are multi-coated.
Manufacturer's Suggested Retail Price: $266
Estimated "Real World" Price: $179

FULLFIELD II 3-9X40 MM ILLUMINATED WITH BALLISTIC PLEX LRS

(also in 2-7x35 mm, 3-9x50 mm, 4.5-14x42 mm, and 6.5-20x50 mm and

with Plex, Ballistic Plex, Ballistic Mil-Dot, and German 3P#4 reticles)
Weight: 13 oz
Length: 12 ¹/₅ in
Main Body Tube Diameter: 1 in
Power: 3-9X
Objective Diameter: 40 mm
Exit Pupil: 13-5 mm
Field of View: 33-13 ft @ 100 yards
Twilight Factor: 10.9-18.9
Eye Relief: 3-3 ⁴/₅ in
Waterproof: Yes
Fogproof: Yes
Limited Lifetime Warranty
Features: The Fullfield II is Burris's line of $200-to-$300 riflescopes. In production for 30 years the scopes are made from a one-piece 1 inch outer tube and with multi-coated optics. Windage and elevation adjustments are in ¼ MOA increments. The illuminated version uses a red-dot crosshair.
Manufacturer's Suggested Retail Price: $416
Estimated "Real World" Price: $279

Burris Fullfield II 3-9x40 MM

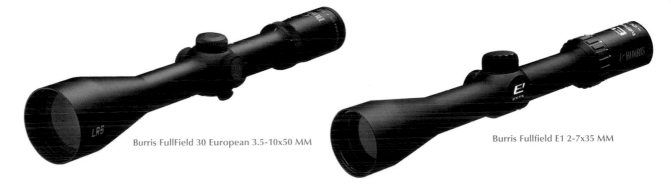

Burris FullField 30 European 3.5-10x50 MM

Burris Fullfield E1 2-7x35 MM

RIFLESCOPES

Burris

www.burrisoptics.com

FULLFIELD II TACTICAL 6.5-20X50 MM WITH BALLISTIC MIL-DOT

(also in 3-9x40 mm and 4.5-14x42 mm and with Ballistic Plex reticle)

Weight: 19 oz
Length: 14 ½ in
Main Body Tube Diameter: 1 in
Power: 6.5-20X
Objective Diameter: 50 mm
Exit Pupil: 7.6-2.5 mm
Field of View: 18-6 ft @ 100 yards
Twilight Factor: 18-31.6
Eye Relief: 3-3 ⅔ in
Waterproof: Yes
Fogproof: Yes
Limited Lifetime Warranty
Features: A tactical version of the Fullfield II scope. Burris notes that their Fullfield II Tacticals weigh 25- to 50-percent less than other scopes in this class. Also includes low profile TAC-2 adjustment knobs with ¼ MOA windage and elevation clicks and resettable to zero. Comes with "easy-on, easy-off" dust covers on adjustment turrets.

Manufacturer's Suggested Retail Price: **$931**
Estimated "Real World" Price: **$589**

FULLFIELD TAC 30 TACTICAL 3-9X40 MM WITH BALLISTIC PLEX RETICLE

(also in 1-4x24mm illuminated, 1-4x24 mm illuminated with Fastfire II reflex sight, 4.5-14x42 mm, 3.5-10x50 mm illuminated, and 6.5-20x50 mm, and with Ballistic CQ 5.56, Ballistic Plex LRS, and Ballistic Mil-Dot)

Weight: 14.1 oz
Length: 12 ⅕ in
Main Body Tube Diameter: 30 mm
Power: 3-9X
Objective Diameter: 40 mm
Exit Pupil: 13-5 mm
Field of View: 33-13 ft @ 100 yards
Twilight Factor: 10.9-18.9
Eye Relief: 3 ¹/₁₀-3 ⅘ in
Waterproof: Yes
Fogproof: Yes
Limited Lifetime Warranty
Features: Fully multi-coated lenses. Includes TAC-2 low-profile tactical-adjustment knobs, with ¼ MOA-click

Burris Fullfield II Tactical 6.5-20x50 MM

Burris Fullfield TAC 30 Tactical 3-9x40 MM

Burris Handgun 3-12x32 MM

windage and elevation adjustments that can be reset to zero using three set screws.

Manufacturer's Suggested Retail Price: **$518**
Estimated "Real World" Price: **$329**

HANDGUN 3-12X32 MM WITH BALLISTIC PLEX RETICLE

(also in 2x20 mm, 1.5-4x26 mm, and 2-7x32 mm, and with Plex reticle)

Weight: 16 oz
Length: 10 ⅘ in
Main Body Tube Diameter: 1 in
Power: 3-12X
Objective Diameter: 32 mm
Exit Pupil: 11-2.7 mm
Field of View: 14-4 ft @ 100 yards
Twilight Factor: 9.7-19.5
Eye Relief: 10-19 in
Waterproof: Yes

Fogproof: Yes
Limited Lifetime Warranty
Features: Burris's handgun scopes use fully multi-coated optics. The scope is available with parallax adjustment and variable power. The Posi-Lock windage-and-elevation adjustment system replaces tension springs with a retractable steel post that is loosened for sighting in, then screwed tight to lock the setting and prevent its being shifted by recoil. (Adjustments on the 3-12X are in ⅛ MOA clicks, ¼ MOA in the 1.5-4X and 2-7X scopes, and ½ MOA on the 2X.) And the Ballistic Plex reticle allows for bullet-drop compensation with specific caliber-load-barrel length combinations.

Manufacturer's Suggested Retail Price: **$656**
Estimated "Real World" Price: **$429**

RIFLESCOPES

SCOUT 2.75X27 MM

Weight: 7 oz
Length: 9 ¹/₅ in
Main Body Tube Diameter: 1 in
Power: 2.75X
Objective Diameter: 27 mm
Exit Pupil: 7.3 mm
Field of View: 15 ft @ 100 yards
Twilight Factor: 8.6
Eye Relief: 8.5-14 in
Waterproof: Yes
Fogproof: Yes
Limited Lifetime Warranty
Features: This is a scope designed for use on a lever rifle or on the Jeff Cooper "Scout Rifle"-style short-action lightweight carbine. The extended eye relief allows easy access to the magazine for reloading, and the low power allows the shooter to maintain his peripheral vision.
Manufacturer's Suggested Retail Price: $399
Estimated "Real World" Price: $249

SIGNATURE SELECT 3-12X44 MM WITH BALLISTIC PLEX RETICLE

(also in 3-10x40 mm and 4-16x44 mm)
Weight: 18 oz
Length: 14 in
Main Body Tube Diameter: 1 in
Power: 3-12X
Objective Diameter: 44 mm
Exit Pupil: 15-3.6 mm
Field of View: 37-10 ft @ 100 yards
Twilight Factor: 11.4-22.9
Eye Relief: 3½-4 in
Waterproof: Yes
Fogproof: Yes
Limited Lifetime Warranty
Features: The Signature Select has index-matched "Hi-Lume" multi-coated lenses. Burris advertises its internal lenses as being 40-percent larger than other competitive 1-inch scopes.
Manufacturer's Suggested Retail Price: $778
Estimated "Real World" Price: $479

SIXX 2-12X50 MM ILLUMINATED WITH GERMAN 3P#4 RETICLE

(also in 2-12x40mm, 2-12x40 mm illuminated, and 2-12x50 mm, and with Ballistic Plex and Ballistic Plex E1 reticles)
Weight: 19 oz
Length: 12 ⁹/₁₀ in
Main Body Tube Diameter: 30 mm
Power: 2-12X
Objective Diameter: 50 mm
Exit Pupil: 25-4.2 mm
Field of View: 50-8.5 ft @ 100 yards
Twilight Factor: 8.9-21.9
Eye Relief: 3 ½-4 in
Waterproof: Yes
Fogproof: Yes
Limited Lifetime Warranty
Features: The SixX scope provides a 6:1 magnification ratio. It uses double-spring tension to lock in place internal components, combined with a 30 mm tube, and steel-on-steel ¼ MOA-click windage and elevation adjustments.
Manufacturer's Suggested Retail Price: $1915
Estimated "Real World" Price: $1199

XTREME TACTICAL XTR 6-24X50 MM WITH BALLISTIC MIL-DOT 14X

(also in 1-4x24 mm illuminated, 1-4x24 mm illuminated with Fastfire II reflex sight, 1.5-6x40 mm illuminated, 3-12x50 mm illuminated, 4-16x50 mm, and 4-16x50 mm illuminated, and with XTR Ballistic 5.56 Gen2, XTR Ballistic 7.62, and Ballistic Mil-Dot 12X)
Weight: 26 oz
Length: 16 ½ in
Main Body Tube Diameter: 30 mm
Power: 6-24X
Objective Diameter: 50 mm
Exit Pupil: 8.3-2.1 mm
Field of View: 19-5.3 ft @ 100 yards
Twilight Factor: 17.3-34.6
Eye Relief: 3 ¹/₅-3 ¾ in
Waterproof: Yes
Fogproof: Yes
Limited Lifetime Warranty

Features: The 30-mm XTR scope has a double-force coil-spring suspension locking the inner tube in place. Comes with side-mounted parallax adjustment; long-range models include tactical turret windage and elevation adjustment knobs with ¼ MOA clicks. Lenses are "index-matched" and multi-coated, and treated with "StormCoat" water repellent.
Manufacturer's Suggested Retail Price: $1628
Estimated "Real World" Price: $1029

Burris Scout 2.75X27 MM

Burris Signature Select 3-12x44 MM

Burris SixX 2-12x50 MM

Burris Xtreme Tactical XTR 6-24x50 MM

RIFLESCOPES

Bushnell

www.bushnell.com

BONE COLLECTOR 3-9X40 MM DOA 600 RETICLE

(also in 3-9x40 mm DOA 250 Reticle)
Weight: 13 oz
Length: 12 ³/₅ in
Power: 3-9X
Objective Diameter: 40 mm
Main Tube Diameter: 1 in
Eye Relief: 3 ¹/₃ in.
Exit Pupil: 13.3-4.4 mm
Field of View: 33.8-11.5 ft @ 100 yds
Twilight Factor: 10.95-18.97
Waterproof: Yes
Fogproof: Yes
Limited Lifetime Warranty
Features: The Bushnell Bone Collector
Edition advertises 90-percent light
transmission with the "Ultra Wide
Band Coating" and RainGuard HD
technologies. Made from a one-piece
aluminum tube with a fast-focus eye-
piece. The Bushnell DOA reticle tech-
nology featuring the Rack Bracket for
ranging distance and judging a buck's
trophy quality is available in two configurations–the DOA 600 for centerfire
rifles and the DOA 250 for muzzleloaders. The scope has ¼ MOA adjustment increments and a 50 MOA range
of adjustment for windage and
elevation.
**Manufacturer's Suggested Retail
Price**:..................**$569.95**
**Estimated "Real World"
Price**:..................**$319.99**

ELITE 3-9X40 MM MULTI-X RETICLE (MATTE FINISH)

*(also in 1.25-4x24 mm, 2.5-10x40
mm, 2.5-10x50 mm, 4-16x40 mm
Multi-X Reticle, 4-16x40 mm DOA 600
Reticle, 4 16x50 mm, 6-24x40 mm
Mil-Dot Reticle, 6-24x40 mm Multi-X
Reticle, 8-32x40 mm, Multi-X Reticle,
2-7x 32 mm, 3-10x40 mm, 3-9x40 mm
Gloss Finish, 3-9x40 mm Silver Finish,
3-9x40 mm FireFly Reticle, 3-9x40 mm
DOA 600 Reticle, 3-9x50 mm Multi-X
Reticle, 3-9x50 mm DOA 600 Reticle,
3-9x50 mm FireFly Reticle)*
Weight: 13 oz
Length: 12.6 in
Power: 3-9X
Objective Diameter: 40 mm
Main Tube Diameter: 1 in
Eye Relief: 3 ²/₅ in

Exit Pupil: 13.33-4.44 mm
Field of View: 33.8-11.5 ft @ 100 yds
Twilight Factor: 10.95-18.97
Waterproof: Yes
Fogproof: Yes
**"No Questions Asked" One-Year Elite
Warranty and Limited Lifetime
Warranty**
Features: The Elite family of one-
piece-tube riflescopes includes fully
multi-coated optics, with Bushnell's
"Ultra Wide Band Coating"; and the
lenses are treated with moisture shed-
ding RainGuard HD. The fingertip
windage and elevation adjustments
are audible and resettable and in ¼
MOA increments. And the Elites are
available in an extensive selection of
variable-power, objective, and reticle
configurations.
**Manufacturer's Suggested Retail
Price**:..................**$398.95**
**Estimated "Real World"
Price**:..................**$249.99**

Bushnell Bone Collector Edition 3-9x40 MM

Bushnell Elite 3-9X40 MM

Bushnell Elite Tactical 3-12x44 MM

Bushnell Elite 6500 2.5-16x50 MM

Bushnell Trophy XLT 3-9x40 MM

ELITE TACTICAL 3-12X44 MM

(also in 10x44 mm, 2.5-16x42 mm, 4.5-30x50 mm, 5-15x40 mm, 6-24x50 mm Mil-Dot Reticle, 6-24x50 mm Illuminated Mil Dot)
Weight: 24.4 oz
Length: 13 in
Power: 3-12X
Objective Diameter: 44 mm
Main Tube Diameter: 30 mm
Eye Relief: 3 ¾ in
Exit Pupil: 14.66-3.66 mm
Field of View: 36-10 ft @ 100 yds
Twilight Factor: 11.48-22.97
Waterproof: Yes
Fogproof: Yes
"No Questions Asked" One-Year Elite Warranty and Limited Lifetime Warranty
Features: This year Bushnell's taken their top-of-the-line Elite 6500 riflescope and offered it to "personnel" (military, police, and to private shooters who want a high-tech, hard-use scope and have a $1000 to spend) by giving it a tactical treatment. Along with the 1 inch fogproof and waterproof 3-12x44 Elite Tactical comes in a variety of configurations from 10x40 mm fixed to 6-24x50 mm variable. Some of the scopes feature 6.5-times magnification range, similar to the Elite 6500. All come with tactical target-adjustment turrets and non-glare black-matte finish as well as "blacked-out" cosmetics for concealment. All the Elite Tacticals have fully multi-coated (with Bushnell "Ultra Wide Band Coating") optics and RainGuard HD moisture-shedding exterior coating, along with illuminated and non-illuminated mildot reticles.
Manufacturer's Suggested Retail Price: $1435.95
Estimated "Real World" Price: $899.99

ELITE 6500 2.5-16X50 MM MIL-DOT RETICLE

(also in 1.25x-8x32 mm, 2.5-16x42 mm Fine Multi-X Reticle, 2.5-16x42 mm Mil-Dot Reticle, 2.5-16x50 mm FMX Reticle, 4.5-30x50 mm DOA 600 Reticle, 4.5-30x50 mm Fine Multi-X Reticle, 4.5-30x50 mm Mil Dot Reticle)
Weight: 21 oz
Length: 13 ½ in
Power: 2.5-16X
Objective Diameter: 50 mm
Mai Tube Diameter: 30 mm
Eye Relief: 3 ⁹/₁₀ in
Exit Pupil: 20-3.12 mm
Field of View: 42-7 ft @ 100 yds
Twilight Factor: 11.18-28.28
Waterproof: Yes
Fogproof: Yes
"No Questions Asked" One-Year Flite Warranty and Limited Lifetime Warranty
Features: The Elite 6500 series features a 6.5-times range of magnification. Lenses have a 60-layer "Ultra Wide Band Coating" with an advertised 91-percent total light transmission through the scope, and are treated with permanent, water-repellent RainGuard HD coating. Windage and elevation adjustments are in ¼ MOA increments and do not require a tool and are audible. The variable Elite 6500s come in a variety of power, objective, and reticle configurations.
Manufacturer's Suggested Retail Price: $1242.95
Estimated "Real World" Price: $779.99

TROPHY XLT 3-9X40 MM MIL-DOT RETICLE

(also in 3-9x40 mm DOA 250 Reticle Matte Finish, 3-9x40 mm DOA 250 Reticle Camo Finish, 3-9x40 mm DOA 600 Reticle, 3-9x40 mm Multi-X Reticle Gloss Finish, 3-9x40 mm Multi-X Reticle Silver Finish, 3-9x40 mm Multi-X Reticle Matte Finish, 3-9x40 mm Circle-X Reticle, 3-9x50 mm, 4-12x40 mm DOA 600 Reticle, 4-12x40 mm Multi-X Reticle, 1-4x24 mm, 1.5-6x42 mm, 1.5-6x44 mm, 3-12x56 mm, 1.75-4x32 mm Camo Finish, 1.75-4x32 mm Matte Finish, 2-6x32 mm Matte Finish, 2-6x32 mm Silver Finish, 2-7x36 mm DOA Crossbow Reticle, 2-7x36 mm DOA 200 Reticle, 3-9x40 mm DOA 200 Reticle, 6-18x50 mm)
Weight: 14.1 oz
Length: 11 ⁹/₁₀ in
Power: 3-9X
Objective Diameter: 40 mm
Main Tube Diameter: 1 in
Eye Relief: 4 in
Exit Pupil: 13.3-4.4 mm
Field of View: 40-13 ft @ 100 yds
Twilight Factor: 10.95-18.97
Waterproof: Yes
Fogproof: Yes
Features: The Trophy XLT features fully multi-coated optics that are advertised to produce 91-percent total-light transmission. It has a one-piece tube with an integrated saddle. Has ¼ MOA fingertip windage and elevation adjustments with a range of adjustment of 80 MOA. Comes with Butler Creek flip-up scope covers.
Manufacturer's Suggested Retail Price: $204.95
Estimated "Real World" Price: $117.99

RIFLESCOPES

Cabela's

www.cabelas.com

Cabela's Alaskan Guide 1 in. 3-10x40 MM EXT

ALASKAN GUIDE 1 INCH 3-10X40 MM EXT– "EXTENDED RANGE"

(also in 4-12x44 mm SF–side-focus parallax adjustment–and 6-18x50 mm SF EXT, and 3-10x40 mm, 4-12x44 mm SF, and 6-18x50 mm SF Duplexes)
Weight: 13.5 oz
Length: 12 ²/₅ in
Power: 3-10X
Objective Diameter: 40 mm
Main Tube Diameter: 1 in
Exit Pupil: 13.33-4 mm
Field of View: 33.65-10.48 ft @ 100 yards
Twilight Factor: 10.95-20
Eye Relief: 3 ¾ in
Waterproof: Yes
Fogproof: Yes
Limited Lifetime Warranty
Features: This scope use "Guidetech" broadband lens coating technology. The body is a three-dimensionally forged one-piece tube. All components are machined to military-grade tolerances. Low-profile turrets with ¼ MOA click windage and elevation adjustments. Hard-blasted anodized finish for durability and corrosion resistance. Moisture- and dust-repelling lenses.
Estimated "Real World" Price: $269.99

ALASKAN GUIDE 30 MM 3-12 SF X52 MM WITH RANGEFINDING RETICLE

(also in 4-16 SF x52 mm, and both with side-focus parallax adjustment and with Duplex and EXT reticles)
Weight: 21.9 oz
Length: 14 in

Power: 3-12X
Objective Diameter: 52 mm
Main Tube Diameter: 30 mm
Exit Pupil: 17.33-4.33 mm
Field of View: 31.5-7.8 ft @ 100 yards
Twilight Factor: 12.48-24.97
Eye Relief: 4 in
Waterproof: Yes
Fogproof: Yes
Limited Lifetime Warranty
Features: The features on these scopes are similar to those on the other Alaskan Guide rifles with the addition of the 30 mm tube and 52 mm objective for added light gathering an enhanced field of view with less aberration.
Estimated "Real World" Price: $269.99

ALASKAN GUIDE PREMIUM 3-9X40 MM

(also in 4-12x40 and 6-20x40 with adjustable objective–AO)
Weight: 13 oz

Length: 12 ²/₅ in
Power: 3-9X
Objective Diameter: 40 mm
Main Tube Diameter: 1 in
Exit Pupil: 13.33-4.44 mm
Field of View: 33.2-11.1 ft @ 100 yards
Twilight Factor: 10.95-18.97
Eye Relief: 3 ½ in
Waterproof: Yes
Fogproof: Yes
Limited Lifetime Warranty
Features: The lens surface is fully multi-coated. A one-piece aluminum tube; power adjustment is rubber coated; positive-click increments on the fast-focus eyepiece; metal-to-metal contact between the windage and elevation adjustments and the erector tube; and ½ MOA adjustments. The AO ring on the higher magnification scopes is knurled.
Estimated "Real World" Price: $299.99

Cabela's Alaskan Guide 30 MM

Cabela's Alaskan Guide Premium 3-9x40 MM

RIFLESCOPES

5X ALPHA 3-15X40 MM
Weight: 12 oz
Length: 12 ²/₅ in
Power: 3-15X
Objective Diameter: 40 mm
Main Tube Diameter: 1 in
Exit Pupil: 13.33-2.66 mm
Field of View: 31.5-6.3 ft @ 100 yards
Twilight Factor: 10.95-24.49
Eye Relief: 4 in
Waterproof: Yes
Fogproof: Yes
Limited Lifetime Warranty
Features: The Alpha riflescopes in 5-times optical zoom and the EXT bullet drop reticle for long-range accuracy out to 500 yards. The other reticles are matched to bullet drop at 300, 400 and 500 yards. Pine Ridge lenses are multicoated for enhanced light transmission and image clarity. Scopes are waterproof, shockproof and fogproof for all-weather performance. Windage and elevation adjustments are ¼ MOA clicks.
**Estimated "Real World"
Price:** $249.99

EURO 3-9X42 MM EXT
(also with Duplex reticle, and in 4-12x50 mm and 6-18x50 mm with EXT and Duplex reticles)
Weight: 16 oz
Length: 12 ²/₅ in
Power: 3-9X
Objective Diameter: 42 mm
Main Tube Diameter: 1 in
Exit Pupil: 14-4.66 mm
Field of View: 36.3-12.1 ft @ 100 yards
Twilight Factor: 11.22-19.44
Eye Relief: 3 ¾ in
Waterproof: Yes
Fogproof: Yes
Limited Lifetime Warranty
Features: Cabela's has partnered with the Czech optics manufacturer Meopta to make its new Euro line of rifle scopes. These 1 inch tube variable scopes are CNC machined from a single billet of aircraft-aluminum and bead blasted before undergoing ELOX (electrolytic oxidation) anodization for a reduced-glare black matte, abrasion-resistant finish. The scopes are available in configurations ranging from 3-9x42 mm to 4-12x50 and 6-18x50

mm, with objectives on the 6-18s equipped with parallax adjustment. Lenses are fully multi-coated using ion-assisted coatings. The scopes is listed as having 3 ¾ inches of eye relief; fields of view that span from 36.3 feet to 6.1 feet at 100 yards, depending on power setting and objective diameter; have fast-focus eyepieces; and are waterproof and fogproof. Elevation and windage turrets are finger adjustable in ¼ MOA clicks. The Euro scopes also offer two reticle options, the "D" for duplex and for $50 more the "EXT" glass-etched hash-marked "extended range" for individual holds out to 500 yards. And the Euro scopes come with Cabela's 60 day free-trial-period guarantee.
**Estimated "Real World"
Price:** $449.99

LEVER ACTION 3-9X40 MM .30-30 WINCHESTER RETICLE
(also in .308 Marlin, .338 Marlin Express, .444 Marlin, .35 Remington, and .45-70 Govt. reticles)
Weight: 14.64 oz
Length: 13 in
Power: 3-9X
Objective Diameter: 40 mm
Main Tube Diameter: 1 in
Exit Pupil: 13.33-4.44 mm
Field of View: 30.55-9.6 ft @ 100 yards
Twilight Factor: 10.95-18.97
Eye Relief: 5 ½ in
Waterproof: Yes
Fogproof: Yes
Limited Lifetime Warranty
Features: These scopes are tailored for use with Hornady LEVERevolution, Flex Tip bullet-technology ammunition. The scopes are outfitted with Ballistic Glass Reticles specifically engineered for use with a particular Hornady LEVERevolution round. An extra-long, 5½ inch eye relief facilitates mounting on traditional lever-action rifles. Comes with 200 and 300 yard horizontal lines to hold dead-on at those ranges with 100 yard zero. Besides the .30-30 Winchester regulated for the 160 grain LEVERevolution round, other models are available for use with LEVERevolution ammunition in .45-70 (modern rifles only) using a 325-grain bullet, .444 Marlin using a 265-grain bullet, .308 Marlin using a 160-grain bullet, .35 Rem. using a 200-grain bullet, .338 Marlin using a 200-grain bullet and .44 Mag. using a 225-grain bullet. The tube is machined aluminum and lenses are multi-coated. Windage and elevation are adjustable in ¼ MOA clicks.
**Estimated "Real World"
Price:** $99.99

Cabela's 5x Alpha 3-15x40 MM

Cabela's Lever Action 3-9x40 MM .30-30 Winchester

Cabela's Euro 3-9x42 MM

Cabela's

www.cabelas.com

POWDERHORN MUZZLELOADER 3-10X40 MM

(also in silver and camo)
Weight: 11.6 oz
Length: 12 ⅕ in
Power: 3-10X
Objective Diameter: 40 mm
Main Tube Diameter: 1 in
Exit Pupil: 13.33-4 mm
Field of View: 31.5-10.5 ft @ 100 yards
Twilight Factor: 10.95-20
Eye Relief: 3 ¾ in
Waterproof: Yes
Fogproof: Yes
Limited Lifetime Warranty
Features: The ballistic reticle of the Powderhorn scope is regulated to match bullet drop. When the scope is sighted in at 100 yards at 10X, the next bar down is calibrated for a drop at 150 yards and the lowest bar down for 250 yards. Loading data is based on the 250-grain saboted bullet and 150 grains of Triple Se7en FFg powder. Scope multi-coated lenses and hand-turn ¼ MOA click adjustments.
Estimated "Real World"
Price:. $119.99

RIMFIRE 3-9X40 MM WITH DUPLEX RETICLE

(also in 4x32 mm)
Weight: 13.4 oz
Length: 12 in
Power: 3-9X
Objective Diameter: 40 mm
Main Tube Diameter: 1 in
Exit Pupil: 13.33-4.44 mm
Field of View: 37.7-12.4 ft @ 100 yards
Twilight Factor: 10.95-18.97
Eye Relief: 4 in
Waterproof: Yes
Fogproof: Yes
Limited Lifetime Warranty
Features: For hunting, target shooting, or plinking with a rimfire rifle. Parallax-free at 50 yards. Multi-coated glass optics. Extended eye relief and an expanded exit pupil. Low-profile windage and elevation turrets.
Estimated "Real World"
Price:. $79.99

SHOTGUN/BLACK-POWDER 2.5-7X32 MM WITH DIAMOND RETICLE

(also with Duplex reticle and in camo, and in 2.5x32 mm fixed power with Diamond reticle)
Weight: 12.2 oz
Length: 11 ⅘ in
Power: 2.5-7X
Objective Diameter: 32 mm
Main Tube Diameter: 1 in
Exit Pupil: 12.8-4.57 mm
Field of View: 40.03-14.15 ft @ 100 yards
Twilight Factor: 8.94-14.96
Eye Relief: 4 in
Waterproof: Yes
Fogproof: Yes
Limited Lifetime Warranty
Features: For use with slug guns an muzzleloading rifles. Has extended eye relief and an expanded exit pupil to promote faster target acquisition.

Uses rigid machined-aluminum tube and has low-profile turrets for windage and elevation adjustments. Also available in Seclusion 3D camouflage.
Estimated "Real World"
Price:. $69.99

Cabela's Shotgun/Black-Powder 2.5-7x32 MM

Cabela's Powderhorn Muzzleloader 3-10x40 MM

Cabela's Rimfire 3-9x40 MM

RIFLESCOPES

PINE RIDGE .17 TACTICAL 3-12 SF X40 MM WITH TARGET DOT RETICLE

(also with Duplex reticle and in 3-9x40 mm with Duplex reticle)
Weight: 16.2 oz
Length: 13 ²/₅ in
Power: 3-12X
Objective Diameter: 40 mm
Main Tube Diameter: 1 in
Exit Pupil: 13.3 3-3.33 mm
Field of View: 29.42-7.33 ft @ 100 yards
Twilight Factor: 10.95-21.9
Eye Relief: 4 in
Waterproof: Yes
Fogproof: Yes
Limited Lifetime Warranty
Features: Redesigned in 2010 with new low-profile knurled turrets for windage and elevation adjustments. Incrementally calibrated to adjust for bullet drop out to 300 yards. Fully coated optics. The 3-12x40 features side-focus parallax adjustment and is available with the Target Dot reticle, with Duplex also available. Uses lighter, smaller "eggshell" eyepiece.
Estimated "Real World" Price: $119.99

30 MM TACTICAL CLASSIC 6-18 SF X50 MM EXT

(also with Duplex reticle and in 2.5-10X50 mm and 8-32 SF x50 mm with both EXT and Duplex reticles)
Weight: 17.5 oz
Length: 13 ¼ in
Power: 6-18X
Objective Diameter: 50 mm
Main Tube Diameter: 30 mm
Exit Pupil: 8.33-2.77 mm
Field of View: 15.88-5.24 ft @ 100 yards
Twilight Factor: 17.32-30
Eye Relief: 4 in
Waterproof: Yes
Fogproof: Yes
Limited Lifetime Warranty
Features: Made with the larger, tactical-grade three-dimensionally forged 30 mm tube and with Guidetech broadband lens technology. All components are machined to military-grade tolerances. Low-profile turrets with ¼ MOA click windage and elevation adjustments for the 2.5-10 power models and a ⅛ MOA click windage and elevation adjustments for the 6-18 and 8-32 power models. Hard-blasted anodized finish and moisture- and dust-repelling lenses.
Estimated "Real World" Price: $369.99

Cabela's Pine Ridge .17 Tactical 3-12 SF x40 MM

Cabela's 30mm Tactical Classic 6-18 SF x50 MM

Hensoldt
www.zeiss.com/sports

ZF 3-12X56 MM

Weight: 28.21 oz
Length: 12 ¾ in
Power: 3-12X
Main Body Tube Diameter: 34 mm
Objective Diameter: 56 mm
Exit Pupil: 14.9-4.6 mm
Field of View: 394-112 (SFP) or 384-112 (FFP) ft @ 1000 m (1094 yds)
Twilight Factor: 12.9-25.9
Eye Relief: 3 ½ in
Waterproof: Yes
Fogproof: Yes
Warranty: Pending
Features: The Hensoldt ZF 3-12x56 mm is available in either first - or second-focal-plane models with illuminated MilDot reticle with range-finding brackets. The 34 mm main tube provides for extended elevation adjustment. Color-coded target knobs for rotation tracking in MRAD adjustments allow for shooting over extended distances. Parallax adjustment is also provided on both models of these scopes. A variety of sunshades, anti-reflective devices (ARD) and filters are available as accessories.
Manufacturer's Suggested Retail Price: $3210.99

Hensoldt ZF 3-12x56 MM

Hensoldt

www.zeiss.com/sports

ZF 4-16X56 MM

Weight: 31.74 oz
Length: 13 ½ in
Power: 4-16X
Objective Diameter: 56 mm
Main Tube Body Diameter: 34 mm
Exit Pupil: 14-3.5 mm
Field of View: 295-82 (FFP) or 285-82 (SFP) ft @ 1000 m (1094 yds)
Twilight Factor: 14.9-29.9
Eye Relief: 3 ½ in
Waterproof: Yes
Fogproof: Yes
Warranty: Pending
Features: The Hensoldt ZF 4-12x56 mm military-grade riflescope is available in either first- or second-focal-plane models with illuminated MilDot reticle with range-finding brackets. The 34 mm main tube provides for extended elevation adjustment. Color-coded target knobs for rotation tracking in MRAD adjustments allow for shooting over extended distances. Parallax adjustment is also provided on both models of these scopes. A variety of sunshades, anti-reflective devices (ARD), and filters are available as accessories.
Manufacturer's Suggested Retail Price: $3463.99

ZF 6-24X56 MM

Weight: 29.98 oz
Length: 15 ½ in
Main Tube Body Diameter: 30 mm
Power: 6-24X
Objective Diameter: 56 mm
Exit Pupil: 9.3-2.3 mm
Field of View: 200-56 ft @ 1000 m (1094 yds)
Twilight Factor: 18.3-36.6
Eye Relief: 3 ½ in
Waterproof: Yes
Fogproof: Yes
Warranty: Pending
Features: The Hensoldt ZF 6-24x56 mm is available in a second-focal-plane model with illuminated MilDot reticle with range-finding brackets. The 30 mm main tube provides for extended elevation adjustment. Large objective lens and extended magnification can be used with night-vision systems. Color-coded target knobs for rotation tracking in MRAD adjustments allow for shooting over extended distances.

Parallax adjustment is also provided with this scope. A variety of sunshades, anti-reflective devices (ARD) and filters are available as accessories.
Manufacturer's Suggested Retail Price: $3503.99

ZF 6-24X72 MM

Weight: 38.8 oz
Length: 15 in
Main Tube Body Diameter: 34 mm
Power: 6-24X
Objective Diameter: 72 mm
Exit Pupil: 12-3 mm
Field of View: 200-56 ft meters @ 1000 meters (1094 yds)
Twilight Factor: 20.7-41.5
Eye Relief: 3 ½ in
Waterproof: Yes
Fogproof: Yes

Warranty: Pending
Features: The Hensoldt ZF 6-24x72 mm is available in a second-focal-plane model with illuminated MilDot reticle with range-finding brackets. The 34 mm main tube provides for extended elevation adjustment. The large 72 mm objective lens offers maximum image resolution over long distances. Can be used with night-vision systems. Color-coded target knobs for rotation tracking in MRAD adjustments allow for shooting over extended distances. Parallax adjustment is also provided with this scope. A variety of sunshades, anti-reflective devices (ARD), and filters are available as accessories.
Manufacturer's Suggested Retail Price: $3771.99

Hensoldt ZF 4-16x56 MM

Hensoldt ZF 6-24x56 MM

Hensoldt ZF 6-24x72 MM

Huskemaw Optics

www.huskemawoptics.com

BLUE DIAMOND 5-20X50 MM

Weight: 23 oz
Length: 13 ¾ in
Main Tube Body Diameter: 30 mm
Power: 5-20X
Objective Diameter: 50 mm
Elevation and Windage Adjustments: ⅓ MOA per click
Exit Pupil: 10-2.5 mm
Field of View: 18.5-5 ft @ 100 yds
Twilight Factor: 15.81-31.62
Eye Relief: 3 ⅖-4 in
Waterproof: Yes
Fogproof: Yes
Lifetime Warranty
Features: The Huskemaw Blue Diamond 5-20X, for varmint, target,

Huskemaw Blue Diamond 5-20 MM

and big-game shooting, includes True BC, Rapid Field Ballistic Compensator, and Hunt Smart rangefinding and windage compensating reticle with side-focus parallax-correction dial.

Ballistic compensation and parallax adjustments can be made without breaking shooting position.
Manufacturer's Suggested Retail Price: $1149.99

Konus

www.konuspro.com

KONUSPRO 3-9X4O MM

(also in 3-9x50 mm, 4x32 mm, 3-9x32 mm, 2-7x32 mm, 2.5x32 mm, 1.5-5x32 mm, and 6-24x44 mm, and with illuminated reticles)
Weight: 17.2 oz
Length: 13 in
Main Tube Body Diameter: 1 in
Power: 3-9X
Objective Diameter: 40 mm
Elevation and Windage Adjustments: ¼ MOA per click
Exit Pupil: 13.3-4.4 mm

Field of View: 380-125 ft @ 1000 yds
Twilight Factor: 11-19
Eye Relief: 3 in
Waterproof: Yes
Fogproof: Yes
Warranty: Lifetime Replacement
Features: The 3-9x40 mm KonusPro (like all KonusPro riflescopes) is equipped with a laser-etched reticle and features multi-coated optics and is finger adjustable for windage and elevation. It is approved for both centerfire rifles and airguns. The scope is

covered by the Konus Lifeline expedited-replacement service program (855-KONUS-4U), which lets you contact a service representative and request that a new scope be shipped, overnight, if your scope is damaged in the field on a hunting trip.
Manufacturer's Suggested Retail Price: $139.99
Estimated "Real World" Price: $109.99

Konuspro 3-9x40 MM

RIFLESCOPES

Konus

www.konuspro.com

KONUSPRO-275 3-9X40

(also in 3-10x44 with illuminated reticle)
Weight: 17.2 0z
Length: 13 in
Main Tube Body Diameter: 1 in
Power: 3-9X
Objective Diameter: 40 mm
Elevation and Windage Adjustments: ¼ MOA per click
Exit Pupil: 13.34.4 mm
Field of View: 390-125 ft @ 1000 yds
Twilight Factor: 11-19
Eye Relief: 3 in
Waterproof: Yes
Fogproof: Yes
Warranty: Lifetime Replacement
Features: The KonusPro 275 features Konus's exclusive ballistic reticle with several aiming points out to 275 yards. The 275 is designed for use with muzzleloaders. Lateral hash marks provide compensation for crosswinds.
Manufacturer's Suggested Retail Price: $179.99
Estimated "Real World" Price: $139-99
Company Address and Phone:

KONUSPRO-550 3-9X40 MM

(also available with an illuminated reticle and in 4-16x50 mm)
Weight: 14.4 0z
Length: 12 ¹/5 in
Main Tube Body Diameter: 1 in
Power: 3-9X
Objective Diameter: 40 mm
Elevation and Windage Adjustments: ¼ MOA per click
Exit Pupil: 13.3-4.4 mm
Field of View: 369 ft-123 ft @1000 yds
Twilight Factor: 11-19
Eye Relief: 3 in
Waterproof: Yes
Fogproof: Yes
Warranty: Lifetime Replacement
Features: The KonusPro 550 3-9x40 mm is designed for use with centerfire rifles for long range. Lateral hash marks provide compensation for cross-winds.
Manufacturer's Suggested Retail Price: $179.99
Estimated "Real World" Price: $139-99

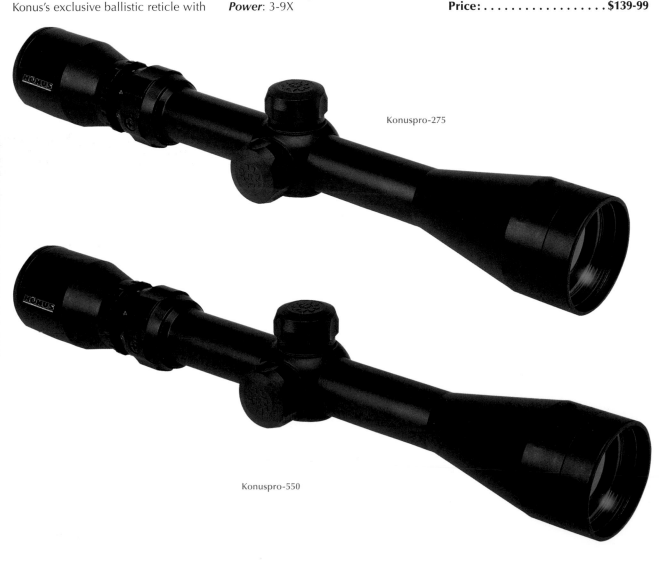

Konuspro-275

Konuspro-550

RIFLESCOPES

KONUSPRO M30 8.5-32X52 MM

(also in 4.5-16x40 mm, 6.5-25x44 mm, 3-12x56 mm, 1-4x24 mm, 1.5-6x44 mm)

Weight: 29.9 0z
Length: 17 in
Main Tube Body Diameter: 30 mm
Power: 8.5-32X
Objective Diameter: 52 mm
Elevation and Windage Adjustments: $^1/_{10}$ mil per click
Exit Pupil: 6.1-1.6 mm
Field of View: 130-33 ft @ 1000 yds
Twilight Factor: 21-41
Eye Relief: 4-3 $^2/_5$ in
Waterproof: Yes
Fogproof: Yes
Warranty: Lifetime Replacement

Konuspro M30 8.5-32x52 MM

Features: The KonusPro M30 line of riflescopes has been tested, used, and recommended by the National Tactical Officers Association (NTOA). The 8.5-32x52 mm is made for extreme long-range shooting, whether tactical, big-game hunting, or varminting. The M30s are said to be able to withstand heavy recoil.

Manufacturer's Suggested Retail Price: $679.99
Estimated "Real World" Price: $529.99

Kruger Optics
www.krugeroptical.com

K4 SERIES 4-16X40 MM

(also in 2-8x32 mm, 3-12x40 mm, 3-12x50 mm)

Weight: 13 oz
Length: 13 in
Main Tube Body Diameter: 1 in.
Power: 4-16X
Objective Diameter: 40 mm
Elevation and Windage Adjustments: ¼ MOA per click
Exit Pupil: 10-2.5 mm
Field of View: 24-6 ft @ 100 yds
Twilight Factor: 12.6-25.3
Eye Relief: 3 ¾ in
Waterproof: Yes
Fogproof: Yes
Transferable limited lifetime
Features: Kruger Optical's K-4 riflescope provides long eye relief and extra-large exit pupil. Built from a one-piece main tube, the K-4 has ¼-minute windage and elevation clicks with low-profile adjutment knobs. The optics are fully broad-band anti-reflection coated.
Manufacturer's Suggested Retail Price: $176.41
Estimated "Real World" Price: $149.95

TACDRIVER TACTICAL 2.5-10X50

(also in 1-4x24 mm, 1.5-5x32 mm, and 10-40x56 mm)

Weight: 24 oz
Length: 13 in
Main Tube Body Diameter: 30 mm
Power: 2.5-10X
Objective Diameter: 50 mm
Elevation and Windage Adjustments: ¼ MOA per click
Exit Pupil: 20-5 mm
Field of View: 38-10.5 ft @ 1000 yds
Twilight Factor: 11-22
Eye Relief: 3 ¼ in

Waterproof: Yes
Fogproof: Yes
Transferable limited lifetime
Features: The Kruger TacDriver Tactical 2.5-10x50 mm riflescope offers locking windage and elevation knobs, glass-etched illuminated Mil-Dot reticle with 11 brightness settings, 30 mm one-piece main tube, and fully multi-coated optics.
Manufacturer's Suggested Retail Price: $258.75
Estimated "Real World" Price: $244.97

Kruger K4 Series 4-16x40 MM

Kruger TacDriver Tactical 2.5-10x50 MM

RIFLESCOPES

Kruger Optics

www.krugeroptical.com

TACDRIVER 3-9X50 MM

(also in 4x32 mm, 3-9x40 mm,
4-12x40mm, and 4-12x50 mm)
Weight: 14 oz
Length: 12 in
Main Tube Body Diameter: 1 in
Power: 3-9 X
Objective Diameter: 50 mm
Elevation and Windage Adjustments:
¼ MOA per click
Exit Pupil: 16.6-5.5 mm
Field of View: 32-10.5 ft @ 100 yds
Twilight Factor: 12.2-21.21
Eye Relief: 3 ¾ in
Waterproof: Yes
Fogproof: Yes
Transferable limited lifetime

Kruger TacDriver Series 3-9x50 MM

Features: The Kruger TacDriver rifle-scope is equipped with Kruger's patented "Rapid Target Technology" (RTT), providing a larger exit pupil and longer eye relief. The one-inch main tube is made from solid aircraft-grade aluminum. Includes multi-coated optics and a fast-focus eyepiece.

Manufacturer's Suggested Retail Price:.....................$94.04
Estimated "Real World" Price:.....................$79.99

Leatherwood/Hi-Lux Optics

www.hi-luxoptics.com

M-1000 AUTO RANGING TRAJECTORY 2.5-10X44 MM

Weight: 25.2 oz
Length: 13 ⅕ in
Main Body Tube Diameter: 1 in
Power: 2.5-10X
Objective Diameter: 44 mm
Exit Pupil: 10.2-4 mm
Field of View: 47.2-11.9 ft @ 100 yards
Twilight Factor: 10.5-21
Eye Relief: 3 ¹⁄₁₀ in
Waterproof: Yes
Fogproof: Yes
Limited Lifetime Warranty
Features: Leatherwood/Hi-Lux M-1000 Auto Ranging Trajectory 2.5-10x44 scope compensate for the bullet drop automatically by using an external cam system. It can be calibrated for most centerfire rifle cartridges–from .223 to .50 BMG. The shooter sets the multi-caliber cam for the different cartridges being used. The M-1000 scope comes with mount and rings. The scope reticle used is the "No-Math Mil-Dot."

Leatherwood-Hi-Lux M-1000

Manufacturer's Suggested Retail Price:.....................$459
Estimated "Real World" Price:.....................$379

RIFLESCOPES

Leatherwood/Hi-Lux Optics

www.hi-luxoptics.com

TOBY BRIDGES SERIES HIGH PERFORMANCE MUZZLELOADING 3-9X40 MM, MATTE BLACK

(also available in silver finish)

Weight: 15.8 oz
Length: 12 ½ in
Main Body Tube Diameter: 1 in
Power: 3-9X
Objective Diameter: 40 mm
Exit Pupil: 13.3-4.4 mm
Field of View: 39-13 ft @ 100 yards
Twilight Factor: 10.95-18.97
Eye Relief: 3 ¼ in
Waterproof: Yes
Fogproof: Yes
Limited Lifetime Warranty
Features: The TB/ML scope is designed in-line ignition muzzleloaders and saboted bullets. It offers multiple reticles for shooting at ranges out to 250 yards. The scope is shipped with a chart providing points of impact at different ranges when using the longer range cross-bar reticles with different bullets at different velocities. All lens surfaces are multi-coated for maximum light transmission.
Manufacturer's Suggested Retail Price: . . . . $179 blue-black; . . . . $189 silver
Estimated "Real World" Price: $159; $169

TOP ANGLE SERIES 7-30X50 MM

(also in 3-12x50 and 4-16x50)

Weight: 29.8 oz
Length: 17 ⅕ in
Main Body Tube Diameter: 30 mm
Power: 7-30X
Objective Diameter: 50 mm
Exit Pupil: 6.9-2.3 mm
Field of View: 10.6-3.5 ft @ 100 yards
Twilight Factor: 18.70-38.72
Eye Relief: 3 ⅛ in
Waterproof: Yes
Fogproof: Yes
Limited Lifetime Warranty
Features: All surfaces of all lenses are fully multi-coated; larger diameter turret housing offers additional windage-elevation adjustment in ¼ MOA clicks; top-angle objective lens focus rather than adjustment on the objective lens bell; and mildot reticle for determining range.

Leatherwood Hi-Lux Toby Bridges High Performance Muzzleloading 3-9x40 MM

Leatherwood Hi-Lux Top Angle Series 7-30x50 mm

Manufacturer's Suggested Retail Price: $449
Estimated "Real World" Price: $399

WM. MALCOLM SERIES LONG 6X 32 IN

(also in 3X 17 in and 6X 18 in Short Malcolms)

Weight: 32.5 oz
Length: 30 ½ in (without front mount extension tube)
Main Body Tube Diameter: ¾ in
Power: 6X
Objective Diameter: 16 mm
Exit Pupil: 5.8 mm

Leatherwood-Hi-Lux Wm. Malcolm Long 6X 32 In.

Field of View: 10 ft @ 100 yards
Twilight Factor: 13.85
Eye Relief: 4 in
Waterproof: Yes
Fogproof: Yes
Limited Lifetime Warranty
Features: A modern copy of the Model 1855 W. Malcolm riflescopes, comes with early-style mounts for scoping original and replica 19th century breechloading rifles (Sharps, rolling block, high wall, etc.) or late period long-range percussion muzzleloading bullet rifles. Objective, ocular and internal lenses are fully multi-coated for maximum light transition through a ¾ inch (steel) scope tube. Interchangeable front extension tubes allow this mid 1800s period-correct scope to be mounted on rifles with barrels of 30 to 34 inches.
Manufacturer's Suggested Retail Price: $439
Estimated "Real World" Price: $399

Leatherwood/Hi-Lux Optics

www.hi-luxoptics.com

CLOSE MEDIUM RANGE - CMR SERIES 1-4X24 MM

Weight: 16.5 oz
Length: 10 ⅕ in
Main Body Tube Diameter: 30 mm
Power: 1-4X
Objective Diameter: 24 mm
Exit Pupil: 11.1-6 mm
Field of View: 94.8-26.2 ft @ 100 yards
Twilight Factor: 4.89-9.79
Eye Relief: 3 in
Waterproof: Yes
Fogproof: Yes
Limited Lifetime Warranty
Features: All surfaces of all lenses are fully multi-coated; zero-locking turrets; large external target-style windage and elevation adjustment knobs; power-ring extended lever handle for power change; fast eye-piece focus; CMR ranging reticle for determining range and also BDC hold over value good for .223, .308, and other calibers; green or red illuminated reticle; turrets adjustable in ½ MOA clicks.
Manufacturer's Suggested Retail Price: **$399**
Estimated "Real World" Price: **$339**

Leatherwood-Hi-Lux CMR Series 1-4x24 MM

Leatherwood-Hi-Lux Malcolm 8X USMC Sniper

MALCOLM 8X USMC SNIPER SCOPE

Weight: 24 oz
Length: 24 in
Main Tube Body Diameter: ¾ in
Power: 8X
Objective Diameter: 31.75 mm
Elevation and Windage Adjustments: ¼ MOA per click based on a 7 ⅕-in spacing between the rings
Exit Pupil: 4 mm
Field of View: 11 ft @ 100 yds
Twilight Factor: 15.93
Eye Relief: 3 ½-4 in
Waterproof: Yes
Fogproof: Yes

Limited Lifetime Warranty
Features: The heritage of the vintage Leatherwood/Hi-Lux Malcolm 8X USMC sniper scope dates back to the sniper scopes of World War II and Korea that were mounted on the .30-'o6 Springfield Model 1903-A1; and in the early days of the Vietnam war famed marksman such as the legendary Marine sniper Carlos Hancock used the original of this scope. This close replica includes fully multi-coated lenses and micrometer click external adjustments.
Manufacturer's Suggested Retail Price: **$549**

Leica Sport Optics

www.leica-sportoptics.com

ER 2.5-10X42 MM

(also in 3.5-14x42 mm)
Weight: 15.1 oz
Length: 12 ½ in
Main Tube Diameter: 30 mm
Power: 2.5-10X
Objective Diameter: 42 mm
Exit Pupil: 14-4.2 mm
Field of View:43.5-11.7 ft @ 100 yds
Eye Relief: 4 in
Waterproof: Yes
Fog proof: Yes
Limited Lifetime Warranty
Features: The Leica ER features 4 inch-es of eye relief throughout the power range, a compact eyepiece, second focal plane reticles, nitrogen filled, waterproof to 13 feet, and a generous straight tube for easy mounting. Adjustments are ¼ MOA, parallax free to 100 meters, and exterior lens coated with Aqua Dura water repellant. Available with German #1, German 4A, Leica Plex, Leica Ballistic Plex, and Leica CDD reticles.
Estimated "Real World" Price: **$1,959**

Leica ER 2.5-10x42 MM

Leupold & Stevens Inc

www.leupold.com

FX-3 6X42 MM ADJUSTABLE OBJECTIVE COMPETITION HUNTER

(also in 12x40mm Adjustable Objective Target, 25x40 mm Adjustable Objective Silhouette, 30x40 mm Adjustable Objective Silhouette and 6x42 mm)

Weight: 15 oz
Length: 12 ⅕ inches
Main Body Tube Diameter: 1 in
Power: 6X
Objective Diameter: 42 mm
Exit Pupil: 7 mm
Field of View: 17.3 ft @ 100 yards
Twilight Factor: 15.87
Eye Relief: 4 ⅖ in
Waterproof: Yes
Fogproof: Yes
Limited Lifetime Warranty
Features: The FX-3 fixed-power riflescope features Leupold's Xtended Twilight Lens System. DiamondCoat 2 helps increase light transmission and provides maximum scratch resistance. Blackened lens edges helps reduce glare and improve resolution and contrast. Windage and elevation adjustments are ¼ MOA.
Manufacturer's Suggested Retail Price: **$469.99**

MARK 4 2.5-8X36 MM MR/T M1

(also in 1.5-5x20 mm, 1.5-5x20 mm M2 and 2.5-8x36 mm M2 models)

Weight: 16 oz
Length: 11 ⅓ in
Main Body Tube Diameter: 30 mm
Power: 2.5-8X
Objective Diameter: 36 mm
Exit Pupil: 14.4-4.5
Field of View: 35.5-13.6 ft @ 100 yds
Twilight Factor: 9.48-16.97
Eye Relief: 3 ⁷⁄₁₀-3.0 in
Waterproof: Yes
Fogproof: Yes
"Leupold Tactical Optical Products Warranty"
Features: The Leupold Mark 4 2.5-8x36 mm Mid Range/Tactical M1 riflescope features the Xtended Twilight Lens System and DiamondCoat 2 for maximum scratch resistance. The M1 dials are ¼ MOA for windage and elevation. They are finger-adjustable with audible, tactile clicks. Illuminated Mil

Dot and Tactical Milling Reticle (TMR) options are offered, along with a non-illuminated TMR version. Flip-open lens covers are standard.
Manufacturer's Suggested Retail Price: **$949.99**
($1099.99 with illuminated reticle)

MARK 4 CQ/T 1-3X14 MM

Weight: 17.5 oz
Length: 8 ⅘ in
Main Body Tube Diameter: 2 ⁹⁄₁₀ in
Power: 1-3X
Objective Diameter: 30 mm
Exit Pupil: 30-10 mm
Field of View: 112-41 ft @ 100 yds
Twilight Factor: 3.74-6.48
Eye Relief: 2 ⅘-2 in
Waterproof: Yes
Fogproof: Yes
"Leupold Tactical Optical Products Warranty"
Features: The Leupold Mark 4 Close Quarters/Tactical (CQ/T) riflescope combines a red dot at close range with a variable-power optic. Its Circle Dot reticle is visible with or without illumination or batteries. Eleven reticle-illumination settings. The CQ/T has slotted ½ MOA click adjustments for windage and elevation.
Manufacturer's Suggested Retail Price: **$899.99**

Leupold FX 3 6x42 MM

Leupold Mark 4 2.5-8x36 MM MRT

Leupold Mark CQ-T 1-3x14 MM

RIFLESCOPES

Leupold & Stevens Inc

www.leupold.com

PRISMATIC 1X14 MM, MATTE BLACK

(also in "Dark Earth" anodized finish and with illuminated, Circle Plex, or DCD reticles)

Weight: 12 oz.
Length: 4 ½ in
Main Body Tube Diameter: 30 mm
Power: 1X
Field of View: 83 ft @ 100 yards
Eye Relief: 3 in
Waterproof: Yes
Fogproof: Yes
Limited Lifetime Warranty with Electronics Warranted Against Defect for Two Years
Features: Leupold's Prismatic 1x14 mm riflescope provides the fast target acquisition of a non-magnifying red dot sight with a wide field of view. Key features include an etched-glass reticle that is visible with or without illumination, ½ MOA finger-adjustable windage and elevation dials, and a focusing eyepiece. In addition to the hunting model, including a National Wild Turkey Federation model, the Prismatic is available in a tactical version.
Manufacturer's Suggested Retail Price:.................**$479.99**

Leupold Prismatic 1x14 MM

RIFLEMAN 3-9X40 MM

(also in 2-7x33 mm, 4-12x40 mm, and 3-9x50 mm)

Weight: 12.6 oz
Length: 12 ⅓ in
Power: 3.3-8.5X
Objective Diameter: 40 mm
Main Tube Diameter: 1 in
Exit Pupil: 12-4.7 mm
Field of View: 329-131 ft @ 1000 yards
Twilight Factor: 10.95-18.97
Eye Relief: 4.2-3.7 in
Waterproof: Yes
Fogproof: Yes
Limited Lifetime Warranty
Features: The Leupold Rifleman series features fully coated lenses for excellent low light brightness, durable waterproof construction.
Estimated "Real World" Price:.................**$199.99**

Leupold Rifleman 3-9x40 MM

Leupold VX-3 3.5-10x40 MM

VX-3 3.5-10X40 MM AND CDS (CUSTOM DIAL SYSTEM) MODEL

(also in 1.5-5x20 mm, 1.5-5x20 mm IR, 1.75-6x32 mm, 2.5-8x36 mm, 4.5-14x40 mm, 4.5-14x40 mm CDS, 4.5-14x40 mm SF, 4.5-14x40 mm AO, 6.5-20x40 mm AO, 6.5-20x40 mm EFR, 6.5-20x40 mm SF, 3.5-10x50 mm, 3.5-10x50 mm CDS, 3.5 10x50 mm IR, 3.5-10x50 mm IR Metric, 4.5-14x50 mm, 4.5-14x50 mm SF, 4.5-14x50 mm SF IR, 6.5-20x50 mm SF Target, and 8.5-23x50 mm SF Target)

Weight: 2.6 oz
Length: 2 in
Power: 3-9.7X (actual)
Objective Diameter: 0 mm
Main Tube Diameter: 1 in
Exit Pupil: 2.1-4.1 mm
Field of View: 98-110ft @ 1000 yards
Twilight Factor:
Eye Relief: .4-3.6 in
Waterproof: Yes
Fogproof: Yes
Limited Lifetime Warranty
Features: The Leupold VX-3 series features Leupold's X-Tended Twilight Lens System for high light transmission, finger adjustable ¼ MOA windage and elevation dials, abrasion-resistant Diamond Coat 2 external lens coatings, a dual spring erector assembly, and available CDS dial options and illuminated reticles.
Estimated "Real World" Price:............**$479.99-559.99**

RIFLESCOPES

Leupold & Stevens Inc

www.leupold.com

VX-3L 3.5-10X50 MM AND CDS MODEL

(also in 3.5-10x50 mm IR, 4.5-14x50 mm SF IR, 3.5-10x56 mm, 3.5-10x56 mm IR, 4.5-14x56 mm SF, 4.5-14x56 mm SF IR, 6.5-20x56 mm SF, 6.5-20x56 mm SF Target, and 6.5-20x56 mm SF Extreme Varmint)

Weight: 16.3 oz
Length: 12 ½ in
Power: 3.3-9.5X (actual)
Objective Diameter: 50 mm
Main Tube Diameter: 1 in
Exit Pupil: 15-5.3 mm
Field of View: 298-110 ft @ 1000 yards
Twilight Factor: 13.22-22.36
Eye Relief: 4 ½-3 ³/₅ in
Waterproof: Yes
Fogproof: Yes
Limited Lifetime Warranty
Features: The VX-3Ls are the longer-range versions of the Leupold VX-3 series.
Estimated "Real World" Price:. **$699.99-779.99**

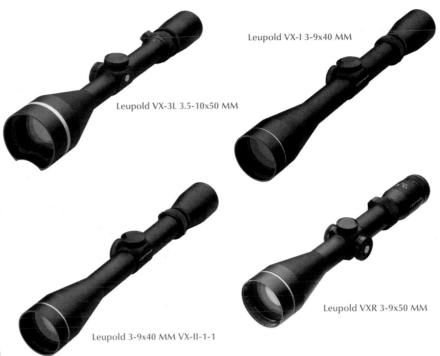

Leupold VX-I 3-9x40 MM

Leupold VX-3L 3.5-10x50 MM

Leupold VXR 3-9x50 MM

Leupold 3-9x40 MM VX-II-1-1

VX-I 3-9X40 MM

(also in 3-9x50 mm)

Weight: 12 oz
Length: 12 ⅕ in
Power: 3.3-8.5x (actual)
Objective Diameter: 40 mm
Main Tube Diameter: 1 in
Exit Pupil: 12-4.7 mm
Field of View: 329-131 ft @ 1000 yards
Twilight Factor: 10.95-18.97
Eye Relief: 4 ⅕-3 ⁷/₁₀ in
Waterproof: Yes
Fogproof: Yes
Limited Lifetime Warranty
Features: The Leupold VX-I series features Leupold's Standard Multicoat Lens system for low-light brightness and microfriction ¼ MOA windage and elevation dials.
Estimated "Real World" Price:. **$229.99**

VX-II 3-9X40 MM

(also in 1-4x20 mm, 4-12x40 mm AO, 6-18x40 mm AO and Target, 3-9x50 mm, 4-12x50 mm)

Weight: 12 oz
Length: 12 ⅖ in
Power: 3.3-8.6X (actual)
Objective Diameter: 40 mm
Main Tube Diameter: 1 in

Exit Pupil: 12-4.6 mm
Field of View: 323-140 ft @ 1000 yards
Twilight Factor: 10.95-18.97
Eye Relief: 4 ⁷/₁₀-3 ⁷/₁₀ in
Waterproof: Yes
Fogproof: Yes
Limited Lifetime Warranty
Features: The Leupold VX-II series features Leupold's Multicoat 4 Lens System for 92% light transmission and coin click ¼ MOA windage and elevation dials.
Estimated "Real World" Price:. **$299.99**

VX-R 3-9X50 MM

(also in 1.25-4x20 mm, 1.25-4x20 mm HOG, 2-7x33 mm, 3-9x40 mm, 4-12x40 mm, and 4-12x50)

Weight: 16.6 oz
Length: 12 ⅓ in
Power: 3.3-8.6X (actual)
Objective Diameter: 50 mm
Main Tube Diameter: 30 mm
Exit Pupil: 15.2-5.8 mm
Field of View: 336-136 ft @ 1000 yards
Twilight Factor: 12.24-21.21
Eye Relief: 4 ⅕-3 ³/₅ in
Waterproof: Yes
Fogproof: Yes

Limited Lifetime Warranty
Features: The Leupold VX-R has a fiber-optic LED illumination system employing the FireDot Reticle System which is available in FireDot Duplex, FireDot Circle, Ballistic FireDot, and FireDot 4, with the dot within the reticle illuminated while the rest of the reticle is non-illuminated. The VX-R uses what Leupold calls its "Motion Sensor Technology" (MST) that employs a single-touch button to activate the illumination, offering eight different intensity settings including a high-low indicator. The reticle will automatically switch to "stand-by mode" after five minutes of inactivity, then reactivate whenever the rifle is moved. The VX-R is powered by a CR-2032 coin cell battery. Windage and elevation are adjustable in ¼ MOA finger clicks, and the erector assembly uses twin bias springs. The extended-focus-range eyepiece is one turn adjustable. The lenses are lead-free glass and the exterior surfaces have an ion-assisted coating to help prevent scratches.
Estimated "Real World" Price:. **$549.99**

Leupold & Stevens Inc

www.leupold.com

COMPETITION SERIES 40X45 MM

(also in 35x45 mm and 45x45 mm)
Weight: 20.3 oz
Length: 15 ⁹/₁₀ in
Main Body Tube Diameter: 30 mm
Power: 40X
Objective Diameter: 45 mm
Exit Pupil: 1.125 mm
Field of View: 2.7 ft @ 100 yds
Twilight Factor: 42.42
Eye Relief: 3 ¹/₅ in
Waterproof: Yes
Fogproof: Yes
Limited Lifetime Warranty
Features: Key features of the Competition Series riflescope include Leupold's Multicoat 4 lens system, side-focus parallax adjustment, ¹/₈ MOA target-style click adjustments for windage and elevation, and ocular adjustments from -2.0 to +1.0. Reticle options include Target Crosshair and ¹/₈ MOA Target Dot. The scope comes with threaded lens covers.
Manufacturer's Suggested Retail Price: **$999**
Estimated "Real World" Price: **$999**

Leupold Competition Series 40x45 MM

FX-3 6X42 MM ADJUSTABLE OBJECTIVE COMPETITION HUNTER

(also available in 12x40 vmm Adjustable Objective Target, 25x40 mm Adjustable Objective Silhouette, 30x40 mm Adjustable Objective Silhouette, and 6x42 mm)
Weight: 15 oz
Length: 12 ¹/₅ in
Main Body Tube Diameter: 1 in
Power: 6X
Objective Diameter: 42 mm
Exit Pupil: 7
Field of View: 17.3 ft @ 100 yds
Twilight Factor: 15.87
Eye Relief: 4 ²/₅ in
Waterproof: Yes
Fogproof: Yes
Limited Lifetime Warranty
Features: The FX-3 fixed-power riflescope features Leupold's Xtended Twilight Lens System and scratch-resistant DiamondCoat 2. Blackened lens edges helps reduce glare and improve resolution and contrast. Windage and elevation adjustments

Leupold FX-3 6x42 MM

are ¼ MOA.
Manufacturer's Suggested Retail Price: **$469.99**

FX-II 4X33 MM

(FX-II also in 2.5x28 mm IER Scout and 6x36mm)
Weight: 9.3 oz
Length: 10 ½ in
Main Body Tube Diameter: 1 in
Power: 4X
Objective Diameter: 33 mm
Exit Pupil: 8.25 mm
Field of View: 24 ft @ 100 yds
Twilight Factor: 11.48

Leupold FX-II 4x33 MM

Eye Relief: 4 in
Waterproof: Yes
Fogproof: Yes
Limited Lifetime Warranty
Features: The FX-II fixed-power riflescope features Leupold's Multi-coat 4 lens system, with a large exit pupil for low-light conditions. Other features include ¼ MOA coin-click adjustments for windage and elevation. Reticle options include Duplex and Wide Duplex.
Manufacturer's Suggested Retail Price: **$299.99**

RIFLESCOPES

Leupold & Stevens Inc

www.leupold.com

MARK 8 1.1-8X24MM CQBSS FRONT FOCAL

Weight: 23.2 oz
Length: 11 ¾ in
Main Body Tube Diameter: 34 mm
Power: 1.1-8X
Objective Diameter: 24 mm
Exit Pupil: 21.81-3
Field of View: 92.0-14.7 ft @ 100 yds
Twilight Factor: 5.13-13.85
Eye Relief: 3 ⁷⁄₁₀-3 ³⁄₁₀ in
Waterproof: Yes
Fogproof: Yes
***Leupold Tactical Optical Products
Warranty***
Features: The Mark 8 CQBSS provides a holographic red-dot sight an 8-power riflescope. The main tube features a fully checkered ocular bell. The front focal plane reticle is accurate at all magnification settings and is combined with a 5-MOA holographic red dot. Eight illumination settings allow for dot contrast with or without night vision. Other key features include Auto-Locking Pinch and Turn turrets with 0.10 mil clicks, an AA53 (77 grain 5.56 NATO) BDC dial and quick-change BDC ring, and Index Matched Lens System with DiamondCoat 2.

**Manufacturer's Suggested Retail
Price:** $3,999.99

Leupold Mark 8 1.1-8x24 MM

ULTIMATE SLAM 2-7X33 MM IN SILVER

(also in 3-9x40 mm in matte black, Mossy Oak Break-Up, and Mossy Oak Treestand finishes)
Weight: 10.5 oz
Length: 10 ⁴⁄₅ in
Main Body Tube Diameter: 1 in
Power: 2-7X
Objective Diameter: 33 mm
Exit Pupil: 16.5-4.7
Field of View: 43.2-17.3 ft @ 100 yds
Twilight Factor: 8.12-15.19
Eye Relief: 4 ¹⁄₅-3 ⁷⁄₁₀ in
Waterproof: Yes
Fogproof: Yes
Limited Lifetime Warranty
Features: The UltimateSlam scope is designed for muzzleloaders and shotguns. Has Leupold's Sabot Ballistics Reticle (SA.B.R.) with a power-selector ring to synchronize with their preferred load. Other features include Leupold's Standard Multi-coat lens system.

Leupold Ultimate Slam 2-7x33 MM

**Manufacturer's Suggested Retail
Price:** $249.99
**Estimated "Real World"
Price:** $249.99

Millett

www.millettsights.com

Millett DMS-1 1-4x24 MM

Millett LRS 6-25x56 MM

Millett TRS-1 4-16x50 MM

DMS-1 1-4X24 MM A-TACS FINISH

(also in 1-4x24 mm matte finish)
Power: 1-4X
Objective Diameter: 24 mm
Main Tube Diameter: 30 mm
Eye Relief: 3 ½ in
Exit Pupil: 24-6 mm
Field of View: 90-23 ft @ 100 yds
Twilight Factor: 4.89-9.79
Waterproof: Yes
Fogproof: Yes
Limited Lifetime Warranty
Features: The low-light Designated Marksman Riflescope (DMS) features a Donut Dot illuminated reticle with the "donut" subtending 18 MOA for ranges as close as three meters, and the illuminated dot 1 MOA for medium to extended ranges out to 500 yards. The featured A-TACS model offers the best in concealment technology.
Manufacturer's Suggested Retail Price: **$450.95**
Estimated "Real World" Price: **$269.95**

LRS 6-25X56 MM ILLUMINATED MIL-DOTBAR RETICLE MATTE FINISH .1 MIL

(also in 6-25x 56 mm Mil-DotBar Reticle .25 Click Value, 6-25x 56 mm Mil-DotBar Reticle .1 Mil Click Value, 6-25x 56 mm Illuminated Mil-DotBar Reticle A-TACS Finish, Millet LRS 6-25x 56 mm Illuminated Mil-DotBar Reticle Matte Finish .25 Click Value)
Power: 6-25X
Objective Diameter: 56 mm
Main Tube Diameter: 35 mm
Eye Relief: 3 in
Exit Pupil: 9.33-2.24 mm
Twilight Factor: 18.33-37.41
Waterproof: Yes
Fogproof: Yes
Limited Lifetime Warranty
Features: The Millet LRS is built for extreme-duty and extended-range for calibers such as the .50 BMG and .338 Lapua. Massively built with a one-piece 35mm tube and 56mm objective, it has precision controls with 140 MOA range of adjustment. The Millett LRS riflescope line features several glass-etched Mil-DotBar reticle and click value configurations. The scope is available in a matte or A-TACS (Advanced Tactical Concealment System) finish.
Manufacturer's Suggested Retail Price: **$854.95**
Estimated "Real World" Price: **$462.95**

TRS-1 4-16X50 MM .1 MIL CLICK VALUE

(also in 4-16x50 mm .25 Click Value Matte Finish, 4-16x50 mm .25 Click Value A-TACS Finish, 10x50 mm .25 Click Value, 10x50 mm .1 mil Click Value)
Power: 4-16X
Objective Diameter: 50 mm
Main Tube Diameter: 30 mm
Eye Relief: 3 ½ in
Exit Pupil: 12.5-3.12 mm
Twilight Factor: 14.14-28.28
Waterproof: Yes
Fogproof: Yes
Limited Lifetime Warranty
Features: The Mil-DotBar reticle system functions as a standard Mil-Dot with the addition of a thin line for easier alignment for rangefinding and holdover. The illuminated reticle is green and adjustable for brightness. The optics are multi-coated and the scope has a side-focus parallax adjustment knob. Five models are available, including a fixed 10x50 mm model and several 4-16x50 mm models finished in either matte or A-TACS (Advanced Tactical Concealment System).
Manufacturer's Suggested Retail Price: **$567.95**
Estimated "Real World" Price: **$323.95**

Minox GmbH

www.minox.com

ZA 3 3-9X40 MM

(also in 3-9x50 mm)
Weight: 12.3 oz
Length: 12 ³⁄₁₀ in
Main Tube Diameter: 1 in
Power: 3-9X
Objective Diameter: 40 mm
Exit Pupil: 13.33-4.44 mm
Field of View: 31.5 ft @ 100 yards
Twilight Factor: 10.95-18.97
Eye Relief: 4.0 in
Waterproof: Yes
Fogproof: Yes
"Full Coverage" Lifetime Warranty
Features: Fully multi-coated Schott-glass lenses with 3-times magnification zoom range.
Manufacturer's Suggested Retail Price:.................... $479
Estimated "Real World" Price:.................... $399

Minox-ZA 3 3-9x40 MM

ZA 5 4-20X50 MM SF

(also in 1.5-8x32 mm, 2-10x40 mm, 2-10x50 mm, 3-15x42 mm, 4-20x56 mm, 6-30x56 mm)
Weight: 19.2 oz
Length: 13 ¹⁄₂ in
Main Tube Diameter: 1 in (30 mm in 6-30x56)
Power: 4-20X
Objective Diameter: 50 mm
Exit Pupil: 0.49 mm
Field of View: 23.6 ft @ 100 yards

Minox-ZA 5 4-20x50 MM SF

Twilight Factor: 14.14-31.62
Eye Relief: 4 in
Waterproof: Yes
Fogproof: Yes
"Full Coverage" Lifetime Warranty
Features: Fully multi-coated Schott-glass lenses with 5-times magnification zoom range.
Manufacturer's Suggested Retail Price:.................... $839
Estimated "Real World" Price:.................... $699

Nightforce Optics

www.nightforceoptics.com

3.5-15X50 MM NXS

Weight: 30 oz
Length: 14 ⁴⁄₅ in
Main Tube Diameter: 30 mm
Power: 3.5-15
Objective Diameter: 50 mm
Exit Pupil: 14.3-3.6 mm
Field of View: 27.6 ft @ 100 yds-7.3 ft @ 100 yds
Twilight Factor: 13.22-27.38
Eye Relief: 3 ⁹⁄₁₀ in
Waterproof: Yes
Fogproof: Yes
Limited Lifetime Warranty *(mechanical defects in materials and workmanship in optical and mechanical components for as long as the original purchaser owns the scope.)*
Features: Developed for use on military small arms, proven in the harshest combat conditions around the globe. An excellent choice for all-around hunting and by professional shooters. Low mounting profile, a full 110 MOA of internal adjustment, applicable to a wide range of applications. Available with .250 MOA and .1 Mil-Radian adjustments, and one of several scopes offered with Nightforce's patented ZeroStop, which provides an instant

Nightforce
3.5-15x50 MM
ZeroStop

return to the shooter's chosen zero point under any conditions, just by feel.
Manufacturer's Suggested Retail Price:.................... $1591
Estimated "Real World" Price:.................... $1527

Nightforce Optics

www.nightforceoptics.com

1-4X24 MM NXS COMPACT

Weight: 17 oz
Length: 8 ⁴/₅ in
Main Tube Diameter: 30 mm
Power: 1-4
Objective Diameter: 24 mm
Exit Pupil: 1-6 mm
Field of View: 100 ft @ 100 yds-25 ft @ 100 yds
Twilight Factor: 4.89-9.79
Eye Relief: 3 ½ in
Waterproof: Yes
Fogproof: Yes
Limited Lifetime Warranty *(mechanical defects in materials and workmanship in optical and mechanical components for as long as the original purchaser owns the scope)*
Features: Originally designed for military and CQB (close-quarters battle) applications, it is ideal for the hunter pursuing dangerous or running game at close quarters. A low profile complements big bore bolt action and double rifles. One of the few true one-power variable scopes in the world, making it as quick as open sights yet vastly more precise. The shooter can keep both eyes open for instant target acquisition in high-stress situations.
Manufacturer's Suggested Retail Price: **$1252**
Estimated "Real World" Price: **$1202**

2.5-10X32 MM NXS COMPACT

Weight: 19 oz
Length: 12 in
Main Tube Diameter: 30 mm
Power: 2.5-10
Objective Diameter: 32 mm
Exit Pupil: 13.3-3.3 mm
Field of View: 44 ft @ 100 yds-11 ft @ 100 yds
Twilight Factor: 8.94-17.88
Eye Relief: 3 ²/₅ in
Waterproof: Yes
Fogproof: Yes
Limited Lifetime Warranty *(mechanical defects in materials and workmanship in optical and mechanical components for as long as the original purchaser owns the scope)*
Features: The optimum in size-to-weight performance. Light in weight, low in profile, it will not overwhelm

Nightforce 1-4x24 MM

Night Force 2.5-10x32 MM NXS Compact

Nightforce 3.5-15x56 MM NXS

even a delicate rifle yet provides low-light performance that exceeds most optics with much larger objective lenses. Large exit pupil for fast target acquisition and no parallax or focusing issues. Available with the Nightforce Velocity 600 yard reticle, which provides precise shot placement to 600 yards with no guessing at holdover.
Manufacturer's Suggested Retail Price: **$1345**
Estimated "Real World" Price: **$1291**

3.5-15 X 56 MM NXS

Weight: 31 oz
Length: 14 ²/₅ in
Main Tube Diameter: 30 mm
Power: 3.5-15
Objective Diameter: 56 mm
Exit Pupil: 14.5-4 mm
Field of View: 27.6 ft @ 100 yds-7.3 ft @ 100 yds
Twilight Factor: 14-28.98
Eye Relief: 3 ⁴/₅ in
Waterproof: Yes
Fogproof: Yes
Limited Lifetime Warranty *(mechanical defects in materials and workmanship in optical and mechanical components for as long as the original purchaser owns the scope)*
Features: The top choice for law enforcement snipers. The large objective lens increases resolution and exit pupil size for quick target acquisition and optimal performance at twilight. Especially appropriate for tactical teams that may not have a dedicated night vision scope. This configuration also makes it ideal for hunters and sport shooters wanting a scope that will perform in the shadows. Large field of view allows quick recovery from recoil for an accurate second shot.
Manufacturer's Suggested Retail Price: **$1591**
Estimated "Real World" Price: **$1527**

5.5-22X50 MM NXS

Weight: 31 oz
Length: 15 ¹/₁₀ in
Main Tube Diameter: 30 mm
Power: 5.5-22
Objective Diameter: 50 mm
Exit Pupil: 9.1-2.3 mm
Field of View: 17.5 ft @ 100 yds-4.7 ft @ 100 yds
Twilight Factor: 16.58-33.16
Eye Relief: 3 ⁴/₅ in
Waterproof: Yes
Fogproof: Yes
Limited Lifetime Warranty (mechanical defects in materials and workmanship in optical and mechanical components for as long as the original purchaser owns the scope)
Features: Originally developed for the U.S. military's extreme long range shooting and hard target interdiction. Plenty of eye relief and 100 MOA of elevation travel make it ideal for use on the .50 BMG, allowing accurate shots to 2000 yards and beyond. Slim profile, easily adaptable to a wide range of mounting systems. Superb resolution at high magnification has made the 5.5-22x50 extremely popular for long-range hunting.
Manufacturer's Suggested Retail Price: **$1751**
Estimated "Real World" Price: **$1681**

5.5-22X56 MM NXS

Weight: 32 oz
Length: 15 ¹/₅ in
Main Tube Diameter: 30 mm
Power: 5.5-22
Objective Diameter: 56 mm
Exit Pupil: 10.2-2.5 mm
Field of View: 17.5 ft. @ 100 yds-4.7 ft. @ 100 yds
Twilight Factor: 17.54-35.09
Eye Relief: 3 ⁹/₁₀ in
Waterproof: Yes
Fogproof: Yes
Limited Lifetime Warranty (mechanical defects in materials and workmanship in optical and mechanical components for as long as the original purchaser owns the scope)
Features: Advanced field tactical riflescope for long-range applications. Maximum clarity and resolution across the entire magnification range, excep-

Nightforce 5.5-22x50 MM

Nightforce 5.5-22x56 MM

tional low-light performance. Available with ZeroStop technology and .125 and .250 MOA or .1 Mil-Radian adjustments.
Manufacturer's Suggested Retail Price: **$1751**
Estimated "Real World" Price: **$1681**

8-32X56 MM NXS

Weight: 34 oz
Length: 15 ⁹/₁₀ in
Main Tube Diameter: 30 mm
Power: 8-32
Objective Diameter: 56 mm
Exit Pupil: 7-1.8 mm
Field of View: 12.1 ft @ 100 yds-3.1 ft @ 100 yds
Twilight Factor: 21.16-42.33
Eye Relief: 3 ⁴/₅ in
Waterproof: Yes
Fogproof: Yes
Limited Lifetime Warranty (mechanical defects in materials and workmanship in optical and mechanical components for as long as the original purchaser owns the scope)

Nightforce 8-32x56 MM

Features: For long-range hunting, competition, and target shooting. A choice of five different reticles for the shooter's chosen application. For pushing the "long-range" envelope to two miles and beyond, maximizing the potential of the newest high-performance cartridges. Offered with .125 MOA, .250 MOA or .1 Mil-Radian Hi-Speed adjustments. ZeroStop also available.
Manufacturer's Suggested Retail Price: **$1883**
Estimated "Real World" Price: **$1808**

Nightforce Optics

www.nightforceoptics.com

8-32X56 MM PRECISION BENCHREST

(also in 12-42x56 mm)
Weight: 36 oz
Length: 16 ³/₅ in
Main Tube Diameter: 30 mm
Power: 8-32
Objective Diameter: 56 mm
Exit Pupil: 5.6-1.7 mm
Field of View: 9.4 ft @ 100 yds-3.1 ft @ 100 yds
Twilight Factor: 21.16-42.33
Eye Relief: 2 ⁹/₁₀ in
Waterproof: Yes
Fogproof: Yes
Limited Lifetime Warranty *(mechanical defects in materials and workmanship in optical and mechanical components for as long as the original purchaser owns the scope)*
Features: A new Heavy Gun World Record was set with this scope in September, 2010, by Matt Kline–10 shots, 2.815 inches. This breaks the previous world record of 3.044 inches, also set with a Nightforce scope. Nightforce Precision Benchrest models are known for superior resolution, allowing fine detail to be distinguished at extreme ranges. An adjustable objective allows extra-fine focus for parallax adjustment from 25 yards to infinity. Target adjustments are calibrated in true .125 MOA (⅛ click) values, and can be re-indexed to zero after sighting in. Includes an eyepiece that allows for fast reticle focusing and a glass-etched illuminated reticle, with eight different reticles for specific applications and maximum precision at extreme ranges.
Manufacturer's Suggested Retail Price: $1275
Estimated "Real World" Price: $1211

12-42X56 MM NXS

Weight: 34 oz
Length: 16 ¹/₁₀ in
Main Tube Diameter: 30 mm
Power: 12-42
Objective Diameter: 56 mm
Exit Pupil: 4.7-1.3 mm
Field of View: 8.2 ft @ 100 yds-2.4 ft @ 100 yds
Twilight Factor: 25.92-48.49
Eye Relief: 3 ⁴/₅ in

Nightforce 8-32x56 MM Precision Benchrest

Waterproof: Yes
Fogproof: Yes
Limited Lifetime Warranty *(mechanical defects in materials and workmanship in optical and mechanical components for as long as the original purchaser owns the scope)*
Features: Optical resolution comparable to the highest quality spotting scopes, with unsurpassed clarity across the entire magnification range. Specifically designed for optimum resolution under all conditions, even at maximum magnification, where other scopes often lose resolving power. A scope for rapidly growing F-Class competitions.
Manufacturer's Suggested Retail Price: $1964
Estimated "Real World" Price: $1885

3.5-15X50 MM F1 NXS

Weight: 30 oz
Length: 14 ⁴/₅ in
Main Tube Diameter: 30 mm
Power: 3.5-15
Objective Diameter: 50 mm
Exit Pupil: 11.5-3.2 mm
Field of View: 28 ft @ 100 yds-8.7 ft @ 100 yds
Twilight Factor: 13.22-27.38
Eye Relief: 3 ¹/₅ in
Waterproof: Yes
Fogproof: Yes
Limited Lifetime Warranty *(mechanical defects in materials and workmanship in optical and mechanical components for as long as the original purchaser owns the scope)*
Features: First focal plane reticle design, developed at the request of the U.S. military for a scope applicable to a wide range of targets at various distances. Five specialized reticles available to maximize first focal plane design. Since the reticle remains in the same visual proportion to the target

Nightforce 12-42x56 MM

Nightforce 3.5-15X50 MM F1 NXS

across the entire magnification range, it is especially appropriate with range-finding reticle designs. The F1 has distinct advantages in high-stress situations and when the user might encounter targets from up close to 1000 yards or more. Offered with .250 MOA or .1 Mil-Radian adjustments, with ZeroStop standard. Also includes Nightforce Ultralight rings.
Manufacturer's Suggested Retail Price: $2410
Estimated "Real World" Price: $2290

RIFLESCOPES

BOLT XR 3X32 MM BDC

Weight: 11.2 oz
Length: 8 ¹/₁₀ in
Main Body Tube Diameter: 1 in
Power: 3x
Objective Diameter: 32 mm
Exit Pupil: 10.7 mm
Field of View: 35.6 ft @ 100 yards
Twilight Factor: 9.79
Eye Relief: 3 ⁴/₅ in
Waterproof: Yes
Fogproof: Yes
Limited Lifetime Warranty
Features: Are you and your crossbow up to the 60-yard challenge? Nikon believes you are when your bow is wearing the all-new Bolt XR. Designed to do what other crossbow scopes do not, the Bolt XR features bright, fully multicoated 3x Nikon optics, a large ocular that makes full use of its wide field of view, 3.4-inches of eye relief and quick focus eye-piece with +4 diopter adjustment. The advanced BDC 60 reticle offers precise aiming points out to very achievable 60 yards based upon velocity of approximately 305 fps. You can match virtually any crossbow velocity and bolt weight using Spot On ballistic Match Technology. Fully multicoated lenses: For maximum brightness and contrast and light transmission up to 92%. Nikon coats all lenses with multiple layers of anti-reflective compounds. Precise ¼ inch @ 20 yds Adjustments: With an incredible 150 MOA adjustment range (@ 100 yds). Quick Focus

Eyepiece: ±4 Diopter
Zero-Reset Turrets: Zero-Reset turrets allow you to sight-in at 20 yards, then lift the spring-loaded adjustment knob, rotate to your "zero", and re-engage. Field adjustments are now as simple as dialing-in your subsequent ranges. Lightweight Compact Design: Fits virtually every crossbow design. Parallax-Free @ 20 yards: For optimum accuracy. Large Ocular with Quick Focus Eye Piece Waterproof, Fogproof & Shockproof
Manufacturer's Suggested Retail Price: **$218.95**
Estimated "Real World" Price: **$149.95**

BUCKMASTERS 1X20 MM BLACK POWDER WITH NIKOPLEX

Weight: 10.6 oz
Length: 9 ¹/₁₀ in
Main Body Tube Diameter: 1 in
Power: 1x
Objective Diameter: 20 mm
Exit Pupil: 20 mm
Field of View: 52 ½ ft @ 75 yards
Twilight Factor: 4.47
Eye Relief: 4 ³/₁₀-13 in
Waterproof: Yes
Fogproof: Yes
Warranty: Lifetime
Features: For muzzleloading hunting where only 1 power scopes are allowed. Uses Nikon's Brightvue multi-coating with a stated 92-percent

light transmission. Has hand-turn ½ MOA positive-click adjustments, plus quick-focus eyepiece.
Manufacturer's Suggested Retail Price: **$252.95**
Estimated "Real World" Price: **$179.95**

BUCKMASTERS 3-9X40 MM REALTREE APG NIKOPLEX

(also in 4.5-14x40 mm, 6-18x40 mm, 3-9x50 mm, and 4-12x50 mm, and in matte and silver with BDC, Mil Dot, and fine crosshair with dot)
Weight: 16.1 oz
Length: 13 ¹/₁₀ in
Main Body Tube Diameter: 1 in
Power: 3x-9x
Objective Diameter: 40 mm
Exit Pupil: 13.3-4.4 mm
Field of View: 35.7-11.9 ft @ 100 yards
Twilight Factor: 10.95-18.97
Eye Relief: 3 ³/₅-3 ³/₅ in
Waterproof: Yes
Fogproof: Yes
Limited Lifetime Warranty
Features: Built for centerfire rifle, muzzleloader, or rimfire,the Buckmasters 3-9x40 has Brightvue multi-coating, quick-focus eyepiece, hand-turn ¼ MOA click adjustments, and is adaptable for a sunshade.
Manufacturer's Suggested Retail Price: **$342.95**
Estimated "Real World" Price: **$239.95**

Nikon Bolt XR 3x32 MM

Nikon Buckmasters 3-9x40 MM

Nikon Buckmaster 1x20 MM Black Powder

Nikon Sport Optics

COYOTE SPECIAL 3-9X40 MM IN MOSSY OAK BRUSH WITH BDC PREDATOR RETICLE

(also in 4.5-14x40 mm and in matte and RealTree Max-1)

Weight: 16 oz
Length: 13 ¹/₁₀ in
Main Body Tube Diameter: 1 in
Power: 3-9x
Objective Diameter: 40 mm
Exit Pupil: 13.3-4.4 mm
Field of View: 35.7-11.9 ft @ 100 yards
Twilight Factor: 10.95-18.97
Eye Relief: 3 ²/₅-3 ²/₅ in
Waterproof: Yes
Fogproof: Yes
Limited Lifetime Warranty
Features: Nikon's 3-9x40 Coyote Special utilizes the BDC Predator Reticle for ranges out to 450 yards and beyond. The open BDC's ballistic circles don't obscure the target. Has multi-coated lenses; hand-turn ¼ MOA click adjustments; quick-focus eyepiece and lead- and arsenic-free "Eco-Glass." Uses the ARD (Anti Reflective Device) scope cover to eliminate glare but permit shooting.
Manufacturer's Suggested Retail Price: **$416.95**
Estimated "Real World" Price: **$279.95**

ENCORE 2.5-8X28 MM EER IN SILVER WITH BDC RETICLE

(also in 2x20 mm and in matte)

Weight: 11.46 oz
Length: 9 ⁴/₅ in
Main Body Tube Diameter: 1 in
Power: 2.5-8X
Objective Diameter: 28 mm
Exit Pupil: 3.5 mm
Field of View: 13.1-4.1 ft @ 100 yards
Twilight Factor: 8.36
Eye Relief: 12-30 (at 2.5x), 9-13 (at 8x) in
Waterproof: Yes
Fogproof: Yes
Limited Lifetime Warranty
Features: The 2.5-8x28 EER (Extended Eye Relief) scope, engineered for arm's length shooting, features Nikon's BDC reticle and is built for the severe recoil of hunting, varmint, and competition

Nikon Coyote Special 3-9X40 MM

Nikon 2.5-8x28 MM EER

Nikon M-223 3-12X42 MM

handgun shooting, advertised to withstand the recoil of calibers up to S&W .500 Magnum. With the Nikon Ultra ClearCoat optical system and quick-focus eyepiece.
Manufacturer's Suggested Retail Price: **$454.95**
Estimated "Real World" Price: **$299.95**

M-223 3-12X42 MM SF NIKOPLEX WITH RAPID ACTION TURRET

(also in 1-4x20 mm and 2-8x32 mm and with BDC 600 reticle)

Weight: 19.93 oz
Length: 13 ¹/₁₀ in
Main Body Tube Diameter: 1 in
Power: 3-12X
Objective Diameter: 42 mm
Exit Pupil: 14-3.5 mm

Field of View: 33.6-8.4 ft @ 100 yards
Twilight Factor: 11.22-22.44
Eye Relief: 4-3 ⁴/₅ in
Waterproof: Yes
Fogproof: Yes
Limited Lifetime Warranty
Features: The M-223 3-12x42 has side-focus parallax adjustment from zero out to 600 yards. With Nikon's Rapid Action Turret technology based on a .22³/₅.56mm 55-grain polymer tipped bullet. Has a 4-time zoom range, one-piece main body tube and "Ultra ClearCoat optics. Variable-magnification reference numbers are viewable from the shooter's position.
Manufacturer's Suggested Retail Price: **$620.95**
Estimated "Real World" Price: **$429.95**

RIFLESCOPES

Nikon Sport Optics

www.nikonhunting.com/products/riflescopes

M-223 LASER IRT 2.5-10X40 MM

Length: 12 ⅕ in
Power: 2.5-10X
Objective Diameter: 40 mm
Exit Pupil: 16-4 mm
Field of View: 23.6-7.3 ft @ 100 yards
Twilight Factor: 10-20
Eye Relief: 3 ½ in
Waterproof: Yes
Fogproof: Yes
Limited Lifetime Warranty on optics, one year on electronics
Features: The M-223 Immediate Ranging Technology riflescope combines a Nikon laser rangefinder with the M-223 BDC 600 reticle. The M-223 IRT provides the equivalent horizontal range to the target and features one-touch laser technology that keeps ranging and displaying distance for 12 seconds with a single push of the button. Low-profile mounts attach to Picatinny Rails. Remote control laser activator can be affixed to most firearms. Has a zoom control with the reference numbers viewable from the shooter's position.
Manufacturer's Suggested Retail Price: $1150.95
Estimated "Real World" Price: $799.95

Nikon M-223 Laser MM

Nikon Monarch
2.5-10x40 MM

Nikon Monarch African
1 - 4X20 MM

MONARCH 2.5-10X42 MM NIKOPLEX

(also in 2-8x30 mm, 3-12x42 mm, 4-16x42 mm, 5-20x44 mm, 2.5-10x50 mm, 4-16x50 mm, 6-24x50 mm, and 8-32x50 mm, in matte and silver with ED glass, SF–side focus–Mil Dot, and fine crosshair with dot)
Weight: 16.6 oz
Length: 12 ⅗ in
Main Body Tube Diameter: 1 in
Power: 2.5-10X
Objective Diameter: 42 mm
Exit Pupil: 16.8-4.2 mm
Field of View: 40.3-10.1 ft @ 100 yards
Twilight Factor: 10.24-20.49
Eye Relief: 4.0-3.8 in
Waterproof: Yes
Fogproof: Yes
Limited Lifetime Warranty
Features: This Monarch offers a wide magnification range and enhanced ring spacing for mounting on rifles including magnum-length actions. The Monarch is available with the see-through "ballistic circle" BDC reticle. With Ultra ClearCoat optical system, the Monarch is adaptable for a sunshade and can be customized with accessory target-style windage and elevation adjustment knobs and caps.
Manufacturer's Suggested Retail Price: $550.95
Estimated "Real World" Price: $389.95

MONARCH AFRICAN 1-4X20 MM WITH GERMAN #4 RETICLE

(also in 1.1-4x24 mm and with illuminated reticle)
Weight: 12.16 oz
Length: 10 ⅖ in
Main Body Tube Diameter: 1 in (30 mm in the 1.1-4x24)
Power: 1-4x
Objective Diameter: 20 mm
Exit Pupil: 20-5 mm
Field of View: 92.9-23.1 ft @ 100 yards
Twilight Factor: 4.47-8.94
Eye Relief: 4 1/10-4 in
Waterproof: Yes
Fogproof: Yes
Limited Lifetime Warranty
Features: Designed for dangerous-game hunting in Africa, the Monarch African 1-4x20's field of view and 20mm-5mm exit-pupil range allow for low-light hunting, while the 1-4 power range lets shooters see the target with both eyes open. Uses Nikon's Ultra ClearCoat optical system, has a enhanced mount ring spacing for mounting on various rifle actions, including magnum length. Windage and elevation adjustments are hand-turn ¼ MOA clicks. Comes with quick-focus eyepiece and with lead- and arsenic-free glass.
Manufacturer's Suggested Retail Price: $400.95
Estimated "Real World" Price: $279.95

RIFLESCOPES

Nikon Sport Optics
www.nikonhunting.com/products/riflescopes

MONARCH GOLD 2.5-10X50 MM SF BDC

(also in 1.5-6x42 mm and 2.5x10x56 mm and with Nikoplex and German #4 reticles)
Weight: 21.2 oz
Length: 13 in
Main Body Tube Diameter: 30 mm
Power: 2.5-10x
Objective Diameter: 50 mm
Exit Pupil: 19.2-5.2 mm
Field of View: 38.8-10 ½ ft @ 100 yards
Twilight Factor: 11.18-22.36
Eye Relief: 4 ¹/₁₀-4 in
Waterproof: Yes
Fogproof: Yes
Limited Lifetime Warranty
Features: The Monarch Gold riflescope advertises an Ultra ClearCoat optical system that offers a bright, sharp, flat sight picture and light transmission up to its theoretical maximum—95 percent. With larger internal lenses for less spherical abberation. The locking side focus adjustment dials out parallax. Milled from aircraft grade aluminum, with a quick-focus eyepiece and hand-turn ¼ MOA windage and elevation adjustments.
Manufacturer's Suggested Retail Price: **$769.95**

MONARCH X 2.5-10X44 MM SF NIKOPLEX

(also in 4-16x50 mm with mildot and dual-illuminated Mil Dot)
Weight: 23.5 oz
Length: 13 ⁹/₁₀ in
Power: 2.5-10X
Objective Diameter: 44 mm
Main Body Tube Diameter: 30 mm
Exit Pupil: 17.6-4.4 mm
Field of View: 42-10 ½ ft @ 100 yards
Twilight Factor: 10.24-20.49
Eye Relief: 3 ½-3 ⁴/₅ in
Waterproof: Yes
Fogproof: Yes
Limited Lifetime Warranty
Features: The Monarch X series offers Nikoplex, Mildot, or Dual Illuminated Mildot reticle options. Lenses use the Ultra ClearCoat system. Four-time magnification range with easy-to-grip adjustment knobs and a one-piece 30 mm body tube milled from aircraft grade aluminum. Hand-turn ¼ MOA

Nikon Monarch Gold 2.5-10x50 MM

Nikon Monarch X 2.5-10x44 MM SF Nikoplex

Nikon Omega 1.65-5x36 MM Muzzleloading in matte with BDC 250 reticle

windage and elevation adjustments and side-focus parallax adjustment.
Manufacturer's Suggested Retail Price: **$1760.95**
Estimated "Real World" Price: **$1199.95**

OMEGA 1.65-5X36 MM MUZZLELOADING IN MATTE WITH BDC 250 RETICLE

(also in 3-9x40 mm and in silver and RealTree APG and with Nikoplex and BDC 300 reticles)
Weight: 13.58 oz
Length: 11 ¹/₇ in
Main Body Tube Diameter: 1 in
Power: 1.65x-5x
Objective Diameter: 36 mm
Exit Pupil: 7.2 (at 5x) mm

Field of View: 45.3-15.1 ft @ 100 yards
Twilight Factor: 7.7-13.41
Eye Relief: 5 in
Waterproof: Yes
Fogproof: Yes
Warranty: Lifetime
Features: At 5X the Omega gives the maximum useful exit pupil of 7.2 mm. Available with a BDC 250 trajectory-compensating reticle, designed specifically for the lower power range and smaller objective, uses "ballistic circles" for aiming points; 100-yard parallax; compact size; with hand-turn ¼ MOA click adjustments and quick-focus eyepiece.
Manufacturer's Suggested Retail Price: **$320.95**
Estimated "Real World" Price: **$209.95**

PROSTAFF 3-9X40 MM MATTE WITH NIKOPLEX

(also in 2-7x32 mm–and in Shotgun Hunter with BDC 200 reticle–3-9x40 mm, 4-12x40 mm, and 3-9x50 mm and in silver, RealTree APG and with BDC reticle)

Weight: N/A
Length: 12 ²/₅ in
Main Body Tube Diameter: 1 in
Power: 3x-9x
Objective Diameter: 40 mm
Exit Pupil: 13.3-4.4 mm
Field of View: 33.8-11.3 ft @ 100 yards
Twilight Factor: 10.95-18.97
Eye Relief: 3 ³/₅-3 ³/₅ in
Waterproof: Yes
Fogproof: Yes
Limited Lifetime Warranty
Features: he ProStaff riflescopes are available in 3-9x40 mm black matte with Nikoplex reticle (also in 2-7x32– and in Shotgun Hunter with BDC 200 reticle–4-12x40, and 3-9x50 and in silver, RealTree APG and with BDC reticle). Has multi-coated lenses and comes with ¼ MOA hand-turn reticle adjustments with "Zero-Reset" turrets and a quick-focus eyepiece.
Manufacturer's Suggested Retail Price: **$232.95**
Estimated "Real World" Price: **$159.95**

Nikon ProStaff 3-9x40 MM

PROSTAFF RIMFIRE 4X32 MM

(also in 3-9x40 mm with BDC 150 reticle)

Length: 11 ½ in
Main Body Tube Diameter: 1 in
Power: 4X
Objective Diameter: 32 mm
Exit Pupil: 8 mm
Field of View: 11.1 ft @ 50 yards
Twilight Factor: 11.31
Eye Relief: 4 ¹/₁₀ in
Waterproof: Yes
Fogproof: Yes
Limited Lifetime Warranty
Features: The new ProStaff 4x32 features an 8 mm exit pupil, compact size, and light weight for hunters and plinkers. Fully multi-coated optics; ¼ MOA hand-turn adjustments; and the ProStaff Rimfire integrates the .22 LR-specific BDC 150 reticle and a 50-yard parallax setting for targets out to 150 yards and beyond.

Nikon ProStaff
Rimfire 4x32 MM

Manufacturer's Suggested Retail Price: **$156.95**

Estimated "Real World" Price: **$99.95**

Nikon Sport Optics

www.nikonhunting.com/products/riflescopes

SLUGHUNTER 1.65-5X36 MM MATTE WITH BDC 200 RETICLE

(also in 3-9x40 mm and in RealTree APG)

Weight: 13.58 oz
Length: 11 ¹/₇ in
Main Body Tube Diameter: 1 in
Power: 1.65-5X
Objective Diameter: 36 mm
Exit Pupil: 7.2 (at 5x) mm
Field of View: 45.3-15.1 ft @ 100 yards
Twilight Factor: 7.7-13.41
Eye Relief: 5 in
Waterproof: Yes
Fogproof: Yes
Limited Lifetime Warranty
Features: The compact SlugHunter 1.65-5x36 features an increased exit pupil for low-light performance and a 75-yard parallax setting. Available with the BDC 200 trajectory-compensating reticle, with "ballistic circle" aiming points, calibrated for the lower power range and smaller objective and for aerodynamic polymer-tipped slugs. Has lead- and arsenic-free "Eco-Glass" multi-coated optics, hand-turn ¼ MOA click adjustments, and quick-focus eyepiece.

Manufacturer's Suggested Retail Price: $320.95
Estimated "Real World" Price: $209.95

TURKEYPRO BTR 1.65-5X36 MM MOSSY OAK BREAK-UP

(also in RealTree APG and matte)

Weight: 13.58 oz
Length: 11 ¹/₇ in
Main Body Tube Diameter: 1 in
Power: 1.65-5X
Objective Diameter: 36 mm
Exit Pupil: 21.8-7.2 mm
Field of View: 45.3-15.1 ft @ 100 yards
Twilight Factor: 7.7-13.41
Eye Relief: 5 in
Waterproof: Yes
Fogproof: Yes
Limited Lifetime Warranty
Features: This is Nikon's dedicated turkey-hunting scope with the Ballistic Turkey Reticle, or BTR, which subtends a turkey's head from crown to wattles

at 5x (larger circle) and at 1.65x (smaller circle) at 40 yards. Also includes the ARD (Anti-Reflective Device) lens cap technology to eliminate glare.

Manufacturer's Suggested Retail Price: $420.95
Estimated "Real World" Price: $279.95

Nikon SlugHunter 1.65-5x36 MM

Nikon TurkeyPro BTR 1.65-5x36 MM

RIFLESCOPES

GAMESEEKER 30 3-10X40MM

(also in 4-16x50 mm, 6-24x50 mm, and 8.5-32x50 mm)
Weight: 15.2 oz
Length: 13 ¹/₁₀ in
Main Tube Diameter: 30 mm
Power: 3x-10x
Objective Diameter: 40 mm
Exit Pupil: 13.3-4 mm
Field of View: 35.6-10.5 ft @ 100 yards
Twilight Factor: 10.95-20
Eye Relief: 4 ²/₅-3 ¹/₅ in
Waterproof: Yes
Fogproof: Yes
Limited Lifetime Warranty
Features: A 30 mm variable scope with fully multi-coated optics and a bullet-drop-compensating "Precision Plex" reticle.
Manufacturer's Suggested Retail Price: $179
Estimated "Real World" Price: $179

GAMESEEKER II 4-16X 50 MM (PP)

(also in 2-7x32 mm, 3-9x40 mm, 4-12x40 mm, 3-9x50 mm, and 5-10x56, and P and LPP reticles)
Weight: 16.1 oz
Length: 13 ⁹/₁₀ in
Main Tube Diameter: 1 in
Power: 4x-16x
Objective Diameter: 50 mm
Exit Pupil: 12.5-3.125 mm
Field of View: 26 ¹/₅ -6 ⁴/₅ ft @ 100 yards
Twilight Factor: 14.14-28.28
Eye Relief: 3 in
Waterproof: Yes
Fogproof: Yes
Limited Lifetime Warranty
Features: This scope features a one-piece, 1-inch tube with finger-adjustable windage and elevation turrets and fully multi-coated optics.
Manufacturer's Suggested Retail Price: $149
Estimated "Real World" Price: $149

LIGHTSEEKER 30 3-10X40 (BP)

(also in 4-16x50 mm and 6-24x50 mm, and with Mil Dot reticle)

Weight: 20 oz
Length: 13 ¹/₁₀ in
Main Tube Diameter: 30 mm
Power: 3-10x
Objective Diameter: 40 mm
Exit Pupil: 13.3-4.0 mm
Field of View: 34-14 ft @ 100 yards
Twilight Factor: 10.95-20
Eye Relief: 3 ¹/₂-4 in
Waterproof: Yes
Fogproof: Yes
Limited Lifetime Warranty
Features: A 30mm tube scope with finger-adjustable windage and elevation turrets, and side parallax adjustment. Fully multi-coated optics.
Manufacturer's Suggested Retail Price: $519
Estimated "Real World" Price: $519

LIGHTSEEKER XL 4-16X44 (BP)

(also in 3-9x40 mm and 2.5-10x50 mm, and with P and Twilight Plex reticles)
Weight: 23 oz
Length: 14 in

Main Tube Diameter: 1 in
Power: 4x-16x
Objective Diameter: 44 mm
Exit Pupil: 11-2.8 mm
Field of View: 24-8 ft @ 100 yards
Twilight Factor: 9.4-26.5
Eye Relief: 3 ¹/₂-4 in
Waterproof: Yes
Fogproof: Yes
Limited Lifetime Warranty
Features: A 1-inch-tube riflescope with finger-adjustable windage and elevation turrets, fully multi-coated optics, and "European-style" eyepieces.
Manufacturer's Suggested Retail Price: $459
Estimated "Real World" Price: $459

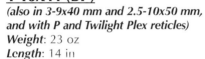

Pentax Gameseeker II 4-16x50 MM

Pentax Gameseeker 30 3-10x40 MM

Pentax Lightseeker 30 3-10x40 MM

Pentax Lightseeker XL 4-16x44 MM BP

RIFLESCOPES

Premier Optics
www.premieroptics.com

HERITAGE 3-15X50 MM LIGHT TACTICAL
Weight: 24.9 oz
Length: 13 in
Main Tube Body Diameter: 30 mm
Power: 3-15X
Objective Diameter: 50 mm
Elevation and Windage Adjustments: ¼ MOA per click
Exit Pupil: 16.7-3.3 mm
Field of View: 360-70 ft @ 1000 yds
Twilight Factor: 12.25–27.4
Eye Relief: 3½ in
Waterproof: Yes (to 33 ft)
Fog proof: Yes
Premier "Transferable Lifetime" Warranty
Features: The Premier Optics Heritage Light Tactical Riflescope is waterproof-submersible to 33 feet with exterior turrets (no caps), fully adjustable for windage and elevation. This lighter-weight tactical scope uses a 30 mm main tube for easier mounting on M-24, M-16, and other MSR-type rifles.
Manufacturer's Suggested Retail Price: $2383
Estimated "Real World" Price: $2145

Premier Heritage 3-15x50 MM Light Tactical

HERITAGE 3-15X50MM VARMINT
Weight: 23.2 oz
Length: 13 ⅔ in
Main Tube Body Diameter: 30 mm
Power: 3-15X
Objective Diameter: 50 mm
Elevation and Windage Adjustments: ¼ MOA per click
Exit Pupil: 16.7-3.3 mm
Field of View: 360-70 ft @ 1000 yards
Twilight Factor: 12.25-27.4
Eye Relief: 3 ½ in
Waterproof: Yes to 3m-10 ft depth
Fog proof: Yes
Premier "Transferable Lifetime" Warranty
Features: Premier's new Varmint riflescope is Waterproof Submersible to three meters or 10 feet. Includes tactical elevation turret, side-focus parallax adjustment, and fast-focus eye piece.
Manufacturer's Suggested Retail Price: $2219
Estimated "Real World" Price: $1997

Premier Heritage 3-15x50 MM Varmint

Premier Heritage 3-15x50 MM Hunter Riflescope

HERITAGE 3-15X50 MM HUNTER
Weight: 23.7 oz
Length: 13 ⅔ in
Main Tube Body Diameter: 30 mm
Power: 3-15X
Objective Diameter: 50 mm
Elevation and Windage Adjustments: ⅓ MOA per click
Exit Pupil: 16.7-3.3 mm
Field of View: 360-70 ft @ 1000 yds
Twilight Factor: 12.25-27.4
Eye Relief: 3½ in
Waterproof: Yes to 3 m-10 ft depth
Fog proof: Yes
Premier "Transferable Lifetime" Warranty

Features: The new first-focal-plane-reticle Premier 3-15x50 mm Heritage Hunter scope offers a 5X magnification range and is waterproof submersible to three meters or 10 feet with turrets caps removed. Comes with turret caps on the windage and elevation adjustments. Includes side-focus parallax adjustment and has an available variety of reticles includng A7, Gen2, XR, and Custom Ballistic, as well as illuminated.
Manufacturer's Suggested Retail Price: $2108
Estimated "Real World" Price: $1897

RIFLESCOPES

Premier Optics

www.premieroptics.com

HERITAGE 3-15X50 MM TACTICAL ILLUMINATED

(also in 5-25x56 mm)

Weight: 35.2 oz
Length: 13 ²/₃ in
Main Tube Body Diameter: 34 mm
Power: 3-15X
Objective Diameter: 50 mm
Elevation and Windage Adjustments: 0.1 MRAD per click
Exit Pupil: 16.7-3.3 mm
Field of View: 360-70 ft @ 1000 yds
Twilight Factor: 12.25-27.4
Eye Relief: 3 ¹/₂ in
Waterproof: Yes to 33 f-10 m of depth
Fog proof: Yes
Premier "Transferable Lifetime" Warranty
Features: The Premier Heritage 3-15x50 mm Tactical Riflescope Illuminated with first-focal-plane reticle is an exact duplicate of the one made for and used by USMC Scout Sniper units worldwide in day or night operations. The 3-15x50 mm Tactical Scope is waterproof submersible to 10 meters or 33 feet with exterior, adjustable turrets (no caps). The 34 mm main tube has increased elevation and windage adjustment along with added strength and resistance to harsh environments. Suitable for long-range rifles in calibers up to .50 BMG.

Premier 3-15x50 MM Tactical Illuminated

Premier V8 1-8x24 MM Tactical

Manufacturer's Suggested Retail Price: $3209
Estimated "Real World" Price: $2888

V8 1-8X24 MM TACTICAL

Weight: 24.7 oz
Length: 11 ²/₃ in
Main Tube Body Diameter: 34 mm
Power: 1-8X
Objective Diameter: 24 mm
Elevation and Windage Adjustments: 0.1 MRAD per click
Exit Pupil: 24-3 mm
Field of View: 119-16 ft @ 100 yds
Twilight Factor: 4.89-13.85
Eye Relief: 3 ¹/₂ in

Waterproof: Yes to 33 ft-10 m of depth
Fog proof: Yes
Premier "Transferable Lifetime" Warranty
Features: The newly introduced Premier V8 1-8x24 mm Tactical CQB scope includes two sighting systems– when the magnification is set at 3X or below, a projected red dot appears on the second focal plane. From 3X to the maximum 8X the illuminated GEN 2 CQB reticle operates from the first focal plane from. These sighting systems work from five feet to 500 yards.
Manufacturer's Suggested Retail Price: $3223

Quigley-Ford Scopes

www.quigleyfordscopes.com

3-12X50 MM .30-'06 165 GRAIN

(also in .25-'06, .264, .270, .270 WSM, 7 mm Remington Magnum, 7 mm RUM, .308, .300 Winchester Magnum, .300 WSM, .300 RUM, .325 WSM, and .338, and in a variety of bullet weights)

Weight: 19 oz
Length: 14 in
Main Tube Body Diameter: 1 in
Power: 3-12X
Objective Diameter: 50 mm

Exit Pupil: 16.66-4.16 mm
Twilight Factor: 12.24-24.49
Eye Relief: 4 in
Waterproof: Yes
Fogproof: Yes
Lifetime Warranty
Features: The Quigley-Ford 3-12x50 mm is built for big-game-hunting-range calibers. Turret adjustments for longer ranges are eliminated by the Quigley-Ford scope which is built to match a specific caliber, bullet weight, ballistic coefficient, and muzzle velocity, with

Quigley-Ford 3-12x50 MM

hashmarks calibrated to the load on the scope's reticle. The caliber, bullet weight, and velocity are then engraved on the scope for the shooter's reference.
Manufacturer's Suggested Retail Price: $649.99

Quigley-Ford Scopes

www.quigleyfordscopes.com

4-16X50 MM 7MM REMINGTON MAGNUM 140 GRAIN

(also in models for .204, .223, .22-250, .243, .270, 7 mm Weatherby, .308, .300 WSM, and .338, and assorted bullet weights)
Weight: 19.5 oz
Length: 15.5 in
Main Tube Body Diameter: 1 in
Power: 4-16X
Objective Diameter: 50 mm
Exit Pupil: 12.5-3.125 mm

Quigley-Ford 4-16x50 MM

Twilight Factor: 14.14-28.28
Eye Relief: 4 in
Waterproof: Yes
Fogproof: Yes
Features: The Quigley-Ford 4-16x50

mm is built for varmint and long-range big-game-hunting calibers. Turret adjustments for longer ranges are eliminated by the Quigley-Ford scope which is built to match a specific caliber, bullet weight, ballistic coefficient, and muzzle velocity, with hashmarks calibrated to the load on the scope's reticle. The caliber, bullet weight, and velocity are then engraved on the scope for the shooter's reference.
Manufacturer's Suggested Retail Price: $689.99

Redfield (Leupold & Stevens, Inc.)

www.redfield.com

REVOLUTION 3-9X40 MM

(also in 2-7x33 mm, 3-9x50 mm and 4-12x40 mm)
Weight: 12.6 oz
Length: 12 ³/₁₀ in
Main Body Tube Diameter: 1 in
Power: 3-9x
Objective Diameter: 40 mm
Exit Pupil: 12.1-4.7 mm
Field of View: 32.9-13.1 ft @ 100 yds
Twilight Factor: 10.95-18.97
Eye Relief: 3 ⁷/₁₀-4 ¹/₅ in

Redfield Revolution 3-9x40 MM

Waterproof: Yes
Fogproof: Yes
Limited Lifetime Warranty
Features: The Redfield Revolution riflescope comes with a black matte finish and either a 4-Plex or Accu-Range reticle. Key features include the

Illuminator Lens System with premium lenses and vapor-deposition multi-coatings. The Accu-Trac windage and elevation adjustment system has resettable stainless steel ¼-MOA finger click adjustments. Includes the Rapid Target Acquisition (RTA) lockable eyepiece.
Manufacturer's Suggested Retail Price: $159.99
(4-Plex reticle), ... $169.99
(Accu-Range reticle)

Schmidt & Bender

www.schmidtbender.com

12.5-50X56 MM FIELD TARGET

Weight: 40.56 oz
Length: 16 ²/₅ in
Power: 12.5-50X
Objective Diameter: 56 mm
Main Tube Diameter: 30 mm
Exit Pupil: 4.55-1.18 mm
Field of View: 10.5 - 2.7 ft @ 100 yards
Twilight Factor: 26.5-53
Eye Relief: 2 ³/₄ in
Waterproof: Yes
Fogproof: Yes
30-Year Parts and Service Warranty
Features: Built for field-target shooting. "Field target" is a form of competitive outdoor air-gun shooting that originated in the United Kingdom. It employs

metallic silhouettes at ranges of 8 to 55 yards. Most shots can be taken freestyle from any position, but a certain number must be taken either standing or kneeling. The "kill zone" on target may be as small as 25 mm, making high-powered telescopic sights necessary. Ranging is also essential; and a high-magnification scope has a shallow depth of field, so the parallax side-focus wheel can be used as a reference for gauging the distance to the target and adjusting the trajectory. The Schmidt & Bender 12.5-50x56 comes with an extra-large focus wheel t0 range distances from 7 to 70 meters. The scope also has an illuminated reticle with brightness settings adjustable from 1 to 11.

Manufacturer's Suggested Retail Price: $3199

Schmidt & Bender 12.5-50x56 MM Field Target

RIFLESCOPES

Schmidt & Bender

3-12X50 MM KLASSIK ILLUMINATED

(also in illuminated-reticle 2.5-10x56 mm and 3-12x42 mm, and in non-illuminated 2.5-10x40 mm, 3-12x42 mm, and 4-16x 50 mm which is also available with the Varmint No. 8 Dot reticle)
Weight: 21.66 oz
Length: 13 ¾ in
Power: 3-12X
Objective Diameter: 50 mm
Main Tube Diameter: 30 mm
Exit Pupil: 4.2-14.4 mm
Field of View: 33.3-11.4 ft @ 100 yards
Twilight Factor: 8.5-24.5
Eye Relief: 3 ¹/₇ in
Waterproof: Yes
Fogproof: Yes
30-Year Parts and Service Warranty
Features: All of the Klassik variables have generous objectives for greater light transmission. Schmidt & Bender offers an variety of reticles in illuminated, non-illuminated, and varmint. Adjustments on the 3-12x50 are ⅓ MOA; the 4-16x50 has ¼ OA increments.
Manufacturer's Suggested Retail Price:. **$2279**

6X42 MM KLASSIK FIXED

(also in 10x42 mm and 8x56 mm)
Weight: 16.67 oz
Length: 13 ⁷/₁₀ in
Width: 2 ¹/₁₀ in
Power: 6X
Objective Diameter: 42 mm
Main Tube Diameter: 1 in
Exit Pupil: 7 mm
Field of View: 21 ft @ 100 yds
Twilight Factor: 15.8
Eye Relief: 3 ¹/₇ in
Waterproof: Yes
Fogproof: Yes
30 Year Parts and Service Warranty
Features: Simple and economical, fixed 6-power magnification applicable to a wide range of hunting situations. indage and elevation adjustments are in ⅓ MOA increments. The classic European 8x56 configuration offers maximum light transmission.
Manufacturer's Suggested Retail Price:. **$1189**

4-16X42 MM PM II/LP

(also in 30 mm 10x42 and 34 mm 3-12x50 with non-illuminated reticle, and in 34 mm tube 4-16x42 mm,

3-12x50 mm, 4-16x50 mm, and 5-25x56 mm with illuminated reticle an LP turret system, and the 5-25x56 mm PMII /LP MTC LT for extreme long ranges, along with illuminated reticle 4-16x50 mm and 12-50x56 mm without LP system)
Weight: 30.86 oz
Length: 15 ½ in
Power: 4-16X
Objective Diameter: 42 mm
Main Tube Diameter: 34 mm
Exit Pupil: 10.5-2.6 mm
Field of View: 22.5-7 ft @ 100 yards
Twilight Factor: 11.3-25.9
Eye Relief: 3 ½ in
Waterproof: Yes
Fogproof: Yes
30-Year Parts and Service Warranty
Features: Designed at the request of the US Military. All models include an illuminated reticle and parallax adjustment, except the 10x42. The LP turret system features a color-coded elevation knob for instant reference to the elevation setting.
Manufacturer's Suggested Retail Price:. **$2999**

Schmidt & Bender 3-12x50 MM Klassik Illuminated

Schmidt & Bender Klassic 6x42 MM

Schmidt & Bender 4-16x42 MM

RIFLESCOPES

Schmidt & Bender

www.schmidtbender.com

POLICE MARKSMAN 1.1-4X20 MM PM LOCKING SHORT DOT

(also in 1.1-4x20 mm and 1-8x24 mm Short Dots and 1.1-4x24 mm PM Zenith Short Dot LE)

Weight: 20.11 oz
Length: 10 ³/₅ in
Power: 1.1-4X
Objective Diameter: 20 mm
Main Tube Diameter: 30 mm
Exit Pupil: 14-5 mm
Field of View: 96-30 ft @ 100 yds
Twilight Factor: 4.69-8.94
Eye Relief: 3 ½ in
Waterproof: Yes
Fogproof: Yes
30-Year Parts and Service Warranty
Features: Includes locking turrets and CQB reticle. M855, 75 gr. TAP, and M118LR calibration rings standard.
Manufacturer's Suggested Retail Price:................. **$2549**

3-12X42 MM KLASSIK PRECISION HUNTER

(also in 3-12x50 mm and 4-16x50 mm)
Weight: 19.90 oz
Length: 13 ²/₃ in
Power: 3-12X
Objective Diameter: 42 mm
Main Tube Diameter: 30 mm
Exit Pupil: 3.5-14 mm
Field of View: 31.5-11.4 ft @ 100 yards
Twilight Factor: 8.5-22.4
Eye Relief: 3 ½ inches
Waterproof: Yes
Fogproof: Yes
30-Year Parts and Service Warranty
Features: An enhanced model 3-12x42 Klassik designed for longer ranges. Features the P3 reticle with bullet-drop compensated elevation knob. Originally designed for military and tactical use, the mil-dots can be used for estimating holdover at longer distances, as well as for windage allowance and for leading moving targets. Adjustments are in ⅓ MOA; the 4-16x50's clicks are ¼ MOA and the scope has a third-turret parallax adjustment.
Manufacturer's Suggested Retail Price:................. **$2099**

2.5-10X40 MM SUMMIT

Weight: 16.8 oz
Length: 13 ⅕ in
Power: 2.5-10X
Objective Diameter: 40 mm
Main Tube Diameter: 1 in
Exit Pupil: 16-4 mm
Field of View: 12.3–40.4 ft @ 100 yards
Twilight Factor: 14-20
Eye Relief: 3.93 in
Waterproof: Yes
Fogproof: Yes
30-Year Parts and Service Warranty
Features: The Summit is built for the American market with its 1 inch tube. Adjustments are ¼ MOA, and the field of view is a wide 40 feet at 100 yards at the 2.5X setting.
Manufacturer's Suggested Retail Price:................. **$1499**

Schmidt & Bender
2.5-10x40 mm Summit

Schmidt & Bender Police Marksman
1.1-4x20 MM PM Locking Short Dot

Schmidt & Bender 3-12x42 mm Precision Hunter

Schmidt & Bender

www.schmidtbender.com

1.5-6X42 MM ZENITH FLASH DOT

(also in 1.1-4x24 mm, 1-8x24 mm, 3-12x50 mm, and 2.5-10x56 mm with Flask Dot and in 1.1-4x24 mm, 1.5-6x42 mm, 1-8x24 mm, 3-12x50 mm, and 2.5-10x56 mm with non-illuminated reticle)

Weight: 21.52 oz
Length: 12 ⅓ in
Power: 1.5-6X
Objective Diameter: 42 mm
Main Tube Diameter: 30 mm
Exit Pupil: 28-7 mm
Field of View: 60-19.5 ft @ 100 yards
Twilight Factor: 4.2-15.9
Eye Relief: 3 ½ inches
Waterproof: Yes

Schmidt & Bender 1.5-6x42 MM

Fogproof: Yes
30-Year Parts and Service Warranty
Features: The Zenith line runs from dangerous-game scopes up through long-range, low-light configurations. The Flash Dot reticle in the center of the crosshairs performs like the front bead sight on a shotgun when illuminated–it comes with adjustable bright-ness levels–that can pick up running or charging game. The Flash Dot can also be shut off to use the scope in the non-illuminated mode. The click values on the windage and elevation adjustments are ½ MOA on the 1.1-4x24 and ⅓ MOA on the rest.

Manufacturere's Suggested Retail Price: $2349

Shepherd Enterprises Inc.

www.shepherdscopes.com

SNIPER 3-10X40 MM

Weight: 17 oz
Length: 14 in
Main Tube Body Diameter: 1 In
Power: 3-10X
Objective Diameter: 40 mm
Exit Pupil: 13.3 3-4 mm
Twilight Factor: 10.95-20
Elevation and Windage Adjustments: ¼ MOA per click
Field of View: 415-150 ft @ 1000 yds
Resolution: 2.1 seconds of angle
Eye Relief: 3-3½ in
Waterproof: Yes
Fogproof: Yes
Shockproof: Yes
Lifetime Warranty
Features: All Shepherd scopes feature a patented dual-reticle system, instant rangefinding circles, and bullet-drop compensation on all powers. Offers one-shot zeroing, visual confirmation of original zero and windage and elevation, and is able to measure antler spread before the shot. All lenses fully multi-coated with four layers of Multi

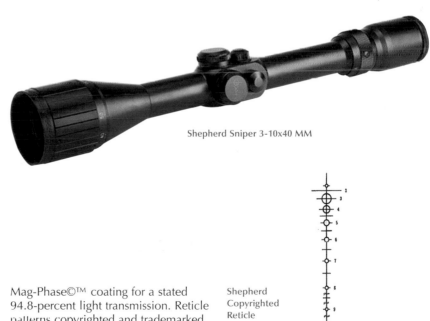

Shepherd Sniper 3-10x40 MM

Shepherd Copyrighted Reticle

Mag-Phase©™ coating for a stated 94.8-percent light transmission. Reticle patterns copyrighted and trademarked, and Shepherd scopes and reticles can be matched to the cartridge and bullet.

Manufacturer's Suggested Retail Price: $799

Shepherd Enterprises Inc.

www.shepherdscopes.com

VARMINTER 6-18X40 MM

Weight: 20.8 oz
Length: 16 ¼ in
Main Tube Body Diameter: 1 in
Power: 6-18X
Objective Diameter: 40 mm
Exit Pupil: 6.66-2.22
Twilight Factor: 15.49-26.83
Elevation and Windage Adjustments:
¼ MOA per click
Field of View: 165-55 ft @ 1000 yds
Resolution: 2.1 seconds of angle
Eye Relief: 3-3 ½ in
Waterproof: Yes
Fogproof: Yes
Shockproof: Yes
Lifetime Warranty
Features: Shepherd scopes feature a patented dual-reticle system, instant rangefinding circles, and bullet-drop compensation on all powers. Offers one-shot zeroing, visual confirmation of original zero and windage and elevation, and is able to measure antler spread before the shot. All lenses fully multi-coated with four layers of Multi Mag-Phase©™ coating for a stated 94.8-percent light transmission. Reticle patterns copyrighted and trademarked, and Shepherd scopes and reticles can be matched to the cartridge and bullet.
Manufacturer's Suggested Retail Price: **$899**

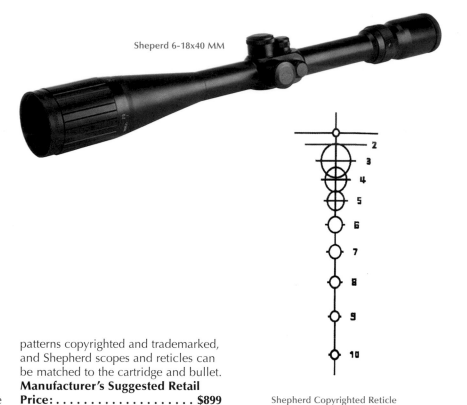

Sheperd 6-18x40 MM

Shepherd Copyrighted Reticle

Simmons

www.simmonsoptics.com

.44 MAG 3-10X44 MM

(also in 4-12x44 mm, 6-21x44 mm .25 Click Value, 6-21x44 mm .125 Click Value TruPlex Reticle, 6-21x44 mm .125 Click Value Mil-Dot Reticle, 6-24x44 mm)
Weight: 11.3 oz.
Power: 3-10x
Objective Diameter: 44 mm
Main Tube Diameter: 1 in
Eye Relief: 3 ¾ in
Exit Pupil: 14.66-4.4 mm
Field of View: 33-9.4 ft @ 100 yds
Twilight Factor: 11.48-20.97
Waterproof: Yes
Fogproof: Yes
Limited Lifetime Warranty
Features: With its 44 mm objective, Simmons Signature .44 Mag riflescope has a wide field of view with brightness delivered via multi-coated optics. The QTA (Quick Target Acquisition) eyepiece makes target acquisition easy and fast. Comes with TrueZero windage and elevation adjustment system.

Simmons .44 Mag 3-10x44 MM

Manufacturer's Suggested Retail Price: **$165.95**
Estimated "Real World" Price: **$94.99**

Simmons

PREDATOR QUEST 6-25X50 MM

(also in 4.5-18x44 mm)
Weight: 17 oz.
Power: 6-25x
Objective Diameter: 50 mm
Main Tube Diameter: 30 mm
Exit Pupil: 8.33-2 mm
Twilight Factor: 17.32-35.35
Field of View: 14-4 ft @ 100 yds
Eye Relief: 3 ⁹/₁₀ in
Waterproof: Yes
Fogproof: Yes
Limited Lifetime Warranty
Features: Inspired by Les Johnson and his popular TV show, the Simmons Predator Quest series. Multi-coated lenses produce bright, high-contrast images and fingertip-adjustable turrets promote quick aim modifications. The Predator Quest has a side focus adjustment for rapid target acquisition and a versatile TruPlex reticle.
Manufacturer's Suggested Retail Price: $364.95
Estimated "Real World" Price: $229.99

PROHUNTER 3-9X40 MM ILLUMINATED TRUPLEX RETICLE

(also in 4x32 mm, 1.5-5x32 mm, 3 9x40 mm TruPlex Reticle, 4x32 mm, 2-6x32 mm Matte Finish, 2-6x32 mm Silver Finish)
Weight: 10.8 oz.
Power: 3-9x
Objective Diameter: 40 mm
Main Tube Diameter: 1 in
Eye Relief: 3 ¾ in
Exit Pupil: 13.33-4.44 mm
Field of View: 31.4-11 ft @ 100 yds
Twilight Factor: 10.95-18.97
Waterproof: Yes
Fogproof: Yes
Limited Lifetime Warranty
Features: Simmons ProHunter has multi-coated optics and is available in seven configurations. The ProHunter series features TrueZero windage and elevation adjustment system for a locked-in zero and raised tab on the power change ring for easy grip and surer adjustments.
Manufacturer's Suggested Retail Price: $186.95
Estimated "Real World" Price: $99.99

Simmons Predator Quest 6-25x50 MM

Simmons ProTarget 3-9x40 MM

PROTARGET 3-9X40 MM

(also in 3-12x40 mm, 6-18x40 mm)
Weight: 20.4 oz.
Power: 3-9x
Objective Diameter: 40 mm
Main Tube Diameter: 1 in
Eye Relief: 3 ⁹/₁₀ in
Exit Pupil: 13.33-4.44 mm
Field of View: 31-10.5 ft @ 100 yds
Twilight Factor: 10.95-18.97
Waterproof: Yes
Fogproof: Yes
Limited Lifetime Warranty
Features: Calibrated for either .22 LR or .17 HMR, the Simmons ProTarget series offers precision optics for mid- to long-range shooting. Multi-coated optics provide bright, sharp images, and the TruPlex Reticle makes it easier to pinpoint the smallest targets with a rimfire rifle. Comes with fingertip-

adjustable turrets with a side focus available on the higher magnification models.
Manufacturer's Suggested Retail Price: $191.95
Estimated "Real World" Price: $104.99

Simmons ProHunter
3-9x40 MM

RIFLESCOPES

Steiner

www.steiner-binoculars.com

MILITARY TACTICAL 3-12X50 MM

(also in 3-12x56 mm and 4-16x50 mm)
Weight: 34.5 oz
Length: 15 ½ in
Main Body Tube Diameter: 34 mm
Power: 3-12X
Objective Diameter: 50 mm
Exit Pupil: 16.7-4.2 mm
Field of View: 34-9.2 ft @ 100 yds
Twilight Factor: 13-24.8
Eye Relief: 3 ⁷/₁₀-3 in
Waterproof: Yes
Fogproof: Yes
Limited Lifetime Warranty on Optics, 3 Year on Illuminated Reticle
Features: The new Steiner Military Tactical scopes are manufactured from a solid one-piece tube of 6061 T-6 aerospace aluminum which offers high strength, good workability, as well as high resistance to corrosion. Uses Steiner HD XP optics with hydrophobic protective coating. Windage and elevation adjustments are .1 mil and guaranteed repeatable with "True-Zero" stop for retune to zero. Has a side-mounted parallax adjustment and a side-mounted illumination control with 11 brightness settings and automatic shutoff. Uses the G2 mildot illuminated reticle suitable for both CQB and long-range conditions.
Manufacturer's Suggested Retail Price: $4182
"Real World" Price: $2549

Steiner Military Tactical 4x16-50 MM

Swarovski Optik North America Ltd

www.swarovskioptik.com

Z3 3-10X42 MM

(also in 3-9x36 mm and 4-12X50 mm)
Weight: 12.7 oz
Length: 12 ³/₅
Main Tube Diameter: 1 in
Power: 3-10X
Objective Diameter: 42 mm
Exit Pupil: 12.6-4.2 mm
Field of View: 33-11.7 ft @ 1000 yds.
Twilight Factor: 11.22-20.49
Eye Relief: 3 ½ in
Waterproof: Yes
Fogproof: Yes
Limited Lifetime Warranty
Features: Z3 riflescopes have a 3X zoom factor and are the lightest riflescopes in the Swarovski Optik line., a perfect fit for many of today's light weight rifles. Available reticles for the Z3 include the 4A, Plex, BRX/BRH (3-10X and 4-12X), and ML in the 3-10X. Ballistic turrets are available in the 4-12X.
Manufacturer's Suggested Retail Price: $1276.67
Estimated "Real World" Price: $1149

Swarovski Z3 3-10x42 MM

Z5 5-25X52 MM

(also in 3.5-18x44 mm)
Weight: 17.5 0z
Length: 14 ³/₅ in
Main Tube Diameter: 1 in
Power: 5-25X
Objective Diameter: 52 mm
Exit Pupil: 9.6-2.1 mm
Field of View: 21.9-4.5 ft @ 100 yards
Twilight Factor: 16.12-36.05
Eye Relief: 3 ³/₄ in
Waterproof: Yes
Fogproof: Yes
Limited Lifetime Warranty
Features: The Z5 Riflescope line features a 5X zoom factor, a third parallax-adjustment turret, and long eye relief, with reticles available in #4, Plex, Fine in the 5-25X, and BRX/BRH. Also available with the ballistic turrets.
Manufacturer's Suggested Retail Price: $1765.56
Estimated "Real World" Price: $1589

Swarovski Z5
5-25x52 MM BT

RIFLESCOPES

Swarovski Optik North America Ltd

www.swarovskioptik.com

Z6 2-12X50 MM

(also in 1-6x24 mm, 1.7-10x42 mm, 2,5-15X44 mm, 2.5-15X56, 3-18X50, and 5-30X50, and in illuminated)
Weight: 18.3 oz
Length: 13 ²/₅ in
Width: in
Main Tube Diameter: 30 mm
Power: 2-12X
Objective Diameter: 50 mm
Exit Pupil: 25-4.17 mm
Field of View: 63.0-10.5 ft @100 yds

Twilight Factor: 10-24.49
Eye Relief: 3.74 in
Waterproof: Yes
Fogproof: Yes
Limited Lifetime Warranty
Features: The Z6 line of riflescopes feature a 6X zoom factor, long eye relief, adjustable parallax, on and HD glass on select high magnification models. Also available with illuminated reticles which have a spare battery stored in the turret cap. Available, as

Swarovski Z6 2-12x50 MM

well, with a wide selection of reticles.
Manufacturer's Suggested Retail Price: $2265.56
Estimated "Real World" Price: $2039

Trijicon Inc.

www.trijicon.com

Trijicon AccuPoint 3-9x40 MM

ACCUPOINT 3-9X40 MM

(also in 1.25-4x24 mm, and in 30 mm in 1-4 x 24, 1.25-4 x 24, 5-20 x 50, and 2.5-10 x 56)
Weight: 13.4 oz
Length: 12 ²/₅ in
Main Tube Diameter: 1 in tube
Power: 3-9X
Objective Diameter: 40 mm
Exit Pupil: 13.3 to 4.4 mm
Field of View: 6.45 to 2.15
Twilight Factor: 10.95-18.97
Eye Relief: 3 ³/₅ in
Waterproof: Yes

Fogproof: Yes
Limited Lifetime Warranty
Features: The Trijicon AccuPoint riflescope combines the illumination characteristics of Tritium with the light-gathering capabilities of fiber for a battery-free dual-illuminated. Has Trijicon's Manual Brightness Adjustment Override, multi-layer-coated, quick-focus eyepiece, long-eye relief, and windage and elevation adjustments. Built from aircraft hard-anodized aluminum with black-matte finish. Available reticles include BAC

Triangle, Standard Cross-Hair with Dot, Mil-Dot Cross-Hair with Dot, and German #4 in red, green and amber illumination.
Manufacturer's Suggested Retail Price: $900
Estimated "Real World" Price: $799

U.S. Optics Inc.

www.usoptics.com

SN-3 3.2-17X44 MM TPAL

SN-3 3.2-17X44 MM TPAL

(also in 1.8-10x37 mm, 1.8-10x44 mm, 3.5-17x44 mm, 3.8-22x44 mm, and 5-25x58 mm)
Weight: 36 oz
Length: 15 ³/₄ in
Main Body Tube Diameter: 30 mm
Power: 3.2-17X
Objective Diameter: 44 mm
Exit Pupil: 13.75-2.58 mm
Field of View: 253-83 ft @ 1000 yds
Twilight Factor: 11.86-27.35
Eye Relief: 3 ½ in
Waterproof: Yes
Fogproof: Yes
Limited Lifetime Warranty
Features: Special-purpose optics manufacturer U.S. Optics builds 100-percent US-made optics for military, police, hunters, and recreational shooters. It considers its low-profile,

highly customizable SN-3 scopes, with fully multi-coated optics, to be the most versatile line it offers. The 3.2-17x44 mm TPAL is designed to meet the needs of hunters, as well as tactical and target shooters. It can be mounted on precision rifles and is also used on AR platforms, M14 type rifles, or any bolt action up to .50 BMG caliber. The 44 mm objective provides low-light ability. Includes an illuminated reticle; and the US No. 1 elevation and windage knobs come standard in ¹/₁₀ MIL click adjustments, with optional ¼ MOA, ½ MOA, and 1 cm, along with a wide variety of available MOA- or MIL-scale reticles. Includes a rapid-focus eyepiece, and a standard side-turret parallax adjustment from 50 yards to infinity. The materials are 6061-T6 aircraft-grade aluminum for

the scope body, and stainless steel, brass, and tungsten carbide for the knobs. All exterior parts and metal surfaces are Type III hard anodized in matte black, and custom coatings and anodizing are available in OD green, earth brown, camouflage patterns, and other colors upon request.
Manufacturer's Suggested Retail Price: $2290

Vortex Optics

www.vortexoptics.com

DIAMONDBACK 4-12X40 MM WITH BDC RETICLE

(also in 4-12x40 mm AO, 3.5-10x50 mm, 3-9x40 mm, 2-7x35 mm, 2-7x35 mm Rimfire, and 1.75-5x32 mm, and with V-Plex reticle)

Weight: 14.6 oz
Length: 12 in
Main Body Tube Diameter: 1 in
Power: 4-12X
Objective Diameter: 40 mm
Elevation and Windage Adjustments: ¼ MOA per click
Exit Pupil: 10-3.33
Field of View: 32.4-11.3 ft @ 100 yds
Twilight Factor: 12.65-21.9
Eye Relief: 3 ²/₅-3 in
Waterproof: Yes
Fogproof: Yes
Unconditional Lifetime Warranty
Features: The Diamondback riflescope is made with solid one-piece aircraft-grade aluminum alloy construction and includes argon purging and fully multi-coated optics. The 4-12x40 mm rifle-scope is suitable for big game, predator and varmint, muzzleloader, slug shot-gun, long range, and target applications.
Manufacturer's Suggested Retail Price: **$269**
Estimated "Real World" Price: **$199.99**

RAZOR 5-20X50 MM FFP WITH EBR-2B MRAD RETICLE

(also in 1-4x24 mm; available reticles include EBR-2 MRAD, EBR-2B MRAD, EBR-3 MRAD, EBR1-MOA, EBR-556 MOA–1-4x24 only–and CQMR MOA– 1-4x24 only).

Weight: 35.2 oz
Length: 15 ⁴/₅ in
Main Body Tube Diameter: 35 mm
Power: 5-20X
Objective Diameter: 50 mm
Elevation and Windage Adjustments: ¹/₁₀ MRAD per click
Exit Pupil: 10-2.5
Field of View: 22.0-5.76 ft @ 100 yds
Twilight Factor: 15.81-31.62
Eye Relief: 4 in
Waterproof: Yes
Fogproof: Yes
Unconditional Lifetime Warranty
Features: Vortex Optics Razor HD 5-20x50 mm riflescope for long-range precision shooting is built with a

Vortex Diamondback Series 4-12x40 MM

Vortex Razor series 5-20x50 MM

Vortex Viper PST 6-24x50 MM

35mm one-piece tube machined from aircraft-grade aluminum, and offers 36 MRAD, 125 MOA adjustment range for windage and elevation. Laser-etched-on-glass, first-focal-plane reticle. Matching reticle and turret subtensions. Vortex's proprietary RZR ("Rapid Zero Return") zero-stop mechanism stops the elevation turret from dialing below sight-in range. Delivers precise return to zero after temporary elevation corrections have been dialed without the need for the user to count clicks.
Manufacturer's Suggested Retail Price: **$2499**
Estimated "Real World" Price: **$1999.99**

VIPER HS LR 4-16X50 MM WITH BDC RETICLE

(also in 4-16x44 mm LR, 4-16x50 mm, 4-16x44 mm, 2.5-10x44 mm, and 1-4x24 mm; available reticles include V-Plex, BDC, and TMCQ–on the 1-4x24 only)

Weight: 22 oz
Length: 13 ⁷/₁₀ in
Main Body Tube Diameter: 30 mm
Power: 4-16X
Objective Diameter: 50 mm
Elevation and Windage Adjustments: ½ MOA per click

Exit Pupil: 12.5-3.125
Field of View: 27.4-7.4 ft @ 100 yds
Twilight Factor: 14.14-28.28
Eye Relief: 4 in
Waterproof: Yes
Fogproof: Yes
Unconditional Lifetime Warranty
Features: Vortex Viper HS LR (Long Range) 4-16x50 mm riflescope provides a 4X-zoom range and increased eye relief gets shooters on target quickly and easily—because shooting opportunities can be measured in fractions of seconds. Has a 30 mm one-piece machined aluminum tube for added windage. The LR 4-16x50 mm model features an exposed tall elevation turret with Vortex's CRS ("Customizable Rotational Stop") zero stop with 75 MOA of elevation travel (24 MOA per revolution). The Viper HS 1-4x24 with the TMCQ ("Tactical Milling Close Quarter") illuminated reticle is suited for AR platform rifles, as well as dangerous game setups. The illuminated reticle has ten intensity levels with an off position between each.
Manufacturer's Suggested Retail Price: **$639**
Estimated "Real World" Price: **$539.99**

VIPER 6.5-20X50 MM WITH BDC RETICLE

(also in 6.5-20x44 mm, 4-12x40 mm, 3.5-10x50 mm, 3-9x40 mm; available reticles include Mil Dot–6.5-20x44 and 6.5-20x50 only–V-Plex Wide–6.5-20x50 only–and V-Plex)

Weight: 21.6 oz
Length: 14 ²/₅ in
Main Body Tube Diameter: 30 mm
Power: 6.5-20X
Objective Diameter: 50 mm
Elevation and Windage Adjustments: ¼ MOA per click
Exit Pupil: 7.69-2.5
Field of View: 17.4-6.2 ft @ 100 yds
Twilight Factor: 18.02-31.62
Eye Relief: 3 ⅓-3 in
Waterproof: Yes
Fogproof: Yes
Unconditional Lifetime Warranty
Features: The Vortex Viper 6.5-20x50 mm BDC, for long-range big game, predator and varmint, and target applications, has fully multi-coated optics with a stated 95-percent light transmission, "Precision Force" spring systems, and "Precision Glide" erector system. Features include "Dead-Hold BDC" reticle, side-knob parallax adjustment with range numbers visible while in the shooting position, and tall capped turrets.
Manufacturer's Suggested Retail Price: **$549**
Estimated "Real World" Price: **$459.99**

Vortex Viper Series 6.5-20x50 MM BDC

Vortex Viper PST 6-24x50 MM

VIPER PST 6-24X50 MM FFP WITH EBR-1 MRAD RETICLE

(also in 6-24x50 mm, 4-16x50 FFP mm, 4-16x50 mm, 2.5-10x44 mm, and 1-4x24 mm; available reticles include EBR-1 MRAD, EBR-1 MOA, TMCQ MRAD–1-4x24 mm only), and TMCQ MOA–1-4x24 only)

Weight: 23 oz
Length: 15 ½ in
Main Body Tube Diameter: 30 mm
Power: 6-24X
Objective Diameter: 50 mm
Elevation and Windage Adjustments: ¹/₁₀ MRAD per click
Exit Pupil: 8.33-2.08
Field of View: 17.8-5.1 ft @ 100 yds
Twilight Factor: 17.32-34.64
Eye Relief: 4 in
Waterproof: Yes
Fogproof: Yes
Unconditional Lifetime Warranty
Features: Vortex Optics's Viper PST ("Precision Shooting Tactical") riflescopes feature matching (MRAD- or MOA-based) turrets and reticles for range calculation. Select models are available in first or second focal plane glass-etched reticles. The target-style, o-ring sealed, waterproof turrets have quick adjustment of elevation and windage. Clicks are audible. The "Radius Bar," a fiber-optic turret-rotation indicator located on top of the elevation turret, aids in keeping track of revolutions, as well as provides a visual zero-reference. Stackable C-shaped shims create a Customizable Rotational Stop under the elevation turret. The one-piece 30 mm tubes are machined from a single solid block of aircraft-grade aluminum. With side parallax adjustment knob. O-ring sealed and purged with argon gas.
Manufacturer's Suggested Retail Price: **$999**
Estimated "Real World" Price: **$899.99**

Weaver

www.weaveroptics.com

GRAND SLAM 3.5-10X50 MM DUAL-X RETICLE, SILVER

(also in 1.5-5x32 mm, 3-10x40 mm, 3.5-10x50 mm, 4.5-14x40 mm AO, and 6-20x40 AO, with Dual-X, Ballistic-X, Varminter, and F/C dot, in silver and matte)

Weight: 16.3 oz
Length: 13 in
Main Body Tube Diameter: 1 in
Power: 3.5-10 X
Objective Diameter: 50 mm
Elevation and Windage Adjustments: ¼ MOA per click
Exit Pupil: 14.25-5 mm
Field of View: 29.6-10.5 ft @ 100 yds
Twilight Factor: 13.2-22.4
Eye Relief: 3 ½ in
Waterproof: Yes
Fogproof: Yes
Limited Lifetime Warranty
Features: The Grand Slam is built from a one-piece, 1-inch tube with fully-multi-coated lenses. Includes "Micro-trac" adjustment system. Higher-power models come with an AO ("adjustable objective" for parallax). A portion of the proceeds from every Grand Slam and Super Slam scope sold goes to benefit the Rocky Mountain Elk Foundation.
Manufacturer's Suggested Retail Price: **$551.49**
Estimated "Real World" Price: **$535.35**

SUPER SLAM EURO-STYLE 1.5-6X24 MM, MATTE, WITH ILLUMINATED GERMAN #4 RETICLE

(also in 3-9x56 mm, and 4-20x50 mm side focus, and in Dual-X and illuminated crosshair German #4 reticles)

Weight: 20 oz
Length: 10 in
Main Body Tube Diameter: 30 mm
Power: 1.5-6X
Objective Diameter: 24 mm
Elevation and Windage Adjustments: ¼ MOA per click
Exit Pupil: 16-4 mm
Field of View: 62.6-16 ft @ 100 yds
Twilight Factor: 6-12
Eye Relief: 3 ¾ in
Waterproof: Yes
Fogproof: Yes

Limited Lifetime Warranty
Features: The Euro-Style incorporates similar features to the Super Slam—such as five-times magnification range in the 4-20x50 mm configuration, fully-multi-coated lenses with hard coating on exteriors, three-point erector system with improved spring design, re-set-to-zero pull-up adjustment turrets, and a wide range of reticle options, including first focal plane—in a 30 mm tube. Higher powers include side-focus parallax adjustment.
Manufacturer's Suggested Retail Price: **$745.49**
Estimated "Real World" Price: **$738.88**

SUPER SLAM 2-10X42 MM IN MATTE WITH BDC RETICLE

(also in 1-5x24 mm for dangerous game with Heavy Dual-X reticle, and in 3-15x42 mm, 3-15x50 mm, and 4-20x50 mm side focus in matte and silver with Dual-X, Fine Crosshair ¼ MOA dot, illuminated Duplex, and EBX glass etched)

Weight: 19 oz
Length: 13 ⅕ in
Main Body Tube Diameter: 1 in
Power: 2-10X
Objective Diameter: 42 mm
Elevation and Windage Adjustments: ¼ MOA per click
Exit Pupil: 21-4.2 mm
Field of View: 49.1-9.9 ft @ 100 yds
Twilight Factor: 9-20
Eye Relief: 4 in
Waterproof: Yes
Fogproof: Yes
Limited Lifetime Warranty
Features: The Weaver Super Slam offers five-times magnification range, fully-multi-coated lenses with hard coating on exteriors, three-point erector system with improved spring design, re-set-to-zero pull-up turrets (no caps) and a wide range of reticle options.
Manufacturer's Suggested Retail Price: **$706.49**
Estimated "Real World" Price: **$699.95**

Weaver Grand Slam 3.5-10x50 MM

Weaver Super Slam Euro-Style 1.5-6x24 MM

Weaver Super Slam 2-10x42 MM

TACTICAL 3-15X50 MM SIDE FOCUS WITH MIL-DOT RETICLE

(also in 1.5x24 mm with illuminated CIRT reticle, 3-15x50 mm with illuminated EMDR reticle, and 4-20x50 mm side focus with Mil-Dot reticle)
Weight: 27.5 oz
Length: 13 ½ in
Main Body Tube Diameter: 30 mm
Power: 3-15 X
Objective Diameter: 50 mm
Elevation and Windage Adjustments: ¼ MOA per click
Exit Pupil: 16.7-3.3 mm
Field of View: 33.9-6.8 ft @ 100 yds
Twilight Factor: 12.2-27.4
Eye Relief: 4 in
Waterproof: Yes
Fogproof: Yes
Limited Lifetime Warranty
Features: The Weaver Tactical 3-15x50 mm offers a five-times magnification range, has a first focal plane Mil-Dot reticle, fully-multi-coated lenses, and tool-free external adjustments turrets that reset to zero. The illuminated 3-15x50 mm has ten brightness settings, five red and five green, and ¹/₁₀ MOA-click adjustments. The other reticles available in the Tacitcal line include the CIRT ("close intermediate ranging tactical") and EMDR ("enhanced mil-dot ranging").
Manufacturer's Suggested Retail Price: $1074.95
Estimated "Real World" Price: $1049.95

40/44 SERIES 2.5-7X32 MM WITH BALLISTIC-X RETICLE

(also in 1x20 mm, 2.8-10x44 mm Aspherical, 3-9x40 mm, 3-9x40 mm 50 yard Parallax, 3-10x44 mm, 3.8-12x44 mm Aspherical AO, 4-12x44 mm AO, and 6.5-20x44 mm AO with Dual-X and Varminter reticles with ⅛ MOA clicks, and in silver)
Weight: 11.2 oz
Length: 11 ⅛ in

Main Body Tube Diameter: 1 in
Power: 2.5-7X
Objective Diameter: 32 mm
Elevation and Windage Adjustments: ¼ MOA per click
Exit Pupil: 13-4.5 mm
Field of View: 44.7-12.7 ft @ 100 yds
Twilight Factor: 8.9-15
Eye Relief: 3 ½ in
Waterproof: Yes
Fogproof: Yes
Limited Lifetime Warranty
Features: Weaver's line of moderately priced rifle scopes, the 40/44 series was originally built around 40- and 44-mm objectives; but it has now expanded into other configurations, such as the 1x20 mm for muzzleloader hunters in states that restrict scoped sights during blackpowder seasons to 1 power, and the 2.5-7x32 mm for shotguns and muzzleloaders. The 2.5-7X has fully-multi-coated lenses, and the available Ballistic-X reticle has holdover marks on the vertical post calculated for shotgun slugs.
Manufacturer's Suggested Retail Price: $191.49
Estimated "Real World" Price: $179.99

Weaver Tactical 3-15x50 MM

Weaver 40-44 Series 2.5-7x 32 MM

RIFLESCOPES

Weaver

www.weaveroptics.com

BUCK COMMANDER SERIES 4-16X42 MM WITH COMMAND-X RETICLE AND SIDE FOCUS PARALLAX ADJUSTMENT IN MATTE

(also in 2-8x36 mm, 2.5-10x42 mm, and 3-12x50 mm, also with Dual-X reticle)

Weight: 15.9 oz
Length: 14 ⅓ in
Main Body Tube Diameter: 1 in
Power: 4-16X
Objective Diameter: 42 mm
Elevation and Windage Adjustments: ¼ MOA per click
Exit Pupil: 10.5-2.6 mm
Field of View: 22-5.5 ft @ 100 yds
Twilight Factor: 13-26
Eye Relief: 3 ½ in
Waterproof: Yes
Fogproof: Yes
Limited Lifetime Warranty
Features: White-tailed-deer scopes with design help from the quondam and still "Duck Commander" Willie Robertson, now the "Buck Commander," the four-times-magnification-range Buck Commander Series scopes are built from one-piece tubes, have fully-multi-coated lenses, and scratch resistant coating. Windage and elevation turrets are finger adjustable and resettable to zero. The 4-16x42 mm includes SF parallax adjustment and the drop-compensating Command-X ballistic reticle.
Manufacturer's Suggested Retail Price: **$413.49**
Estimated "Real World" Price: **$399.95**

CLASSIC HANDGUN 2X28 MM WITH DUAL-X RETICLE, SILVER

(also in 1.5-4x20 mm, 2.5-8x28 mm, and 4x28 mm, and in gloss and matte)

Weight: 6.7 oz
Length: 8 ½ in
Main Body Tube Diameter: 1 in
Power: 2X
Objective Diameter: 28 mm
Elevation and Windage Adjustments: ¼ MOA per click
Exit Pupil: 15.7 mm
Field of View: 21 ft @ 100 yds
Twilight Factor: 7.5
Eye Relief: 26 ⅘ in

Waterproof: Yes
Fogproof: Yes
Limited Lifetime Warranty
Features: Said to be built to withstand the recoil of a thousand rounds of .454 Casull ammunition, Weaver Classic Handgun scopes have some 2 feet of eye relief and are set to be parallax free out to 50 yards.
Manufacturer's Suggested Retail Price: **$239.49**

Weaver Buck Commander Series

Weaver Classic Handgun 2x28 MM

RIFLESCOPES

CLASSIC-K SERIES 6X38 MM WITH DUAL-X RETICLE, IN MATTE

(also in 4x28 mm Scout, 4x38 mm, 4x38 mm Steel Tube, and 8x56 mm)

Weight: 9.8 oz
Length: 11 ¹/₃ in
Main Body Tube Diameter: 1 in
Power: 6X
Objective Diameter: 38 mm
Elevation and Windage Adjustments: ¼ MOA per click
Exit Pupil: 6.33 mm
Field of View: 18.3 ft @ 100 yds
Twilight Factor: 15
Eye Relief: 3 ¹/₇ in
Waterproof: Yes
Fogproof: Yes
Limited Lifetime Warranty
Features: William Ralph Weaver began producing handmade ¾-inch 3X rifle-scopes back in 1930 in a small shop in Kentucky. He later moved the W. R. Weaver Company to El Paso, Texas, where he built the classic K-4 scope. The fixed-power K-Series scopes built on a one-piece aircraft-grade aluminum tube are based on the K-4 and include a steel-tube model like the ones made generations ago. The current K-Series uses fully-multi-coated lenses and are claimed to be able to absorb 10,000 rounds of .375 H&H Magnum ammunition and hold a zero.
Manufacturer's Suggested Retail Price: **$224.49**
Estimated "Real World" Price: **$214.95**

CLASSIC RIMFIRE 2.5-7X28 MM WITH DUAL-X RETICLE

(also in 3-9x32 mm AO and 4x28 mm, in matte and silver)

Weight: 9.75 oz
Length: 11 in
Main Body Tube Diameter: 1 in
Power: 2.5-7X
Objective Diameter: 28 mm
Elevation and Windage Adjustments: ¼ MOA per click
Exit Pupil: 9.9-4 mm
Field of View: 40.3-14.6 ft @ 100 yds
Twilight Factor: 8.3-14
Eye Relief: 3 ²/₃ in
Waterproof: Yes
Fogproof: Yes

Limited Lifetime Warranty
Features: Available in both variable and fixed-power models, the Weaver Classic Rimfire is made from an air-craft-grade one-piece aluminum tube with fully-multi-coated lenses. Suitable for rimfire calibers .17 through .22 and for the multi-directional recoil of heavy spring-loaded precision airguns. Parallax free to 50 yards.
Manufacturer's Suggested Retail Price: **$220.49**
Estimated "Real World" Price: **$205.99**

CLASSIC T-SERIES 36X40 MM AO WITH SUNSHADE, FINE CROSSHAIR, IN SILVER

(also in 24x40 mm AO, with sunshade and ¹/₈ MOA Dot)

Weight: 17 oz
Length: 15 in
Main Body Tube Diameter: 1 in
Power: 36X
Objective Diameter: 40 mm
Elevation and Windage Adjustments: ¹/₈ MOA per click
Exit Pupil: 1.1 mm
Field of View: 3 ft @ 100 yds
Twilight Factor: 38
Eye Relief: 3 in
Waterproof: Yes
Fogproof: Yes
Limited Lifetime Warranty
Features: Weaver's T-Series fixed rifle-scopes have ¹/₈ MOA Micro-Trac independent windage and elevation adjustment system for long-range target and varmint shooting. The optics are fully multi-coated, the objective is adjustable for parallax, the eyepiece uses traditional focus, comes with a sunshade, screw-in metal lens caps, and an extra pair of oversized benchrest adjustment knobs.
Manufacturer's Suggested Retail Price: **$678.49**
Estimated "Real World" Price: **$659.99**

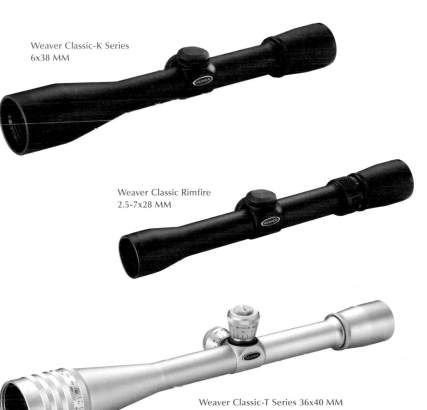

Weaver Classic-K Series
6x38 MM

Weaver Classic Rimfire
2.5-7x28 MM

Weaver Classic-T Series 36x40 MM

Weaver

www.weaveroptics.com

CLASS V-SERIES 6-24X42 MM WITH AO AND SEMI TARGET TURRET (STT) WITH .223 BALLISTIC-X RETICLE, IN MATTE

(also in 1-3x20 mm, 2.5-7x32 mm, 3-9x38 mm, 2-10x38mm, and 4-16x42 mm, in matte and silver, and with Dual-X, Fine Crosshair, F-C ¼ MOA Dot, Mil-Dot, Varminter, and Ballistic-X reticles)

Weight: 17.6 oz
Length: 14 in
Main Body Tube Diameter: 1 in
Power: 6-24X
Objective Diameter: 42 mm
Elevation and Windage Adjustments: ⅛ MOA per click
Exit Pupil: 7-1.75 mm
Field of View: 15.3-4 ft @ 100 yds
Twilight Factor: 15.9-31.7
Eye Relief: 7 ¾-3 ¹/₇ in
Waterproof: Yes
Fogproof: Yes

Weaver Classic V Series 6-24x42 MM

Limited Lifetime Warranty
Features: The Weaver V-Series offers a wide assortment of configurations, reticles, and finishes. Has fast power-change adjustments, fully-multi-coated lenses, and hard coating on exterior lens surfaces. The 6-24x42 mm has a parallax-adjustment objective and semi-target turrets.
Manufacturer's Suggested Retail Price: $601.95
Estimated "Real World" Price: $595.99

Carl Zeiss Sports Optics

www.zeiss.com/sports

CONQUEST 3-9X40 MM, WITH #20 RETICLE

(also in 3-9x40 mm, 3.5-10x44 mm, 4.5-14x44 mm, 3-9x50 mm, 3.5-10x50 mm, 4.5-14x50 mm, 6.5-20x50 mm, 3-12x56 mm)

Weight: 15.17 oz
Length: 12 ⁹/₁₀ in
Main Body Tube Diameter: 1 in
Power: 3-9X
Objective Diameter: 40 mm
Exit Pupil: 13.3-4.4 mm
Field of View: 34-11 ft @ 100 yards
Twilight Factor: 8.5-19.0
Eye Relief: 4 in
Waterproof: Yes
Fogproof: Yes
Transferable Limited Lifetime Warranty

Features: A one-piece 1-inch tube riflescope. Zeiss's moderately priced line. The Conquest 3-9x40 is a classic, all-purpose scope with excellent light gathering ability. It offers wide fields of view, brilliant contrast and high resolution images and is perfect for shotguns, muzzle loaders and centerfire rifles. Conquest riflescopes are available with a variety of reticles including the Rapid-Z® Ballistic Reticle.
Manufacturer's Suggested Retail Price: $399.99
Estimated "Real World" Price: $399.99

Zeiss Conquest 3-9x40 MM

Carl Zeiss Sports Optics

www.zeiss.com/sports

CONQUEST 6.5-20X50 MM

Weight: 21.83 oz
Length: 15 ³/₅ in
Main Body Tube Diameter: 1 in
Power: 6.5-20X
Objective Diameter: 50 mm
Exit Pupil: 7.7-2.5 mm
Field of View: 18-6 ft @ 100 yards
Twilight Factor: 18-31.6
Eye Relief: 3 ¹/₂ in
Waterproof: Yes
Fogproof: Yes
Transferable Limited Lifetime Warranty
Features: The high-magnification Zeiss Conquest 6.5-20x50 includes parallax adjustment for varmints or long-range shooting. Available with either target or hunting turret and with a variety of reticles including the Rapid-Z® 800 and Rapid-Z 1000® Ballistic Reticles.
Manufacturer's Suggested Retail Price: Starting at $999.99 (with #4 or #20 reticle)
Estimated "Real World" Price: $999.99

CONQUEST DURALYT 3-12X50 MM, ILLUMINATED RETICLE

(also in non-illuminated reticle, and in 1.2-5x36 mm and 2-8x42 mm, with illuminated or non illuminated reticles)
Weight: 20.45 oz
Length: 13 ²/₃ in
Main Tube Body Diameter: 30 mm
Power: 3-12X
Objective Diameter: 50 mm
Elevation and Windage Adjustments: ¹/₃ MOA per click
Square Adjustment Range: 43 ¹/₃ in @ 100 yds
Exit Pupil: 16.6-4.2 mm
Field of View: 360-105 ft @ 1000 yards
Twilight Factor: 12.24-24.5
Eye Relief: 3 ¹/₂ in
Waterproof: Yes
Fogproof: Yes
Warranty: Limited Lifetime Transferable
Features: Zeiss's new 30 mm-tube Conquest Duralyt comes with a #60 illuminated (and also available in #6 non-illuminated) second-image-plane reticle. The illuminated reticle employs a fine red dot (just ¹/₃ inch of target

Conquest Duralvt 3-12x50 MM.
Illuminated Reticle

Zeiss Conquest 6.5-20x50 MM

Zeiss Victory Diavari 1.5-6x42 MM

coverage at 100 yards at 12X) in the center of the crosshairs, and are push-button activated with automatic shut-off after four hours of uninterrupted use. And the scope body is an anodized gray for a neutral, unobtrusive appearance in the field.
Manufacturer's Suggested Retail Price: $1499.99
Estimated "Real World" Price: $1349.99

VICTORY DIAVARI 1.5-6X42 T*

(also in 2.5-10x50 mm T, 3-12x56 mm T*, 4-16x50 mm T* FL, 6-24x56 mm T* FL and 6-24x72 mm T* FL)*
Weight: 15.52 oz
Length: 12 ¹/₄ in.
Main Body Tube Diameter: 30 mm
Power: 1.5-6X
Objective Diameter: 42 mm

Exit Pupil: 15.0 mm-7.0 mm
Field of View: 72-23 ft @ 100 yards
Twilight Factor: 4.2-15.9
Eye Relief: 3 ¹/₂ in
Waterproof: Yes
Fogproof: Yes
Transferable Limited Lifetime Warranty
Features: Zeiss Victory Diavari riflescopes come with LotuTec® lens coating and ZEISS T* multi-coating. The 1.5-6x42 is an compact, lightweight, low profile scope designed for fast target acquisition. Available with rail mount and with illumination on select models. And with FL glass where shown.
Manufacturer's Suggested Retail Price: $1649.99
Estimated "Real World" Price: $1649.99

RIFLESCOPES

Carl Zeiss Sports Optics

www.zeiss.com/sports

Zeiss Diarange 2.5-10x50 MM

Zeiss Victory Diavari 6-24x72 MM

Zeiss Victory Varipoint 1.1-4x24 MM

Zeiss Victory Varipoint 3-12x56 MM

DIARANGE M 2.5-10X50 MM T*

(also in 3-12x56 mm T)*
Weight: 31.75 oz
Length: 13 ¹/₅ in
Width: 56.5 mm (rail mount)
Power: 2.5-10X
Objective Diameter: 50 mm
Exit Pupil: 15-5 mm
Field of View: 43 ¹/₂-12 ft @ 100 yards
Twilight Factor: 7.1-22.4
Eye Relief: 3 ¹/₂ in
Waterproof: Yes to 400 mbar
Fogproof: Yes
Transferable Limited Lifetime Warranty on optics and mechanics.
Electronics: 5 Years
Features: The Victory Diarange M series riflescope laser-ranges from 10 yds to 999 yds (depending on the size of the object, reflectivity, angle of impact and weather conditions) with a measuring accuracy of ± 1 yd at ranges up to 600 yards and ± 0.5% at ranges beyond 600 yards in a measuring time of 0.5 seconds. The Diarange can be used in temperatures between -13° to 122° F. Available with illuminated #43 Mil Dot and illuminated Rapid-Z® 600 & 800 reticles.
Manufacturer's Suggested Retail Price: **$3949.99**
Estimated "Real World" Price: **$3949.99**

VICTORY DIAVARI 6-24X72 MM T* FL

Weight: 37.39 oz
Length: 14 ⁹/₁₀ in.
Main Body Tube Diameter: 34 mm
Power: 6-24X
Objective Diameter: 72 mm
Exit Pupil: 12.-3. mm
Field of View: 18 ³/₁₀- 5 ¹/₁₀ ft @ 100 yards
Twilight Factor: 16.9-41.6
Eye Relief: 3 ¹/₂ in
Waterproof: Yes
Fogproof: Yes
Transferable Limited Lifetime Warranty
Features: The 6-24x72 T* Diavari FL riflescope uses a FL glass objective and LotuTec® coating. Available with two ballistic-compensation options— BDC Ballistic Turret and Rapid Z® Ballistic reticle. The Victory 6-24x72 T* FL is designed for tactical marksmen, varmint or predator hunters, and long-range hunters and shooters. This scope also features parallax compensation and ¼ MOA lockable windage and elevation turrets. Available with illumination on select models.
Manufacturer's Suggested Retail Price: **$3399.99**
Estimated "Real World" Price: **$3399.99**

VICTORY VARIPOINT 1.1-4X24 MM T*

(also in 1.5-6x42 mm T, 2.5-10x50 mm T* and 3-12x56 mm T*)*
Weight: 15.87 oz
Length: 11 ⁴/₅ in
Main Body Tube Diameter: 30 mm
Power: 1.1-4X
Objective Diameter: 24 mm
Exit Pupil: 14 8-6.0 mm
Field of View: 108-31 ft @ 100 yards
Twilight Factor: 3.1-9.8
Eye Relief: 3 ¹/₂ in
Waterproof: Yes
Fogproof: Yes
Transferable Limited Lifetime Warranty
Features: The Zeiss Victory Varipoint has an illuminated red-dot reticle for fast target acquisition. It also uses LotuTec® "hydrophobic" lens coating.
Manufacturer's Suggested Retail Price: **$2199.99**
Estimated "Real World" Price: **$2199.99**

VICTORY VARIPOINT 3-12X56 MM T*

Weight: 21.34 oz
Length: 14 in
Main Body Tube Diameter: 30 mm
Power: 3-12X
Objective Diameter: 56 mm
Exit Pupil: 14.7 mm-4.7 mm
Field of View: 37 ¹/₂-10 ¹/₂ ft @ 100 yards
Twilight Factor: 8.5-25.9
Eye Relief: 3 ¹/₂ in
Waterproof: Yes
Fogproof: Yes
Transferable Limited Lifetime Warranty
Features: The large objective lens of the Victory Varipoint 3-12x56 T* is traditional for European scopes that are often used from shooting towers in low light. With illuminated red-dot reticle.
Manufacturer's Suggested Retail Price: **$2399.99**
Estimated "Real World" Price: **$2399.99**

SPOTTING SCOPES

The pedigree of the spotting scope is the oldest among all the optical devices, dating back perhaps as much as three millennia to a rock-crystal lens found in Assyrian ruins that may have been a component of a viewing instrument (the Assyrians supposedly had an advanced knowledge of astronomy, scarcely possible to obtain with the naked eye, that included the description of the rings, which they called "serpents," encircling Saturn).

The certain origins of the spotting scope can be traced to the end of the sixteenth and the beginning of the seventeenth centuries, Anno Domini, to the inventions claimed by many fathers, primarily Dutch, with the Venetian Galileo something of a latecomer with a device fashioned from a leather and wood tube using a convex lens at the objective and a concave at the eyepiece, which he called by the Italian, via Greek, name *telescopio*. Within a year or two of this the German astronomer Johannes Kepler had improved on Galileo's instrument by building a telescope made with two convex lenses, front and back, providing increased magnification, a much larger field of view, and longer eye relief. The drawback of the original Keplerian telescope was that the image emerging from the eyepiece was inverted instead of upright–fine for astronomical, but something more than annoying for terrestrial, observation. Kepler later demonstrated that the addition of a third convex lens, an erector, could revert the image. It is this basic Kepler's refracting or dioptric (again from the Greek, meaning "viewing through") telescope that we use, for the most part, as spotting scopes.

For hunters and shooters a spotting scope must be portable and durable (which is why the other type of telescope, the catadioptric which employs a system of lenses and fragile reflecting mirrors and can produce excellent image quality, may not be well suited for field use if there's a possibility of rough handling). In addition, a spotting scope must be steady, which means either a tripod or a means of mounting it to a solid object, such as the window of a vehicle.

Shooters and hunters often believe that more, rather than less, is more, and so opt for maximum magnifying power without regard to field of view, exit pupil, twilight factor, or resolution, when in fact far more might be seen, and identified, with a, say, 45X scope of the best quality, which includes fine focus adjustments, rather than a mediocre 75X. The spotting scope can also perform other tasks besides spotting, such as doping the wind (through the reading of mirage) or with a mil-dot or MOA scale built in, finding the range. And though hardly a technical or empirical judgment, there is something just clearly exciting, even more exciting than with a binocular or riflescope, about seeing and recognizing things so far away out there with a spotting scope.

Alpen Optics
www.alpenoptics.com

18-36X60 MM

(also in 15-45x60 mm angled and straight, and available in a kit including a tripod, window mount, and foam-lined aluminum hard case)
Weight: 30 oz
Length: 13 ½ in
Width: 4 in
Power: 18-36X
Objective Diameter: 60 mm
Exit Pupil: 3.3-1.7 mm
Field of View: 120-90 ft @ 1000 yds
Twilight Factor: 33-46
Eye Relief: 18 mm
Waterproof: Yes
Fogproof: Yes
Limited Lifetime Warranty
Features: The composite body of the 18-36x60 mm Alpen® spotting scope is rubber armored. It features multi-coated BaK-4 optical design and comes with a nylon field carrying case and tabletop tripod. Also includes an extendable sun shade.
Manufacturer's Suggested Retail Price: **$205**
Estimated "Real World" Price: **$145**

Alpen 18-36x60 MM

Alpen 20-60x60 MM with tripod

20-60X60 MM WITH 45-DEGREE EYEPIECE

(also in straight and in 20-60x80 mm angled and straight)
Weight: 39 oz
Length: 14 ⅓ in
Width: 4 in
Power: 20-60X
Objective Diameter: 60 mm
Exit Pupil: 3-1 mm
Field of View: 113-55 ft @ 1000 yds
Twilight Factor: 35-60
Eye Relief: 17 mm
Waterproof: Yes
Fogproof: Yes
Limited Lifetime Warranty
Features: This Alpen spotting scope features fully multi-coated BaK-4 optical design combined with a rubber-armored composite body. Comes with a nylon field carrying case and table top tripod. Also includes an extendable sun shade and is available with an aluminum foam-filled case.
Manufacturer's Suggested Retail Price: **$290**
Estimated "Real World" Price: **$205**

Alpen 20x50 MM Mini Compact

20X50 MM MINI COMPACT

Weight: 10 oz
Length: 7 ¼ in
Width: 3 in
Power: 20x
Objective Diameter: 50 mm
Exit Pupil: 2.5 mm
Field of View: 147 ft @ 1000 yds
Twilight Factor: 32
Eye Relief: 15 mm
Waterproof: Yes

Fogproof: Yes
Limited Lifetime Warranty
Features: The 20x50 mm Mini Compact Alpen® spotting scope features multi-coated optics. Includes a belt-loop carrying case and compact table-top tripod.
Manufacturer's Suggested Retail Price: **$90**
Estimated "Real World" Price: **$65**

SPOTTING SCOPES

RAINIER 25-75X85 SPOTTING SCOPE WITH 45-DEGREE EYEPIECE

(also in 20-60x80 mm ED HD angled and straight)

Weight: 60 oz
Length: 17 in
Width: 4 ½ in
Power: 25-75X
Objective Diameter: 85 mm
Exit Pupil: 3.4-1.1 mm
Field of View: 84-42 ft @ 1000 yds
Twilight Factor: 46-79
Eye Relief: 16 mm
Waterproof: Yes
Fogproof: Yes
Limited Lifetime Warranty
Features: The Alpen Rainier spotting scope features ED (extra-low-dispersion) fully multi-coated optics, BaK-4 prism, and metallic coatings. Has an adjustable body collar allowing the scope to be turned for varied viewing positions. O-ring sealed.
Manufacturer's Suggested Retail Price: **$1406**
Estimated "Real World" Price: **$900**

Alpen Rainier 25-75x85 MM

Brunton
www.bruntonhunting.com

ICON STRAIGHT 20-60X80 MM

(also angled and in 20-50x80 mm straight and angled)

Weight: 70.4 oz
Length: 16 in
Power: 20-60X
Objective Diameter: 80 mm
Exit Pupil: 4-1.3 mm
Field of View: 115-84 ft @ 1000 yds
Twilight Factor: 40-69.28
Eye Relief: 17 mm
Waterproof: Yes
Fogproof: Yes
Unconditional "HALO" Warranty
Features: The Brunton ICON straight spotting scope uses "super low dispersion" fluorite glass. Has an armored polymer frame with gunsight alignment system. Includes multi-step twist-up eyecup, extendable sunshade, locking center ring for varied viewing angles, and is tripod adaptable.
Manufacturer's Suggested Retail Price: **$3900**

Brunton ICON Straight 20-60x80 MM

Burris

www.burrisoptics.com

HIGH COUNTRY 20-60X60 MM WITH TRIPOD (ALSO IN 15-45X50 MM WITH TRIPOD)

Weight: 35 oz
Length: 14 ²/₅ in
Power: 20-60X
Objective Diameter: 60 mm
Exit Pupil: 3-1 mm
Field of View: 80-48 ft @ 100 yds
Twilight Factor: 34.6-60
Eye Relief: 18 mm
Waterproof: Yes
Fogproof: Yes
Limited Lifetime Warranty:
Features: The Burris High Country straight spotting scope has fully multi-coated lenses and a rubber-armored body. Comes with an integrated lens cap on a slide-out sun shade. Both configurations also include a tripod.
Manufacturer's Suggested Retail Price: **$252**
Estimated "Real World" Price: **$175**

Burris High Country 20-60x60 MM

Burris Landmark Spotter 20-60x80 MM Tripod

LANDMARK 20-60X80 MM WITH TRIPOD AND HARD CASE

(also in 15-45x60 mm, 15-45x60 mm with tripod and hard case, and 20-60x80 mm spotter alone)
Weight: 42 oz
Length: 17 ½ in
Power: 20-60X
Objective Diameter: 80 mm
Exit Pupil: 4-1.3 mm
Field of View: 105-52 ft @ 100 yds
Twilight Factor: 40-69.3
Eye Relief: 20-15 mm
Waterproof: Yes
Fogproof: Yes
Limited Lifetime Warranty:
Features: The Landmark spotting scope has fully multi-coated lenses and a charcoal-colored rubber exterior armor coating to protect against noise, scratches, and moisture. An extension mounting bracket is included with the 20-60X to center the scope's weight on a tripod.
Manufacturer's Suggested Retail Price: **$447**
Estimated "Real World" Price: **$300**

Burris Landmark Spotter 20-60x80 MM Hard Case

Burris Landmark Spotter 20-60x80 MM

XTS-2575 SPOTTER
Weight: 33 oz
Length: 10 in
Power: 25-75X
Objective Diameter: 70 mm
Exit Pupil: 2.8-1 mm
Field of View: 58-33 ft @ 100 yds
Twilight Factor: 41.8-72.5
Eye Relief: 23-18 mm
Waterproof: Yes
Fogproof: Yes
Limited Lifetime Warranty:
Features: A catoptric ("mirror" in Greek) or "reflective" spotting scope, an invention of Sir Isaac Newton. Uses a Cassegrain-style mirror system, usually described as "a folded two mirror" scope, invented by a 17th century Chartres, France, priest Laurent Cassegrain. The telescope has two mirrors, a primary concave parabolic mirror and a secondary convex hyperbolic mirror. The primary mirror focuses light onto the secondary mirror, which light is then reflected through a hole in the primary mirror into the eyepiece. This not only allowed for a more compact, in length, telescope housing but was a way of reducing the "color fringing" seen in the early, crudely ground lenses of Galilean

Burris XTS 2575 Spotter 25x75 MM

dioptric or "refracting" ("see through") telescopes. The XTS-2575 is a variable-power scope, adjustable between 25 and 75X. The lenses are multi-coated and the eyepiece is angled.

Manufacturer's Suggested Retail Price: $388
Estimated "Real World" Price: $260

Bushnell

www.bushnell.com

ELITE 15-45X60 MM
(also in 20-60x80 mm straight and 45-degree angled)
Weight: 26.5 oz
Length: 12 1/5 in
Power: 15-45X
Objective Diameter: 60 mm
Exit Pupil: 4-1.3 mm
Field of View: 125-65 ft @ 1000 yds
Twilight Factor: 30-52
Eye Relief: 15 mm
Waterproof: Yes

Fogproof: Yes
Limited Lifetime Warranty
Features: The straight-through Bushnell Elite 15-45x 60 mm spotting scope has PC-3 phase-corrected BaK-4 prisms and fully-multi-coated lenses. Waterproof construction with RainGuard HD exterior lens coating.
Manufacturer's Suggested Retail Price: $701.95
Estimated "Real World" Price: $379.99

Bushnell Elite 15-45x60 MM

SPOTTING SCOPES

Bushnell
www.bushnell.com

EXCURSION 15-45X60 MM
Weight: 47.2 oz
Length: 11 ¾ in
Power: 15-45X
Objective Diameter: 60 mm
Exit Pupil: 4-1.3 mm
Field of View: 176 -58 ft @ 1000 yds
Twilight Factor: 30-52
Eye Relief: 20 mm
Waterproof: Yes
Fogproof: Yes
Limited Lifetime Warranty
Features: The Bushnell waterproof, fogproof Excursion tactical spotter has a "Folded Light Path System" for a more compact housing. The extra-low-dispersion fluorite glass is fully-multi-coated. Has a blacked-out interior and a "Mil-Hash" reticle for ranging at any magnification. Includes a tripod and a soft-sided, fitted case that can be left on or removed during glassing.
Manufacturer's Suggested Retail Price: **$662.95**
Estimated "Real World" Price: **$399.99**

Bushnell Excursion 15-45x60 MM

Bushnell Legend Ultra HD 15-45x60 MM

LEGEND ULTRA HD 15-45X60 MM
(also in 12-36x50 mm straight and 45-degree angled, and in 20-60x80 mm 45-degree angled)
Weight: 40.4 oz.
Length: 11 in.
Power: 15-45X
Objective Diameter: 60 mm
Exit Pupil: 3.7-1.3 mm
Field of View: 140-63 ft@ 1000 yards
Twilight Factor: 30-52
Eye Relief: 20 mm
Waterproof: Yes
Fogproof: Yes
Limited Lifetime Warranty
Features: The mid-sized 15-45x60 mm Bushnell Legend Ultra HD spotter uses extra-low-dispersion glass, fully-multi-coated lenses, and BaK-4-glass Porro prisms. Dual-focus controls allow rapid and fine adjustments. Includes RainGuard HD water-repellent coating, long eye relief, zoom eyepiece, a retractable sunshade, twist-up eye-cups, and a rotating tripod mount.
Manufacturer's Suggested Retail Price: **$558.95**
Estimated "Real World" Price: **$309.99**

Bushnell Trophy 20-60x65 MM

XLT 20-60X65 MM
(also in 15-45x50 mm)
Weight: 42.3 oz
Length: 13 ⅖ in
Power: 20-60X
Objective Diameter: 65 mm
Exit Pupil: 3.25-1.1 mm
Field of View: 110-55 ft @ 1000 yds
Twilight Factor: 36.1-62.4
Eye Relief: 18.3 mm
Waterproof: Yes
Fogproof: No

Limited Lifetime Warranty
Features: The Bushnell Trophy XLT 20-60x65 mm is a rubber-armored, Porro-prism, zoom spotter. Has fully-multi-coated lenses and comes with a compact tripod, premium hard-sided case, and a soft-sided case.
Manufacturer's Suggested Retail Price: **$364.95**
Estimated "Real World" Price: **$214.99**

SPOTTING SCOPES

Hensoldt

www.zeiss.com/sports

HENSOLDT SPOTTER 20-60X60 MM

Weight: 56.43 oz
Length: 13 ¹/₇ in
Width: 4 in
Power: 20-60X
Objective Diameter: 60 mm
Exit Pupil: 3.6-1.2 mm
Field of View: 161-62 ft @ 1000 m (1094 yds)
Twilight Factor: 34.6-60
Eye Relief: ½ in
Waterproof: Yes
Fogproof: Yes
Warranty: Pending

Features: The Hensoldt Spotter 20-60x60 mm is available in a first-focal-plane model with illuminated MilDot. Adjustable illumination intensity also auto-adjusts to changes in background light. Has a one-piece mono-block design and is nitrogen purged. Features Zeiss FL glass. Includes attachment points for Picatinny rails. Night-vision compatible. Offset optical path to prevent direct visibility of spotter to subject.
Manufacturer's Suggested Retail Price:. $4999.99

Hensoldt Spotter 20-60x60 MM

Konus USA

www.konususa.com

KONUSSPOT-80 20-60X80 MM

(also in 20-60x70 mm, 20-60x100 mm, 15-45x50 mm, 15-45x65 mm, and 9-45x60)
Weight: 54.6 oz
Length: 16 ½ in
Power: 20X-60X
Objective Diameter: 80 mm
Exit Pupil: 4 mm-1.3 mm
Field of View: 79 ft-41 ft @ 1000 yards
Twilight Factor: 40-69.3
Waterproof: Water Resistant

Fogproof: Yes
Warranty: Lifetime Replacement
Features: The KonusSpot-80 spotting scope offers high image definition and brightness. Zoom range is 20X to 60X with a large 80 mm objective. Comes with forward-extending lens, metal table tripod, camera adapter, and carrying case.
Manufacturer's Suggested Retail Price:. $439.99
Estimated "Real World" Price:. $349.99

KonusSpot-80

Kowa Sporting Optics

www.kowa-usa.com

HIGHLANDER PROMINAR PURE FLUORITE CRYSTAL 32X82 MM BINOCULAR

Weight: 14 lb
Length: 16 ⁹/₁₀ in
Width: 9 ²/₅ in
Power: 32X
Objective Diameter: 82 mm
Exit Pupil: 2.6 mm
Field of View: 125 ft @ 1000 yards
Twilight Factor: 51.2
Eye Relief: 20 mm
Waterproof: Yes

Fogproof: Yes
Limited Lifetime Warranty
Features: Die-cast aluminum-housing tripod-mounted fully multi-coated fluorite crystal binocular spotting scope with 32x wide angle eyepieces and twin 82 mm objectives. Eyepieces in 21x and 50x are also available.
Manufacturer's Suggested Retail Price:. $5,560
Estimated "Real World" Price:. $5,000

Kowa Highlander Prominar 32x82 MM Binocular

SPOTTING SCOPES

Kowa Sporting Optics
www.kowa-usa.com

77MM PROMINAR WITH PROMINAR XD LENS – TSN-773 (ANGLED) AND TSN-774 (STRAIGHT) W/20X-60X ZOOM EYEPIECE (TE-10Z)

Weight: 46.9 oz (excluding eyepiece)
Length: 12 ½ in (excluding eyepiece)
Power: 20-60X zoom eyepiece
Objective Diameter: 77 mm
Exit Pupil: 3.9-1.3 mm for zoom eyepiece
Field of View: 118-60 ft @ 1000 yards for zoom eyepiece
Twilight Factor: 39.2-68.0 for zoom eyepiece
Eye Relief: 17.0-16.5 mm
Waterproof: Yes
Fogproof: Yes
Limited Lifetime Warranty
Features: A magnesium-alloy body 77 mm spotting scope, available in angled or straight body, with extra-low-dispersion Prominar XD lenses to correct chromatic aberration. Mountable to ¼ and ⅜ inch tripods plates, with a dual speed focus wheel and a locking eyepiece mechanism. Eyepieces available in 20x-60x zoom, 30x wide angle, and 25x long eye relief.
Manufacturer's Suggested Retail Price: . . . .**$1970, plus $660 for eyepiece**
Estimated "Real World" Price: . . . .**$1770 and $595**

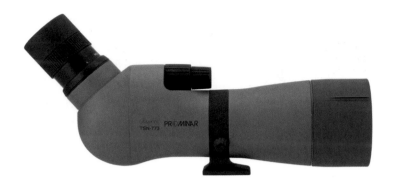

Kowa TSN-773

82MM HIGH PERFORMANCE ANGLED BODY: TSN-82SV W/20X-60X ZOOM EYEPIECE (TE-9Z)

Weight: 52.2 oz (excluding eyepiece)
Length: 15 ¹/₁₀ in (excluding eyepiece)
Power: 20X-60x
Objective Diameter: 82 mm
Exit Pupil: 3.9-1.3 mm
Field of View: 100-54 ft @ 1000 yards
Twilight Factor: 40.49-70.14
Eye Relief: 16.5-16 mm

Kowa TSN-82SV

Waterproof: Yes
Fogproof: Yes
Limited Lifetime Warranty
Features: An angled-bodied scope with a 82mm objective lens and a selection of four different eyepieces.
Manufacturer's Suggested Retail Price: . . . .**$775, plus $415 for eyepiece**
Estimated "Real World" Price: . . . .**$695 and $370**

66MM HIGH PERFORMANCE SPOTTING SCOPE: ANGLED BODY – TSN-661, STRAIGHT BODY – TSN-662 W/ 20X-60X ZOOM EYEPIECE (TE-9Z)

Weight: 35.6 oz (excluding eyepiece)
Length: 12 ¹/₅ in (excluding eyepiece)

Kowa TSN-661

Power: 20X-60x eyepiece
Objective Diameter: 66 mm
Exit Pupil: 3.3-1.1 mm
Field of View: 100-55 ft @ 1000 yards
Twilight Factor: 36.3-62.9
Eye Relief: 16.5-16 mm
Waterproof: Yes
Fogproof: Yes
Limited Lifetime Warranty
Features: A 2 ¼-pound (without eyepiece) spotting scope with fully multi-coated lenses. Optional 30x and 45x fixed wide angle, and 25x long eye relief eyepieces are available for these models.
Manufacturer's Suggested Retail Price: . . . .**$615, plus $415 for eyepiece**
Estimated "Real World" Price: . . . .**$555 and $370**

SPOTTING SCOPES

Kowa Sporting Optics

www.kowa-usa.com

66MM HIGH PERFORMANCE WITH PROMINAR XD LENS: ANGLED BODY – TSN-663, STRAIGHT BODY – TSN-664 W/ 20X-60X ZOOM EYEPIECE (TE-9Z)

Weight: 36.7 oz (excluding eyepiece)
Length: 12 ⅕ in (excluding eyepiece)
Power: 20X-60x eyepiece
Objective Diameter: 66 mm
Exit Pupil: 3.3-1.1 mm
Field of View: 100-55 ft @ 1000 yards
Twilight Factor: 36.3-62.9
Eye Relief: 16.5-16 mm
Waterproof: Yes
Fogproof: Yes
Limited Lifetime Warranty
Features: The spotting scope body (without eyepiece) weighs 36.7 oz with fully multi-coated XD lenses provide crystal clear images. Available eyepieces for these models include 20x-60x zoom, 30x and 45x fixed wide angle, and 25x long eye relief.
Manufacturer's Suggested Retail Price: . . . . $1080 and $415
Estimated "Real World" Price: . . . . $970 and $370

88MM PROMINAR WITH PURE FLUORITE LENS – TSN-883 (ANGLED) AND TSN-884 (STRAIGHT) W/20X-60X ZOOM EYEPIECE (TE-10Z)

Weight: 53.6 oz (excluding eyepiece)
Length: 13 ½ in (excluding eyepiece)
Power: 20-60X zoom eyepiece
Objective Diameter: 88 mm
Exit Pupil: 4.4-1.5 mm for zoom eyepiece
Field of View: 118-60 ft @ 1000 yards for zoom eyepiece
Twilight Factor: 42.0-72.7 for zoom eyepiece
Eye Relief: 17.0-16.5 mm

Waterproof: Yes
Fogproof: Yes
Limited Lifetime Warranty
Features: Large 88mm objective-lens spotting scope available in angled and straight body. With fluorite crystal lenses, dual speed focus wheel and eyepiece. Available eyepieces include 20x-60x zoom, 30x wide angle, and 25x long eye relief.
Manufacturer's Suggested Retail Price: $2570
plus $660 for eyepiece
Estimated "Real World" Price: . . . . $2310 and $595

Kowa TSN-664

Kowa TSN-883

SPOTTING SCOPES

Kruger Optical

www.Krugeroptical.com

BACKCOUNTRY 20-60X80 STRAIGHT

(also in angled and in 15-45x60 mm angled and straight)
Weight: 43 oz
Length: 16 ¹/₇ in
Width: 3 ¾ in
Power: 20-60X
Objective Diameter: 80 mm
Exit Pupil: 4-1.33 mm
Field of View: 100-47.5 ft @ 1000 yds
Twilight Factor: 40-69.28
Eye Relief: 21-15 mm
Waterproof: Yes
Fogproof: Yes
Transferable Limited lifetime
Features: The Kruger Backcountry 20-60x80 mm straight spotting scope

Kruger Backcountry 20-60x80 Straight

features broadband anti-reflection high-fidelity lens coatings, BaK-4 prisms, a close focus of 3 meter, long eye-relief, and hermetically sealed rubber-armored body.

Manufacturer's Suggested Retail Price:................$323.47
Estimated "Real World" Price:................$274.95

Leica Sport Optics

www.leica-sportoptics.com

APO -TELEVID 20-50X WW X 82 MM ANGLED

(also in straight and in 20-50X WW x 65 mm angled and straight)
Weight (with eyepiece): 51.8 oz
Length: 12 1³/₁₆ in
Width: 4 ¼ in
Power: 20x to 50x WW
Objective Diameter: 82 mm
Exit Pupil: 3.28-1.64
Field of View: 92-35 ft @ 1000 yds
Twilight Factor: 40.5-64
Eye Relief: 19 mm
Waterproof: Yes
Fogproof: Yes
Limited Lifetime Warranty
Features: The Leica APO Televid uses a four-part fluoride objective lens group with an optically neutral protective front lens. The body is die-cast magnesium armored in black rubber.

Leica Televid 20-50X WW x 82 MM

Exterior lenses are treated with Leica Aqua Dura coating to repel dust and water. Waterproof to 17 feet. The ASPH wide-angle 20-50X lens reduces spherical aberration. Includes micro-focusing.

Manufacturer's Suggested Retail Price:................ $4300
Estimated "Real World" Price:................ $3899

SPOTTING SCOPES

Leupold & Stevens, Inc

www.leupold.com

LEUPOLD SX-1 VENTANA 15-45X60 MM

(also in 20-60x80 mm; other Leupold spotting scopes include the SX-2 Kenai, Golden Ring HD, Golden Ring HD Boone and Crockett Edition, Golden Ring, Golden Ring Compact, and Mark 4 Tactical)

Weight: 30.6 ounces
Length: 13 ½ inches
Width:
Power: 15-45X
Objective aperture: 60 mm
Exit Pupil: 4.0-1.3 mm
Field of View: 121-63 ft @ 1000 yds
Twilight Factor: 30.0-52.0
Eye Relief: 26.7-24.0 mm
Waterproof: Yes
Fogproof: Yes
Limited Lifetime Warranty
Features: Leupold's SX-1 Ventana comes with both a straight and 45-degree angled eyepiece. It is also available in a kit that includes a hard-side carrying case, soft case, and compact adjustable tripod. The SX-1 Ventana has a Multicoat 4® Lens System. Knurling on the black body assists grip and operation. Other features include a retractable lens shade and twist-up eyecups.
Manufacturer's Suggested Retail Price: $299.99

Leupold SX-1 Ventana 15-45x60 MM

Minox GmbH

www.minox.com

MD 50

Weight: 23.28 oz
Length: 8 ²/₅ in
Width: 4 ⁴/₅ in
Power: 16-30X
Objective Diameter: 50 mm
Exit Pupil: 3.33-1.67 mm
Field of View: 160-100 ft @ 1000 yards
Twilight Factor: 27.4-38.7
Eye Relief: 15-11 mm

Waterproof: Yes
Fogproof: Yes
Five-Year Warranty
Features: Compact straight scope with fully adjustable eyepiece from 16x to 30x magnification.
Manufacturer's Suggested Retail Price: $339
Estimated "Real World" Price: $299

Minox MD 50

Minox GmbH

www.minox.com

MD 50 W
Weight: 21.69 oz
Length: 8 ²/₅ in
Width: 4 ⁴/₅ in
Power: 16-30X
Objective Diameter: 50 mm
Exit Pupil: 3.13-1.67 mm
Field of View: 142-100 ft @ 1000 yards
Twilight Factor: 28.3-38.7
Eye Relief: 15-11 mm
Waterproof: Yes
Fogproof: Yes
Five-Year Warranty
Features: Compact angled scope with fully adjustable eyepiece from 16x to 30x magnification.
Manufacturer's Suggested Retail Price:................... **$339**
Estimated "Real World" Price:................... **$299**

MD 88 W APO
Weight: 66.62 oz

Minox MD 50W

Minox MD 88 W APO

Length: 16 ¹/₃ in
Width: 5 ½ in
Power: 20-60X
Objective Diameter: 88 mm
Exit Pupil: 4.4-1.4 mm
Field of View: 137-62 ft @ 1000 yards
Twilight Factor: 42-73

Eye Relief: 21.76-20.27 mm
Waterproof: Yes
Fogproof: Yes
Limited Lifetime Warranty
Features: Lenses are high-resolution, apochromatically corrected, multi-coated glass and multi-coating. With integrated eyepiece.
Manufacturer's Suggested Retail Price:................... **$1899**
Estimated "Real World" Price:................... **$1599**

Nikon Sport Optics

www.nikonhunting.com/products/fieldscopes

FIELDSCOPE 82 MM ED STRAIGHT
(also in angled)
Weight: 55.5 oz
Length: 12 ⁹/₁₀ in
Width: 4 ¹/₅ in
Power: 25-75X
Objective Diameter: 82 mm
Exit Pupil: 3.3-1.1 mm
Field of View: 84 ft @ 1000 yds
Twilight Factor: 45.27-78.42
Eye Relief: 14.1 mm
Waterproof: Yes
Fogproof: Yes
25-Year Warranty
Features: The Nikon Fieldscope 82 mm uses extra-low dispersion glass. Features aspherical ocular lenses, extended eye relief, dielectric multi-layer prism coating, fully multi-coated optics, and apochromatic lens system to correct chromatic aberration in the violet, as well as red, blue, and green color ranges.
Manufacturer's Suggested Retail Price:................. **$2598.95**
Estimated "Real World" Price:................. **$1799.95**

Nikon Fieldscope 82 MM ED

EDG FIELDSCOPE 65MM STRAIGHT

(also in angled)
Weight: 55 oz
Length: 12 ³/₁₀ in
Width: 3 ½ in
Power: 16-48X
Objective Diameter: 65 mm
Exit Pupil: 4.1-1.4 mm
Field of View: 147-73 ft @ 1000 yds
Twilight Factor: 32.24-55.85
Eye Relief: 18.4-16.5 mm
Waterproof: Yes
Fogproof: Yes
25-Year Limited Warranty
Features: Nikon's top-of-the-line roof-prism spotting scope uses extra-low dispersion glass (EDG). Features aspherical ocular lenses, extended eye relief, dielectric multi-layer prism coating, fully multi-coated optics, and apochromatic lens system to correct chromatic aberration in the violet, as well as red, blue, and green color ranges. The mount include three mounting holes for variations in tripod balance.
Manufacturer's Suggested Retail Price: **$4400.95**
Estimated "Real World" Price: **$2889.95**

FIELDSCOPE 50MM ED ANGLED

(also in straight)
Weight: 16.6 oz
Length: 8 ¹/₁₀ in
Width: 2 ⁴/₅ in
Power: 13-30X
Objective Diameter: 50 mm
Exit Pupil: 3.8-1.4 mm
Field of View: 157 ft @ 1000 yds
Twilight Factor: 25.49-38.72
Eye Relief: 12.9 mm
Waterproof: Yes
Fogproof: Yes
25-Year Limited Warranty
Features: The compact Fieldscope 50 mm ED has fully-multi-coated, extra-low-dispersion-glass lenses.
Manufacturer's Suggested Retail Price: **$1198.95**
Estimated "Real World" Price: **$799.95**

Nikon EDG Fieldscope 65 MM ED

Nikon Fieldscope III 60 MM ED

FIELDSCOPE III 60 MM ED ANGLED

(also in straight, and in non-ED straight and angled)
Weight: 42 oz
Length: 11 ½ in
Width: 3 ⁷/₁₀ in
Power: 20-60X
Objective Diameter: 60 mm
Exit Pupil: 3-1 mm
Field of View: 105 ft @ 1000 yds
Twilight Factor: 34.64-60
Eye Relief: 14.1 mm
Waterproof: Yes
Fogproof: Yes
25-Year Limited Warranty
Features: This Nikon Fieldscope III 60 mm ED contains features similar to the other ED, and EDG, spotting scopes: extra-low dispersion glass, aspherical ocular lenses, extended eye relief, dielectric multi-layer prism coating, fully multi-coated optics, and apochromatic lens system to correct chromatic aberration in the violet, as well as red, blue, and green color ranges. The non-ED Fieldscope III's come without the aspherical lenses and apochromatic lens system.

Nikon Fieldscope 50 MM ED

Nikon ProStaff 16-48x65 MM

Manufacturer's Suggested Retail Price: **$2398.95**
Estimated "Real World" Price: **$1699.95**

PROSTAFF 16-48X65 MM ANGLED

(also in straight)
Weight: 32.5 oz
Length: 12 in
Width: 4 ¹/₁₀ in
Power: 16-48X
Objective Diameter: 65 mm
Exit Pupil: 4.1-1.35 mm
Field of View: 126 ft @ 1000 yds
Twilight Factor: 32.24-54.08
Eye Relief: 15.2 mm
Waterproof: Yes
Fogproof: Yes
25-Year Limited Warranty
Features: The Nikon ProStaff 16-48x65 mm spotting scope is waterproof, has multi-coated lenses, and is equipped with a sliding sunshade and removable peep sight.
Manufacturer's Suggested Retail Price: **$582.95**
Estimated "Real World" Price: **$429.95**

SPOTTING SCOPES

Nikon Sport Optics

www.nikonhunting.com/products/fieldscopes

SPOTTER XL II ZOOM OUTFIT WATERPROOF 16-48X60 MM

Weight: 31.2 oz
Length: 12 ³/₁₀ in
Width: 2 ⁹/₁₀ in
Power: 16-48X
Objective Diameter: 60 mm
Exit Pupil: 3.8-1.25 mm
Field of View: 120 ft @ 1000 yds
Twilight Factor: 28.28-48.98
Eye Relief: 3.8 mm
Waterproof: Yes
Fogproof: Yes
25-Year Limited Warranty
Features: Zoom spotting scope includes a rubber body coating and a sliding sunshade with sighting notch.
Manufacturer's Suggested Retail Price: **$900.95**
Estimated "Real World" Price: **$499.95**
SPOTTING SCOPE
Pentax PF-65 ED A II

Nikon Spotter XL II Outfit

Pentax

www.pentaxsportoptics.com

PF-65 ED A II

(also in straight body)
Weight: 37.7 oz
Length: 10 ³/₅ in
Width: 4 ⁷/₁₀ x 3 ³/₁₀ in
Power: Eyepiece variable
Objective Diameter: 65 mm
Exit Pupil: Eyepiece variable
Field of View: Eyepiece variable
Twilight Factor: Eyepiece variable
Eye Relief: 18 mm with PENTAX XF series prime eyepieces
Waterproof: Yes
Fogproof: Yes
Limited Lifetime Warranty
Features: An angled porro-prism spotting scope with a 65mm objective lens with extra-low dispersion (ED) optical elements.
Manufacturer's Suggested Retail Price: **$659**
Estimated "Real World" Price: **$659**

Pentax PF-65 ED A II

Pentax

www.pentaxsportoptics.com

PF-80 ED

(also in angled body)
Weight: 49.4 oz
Length: 15 ³/₅ in
Width: 4 ⁷/₁₀ x 3 ⁹/₁₀ in
Power: Eyepiece variable
Objective Diameter: 80 mm
Exit Pupil: Eyepiece variable
Field of View: Eyepiece variable
Twilight Factor: Eyepiece variable
Eye Relief: 20 mm with PENTAX XW
series eyepieces
Waterproof: Yes
Fogproof: Yes
Limited Lifetime Warranty
Features: A straight spotting scope
with porro-prism optics and an 80mm
objective lens with extra-low disper-
sion (ED) optical elements. Available
with variable eyepieces.
**Manufacturer's Suggested Retail
Price:** **$849**
**Estimated "Real World"
Price:** **$849**

Pentax PF-80 ED

Redfield

www.redfield.com

SPOTTING SCOPES

RAMPAGE 20-60X60 MM

Weight: 37.2 oz
Length: 14 ⁷/₅ in
Power: 20-60X
Objective Diameter: 60 mm
Exit Pupil: 3.0-1.0 mm
Field of View: 114-51 ft @ 1000 yds
Twilight Factor: 34.6-60
Eye Relief: 17-14 mm
Weatherproof: Yes
Fogproof: Yes
Redfield Limited Lifetime Warranty
Features: The Redfield Rampage spot-
ting scope features fully multi-coated
lenses and a BaK-4 prism. The scope's
body is black polycarbonate and
includes a twist-up-down eyecup, a
compact tripod, view-through soft
case, neoprene neck strap, and lens
caps. It also comes with a retractable
lens shade.
**Manufacturer's Suggested Retail
Price:** **$229.99**

Redfield Rampage 20-60X60 MM

Simmons

www.bushnell.com

PROSPORT 12-36X50 MM
Weight: 23.1 oz
Length: 11 $^7/_{10}$ in
Power: 12-36X
Objective Diameter: 50 mm
Exit Pupil: 4.1-1.3 mm
Field of View: 132 ft-68 ft @ 1000 yds
Twilight Factor: 24.49-42.42
Eye Relief: 17-13.5 mm
Waterproof: Yes
Fogproof: Yes

Limited Lifetime Warranty
Features: The Simmons ProSport Spotting Scope has a built-in sliding sunshade and fully-coated. Comes with a hard-shell aluminum case for transport. Soft-sided case and tripod are included.
Manufacturer's Suggested Retail Price:.................$163.95
Estimated "Real World" Price:.................$109.99

Simmons ProSport 12-36x50 MM

Swarovski Optik North America LTD

www.Swarovskioptik.com

ATM 80 HD
(also in ATM 65, STM 65, STM 80)
Body Only
Weight: 45.2 oz
Length: 12 $^4/_5$ in
Width: in
Power: See Eyepiece Options Below
Objective Diameter: 80 mm
Exit Pupil: See Eyepiece Options Below
Field of View: See Eyepiece Options Below
Twilight Factor: See Eyepiece Options Below
Eye Relief: See Eyepiece Options Below
Waterproof: Yes
Fogproof: Yes
Limited Lifetime Warranty
Features: The ATM/STM (angled and straight) spotting scopes have a magnesium body, full rubber armoring, and large focus ring. Available with or without HD glass.
Manufacturer's Suggested Retail Price:................. $3110
Estimated "Real World" Price:................. $2799
Eyepiece Options: The ATM and STM spotting scopes have a variety of optional eyepieces. All are fogproof, waterproof, and carry limited-lifetime warranties. The data on each is shown below—

Swarovski ATM 80 HD

Swarovski Optik North America LTD

www.Swarovskioptik.com

25-50X

Exit Pupil: (65 mm Objective) 2.6-1.3 mm; (80 mm Objective) 3.2-1.6 mm
Twilight Factor: 40-56.5; 44-63
Field of View: 138-89 ft @ 1000 yards
Eye Relief: 17 mm
Manufacturer's Suggested Retail Price:. **$865.56**
Estimated "Real World" Price:. **$779**

20-60X

Exit Pupil: (65 mm Objective) 3.3-1.1 mm; (80 mm Objective) 4-1.3 mm
Twilight Factor: 36-62; 40-69
Field of View: 118-66 ft @ 1000 yards
Eye Relief: 17 mm
Manufacturer's Suggested Retail Price:. **$665.56**
Estimated "Real World" Price:. **$599**

30X

Exit Pupil: (65 mm Objective) 2.2 mm; (80 mm Objective) 2.7 mm
Twilight Factor: 44; 49
Field of View: 138 ft @ 1000 yards
Eye Relief: 20 mm
Manufacturer's Suggested Retail Price:. **$521.11**
Estimated "Real World" Price:. **$469**

Vortex Optics

www.vortexoptics.com

Vortex Nomad 20-60x60 MM

Vortex Razor 20-60x85 MM

NOMAD SPOTTING SCOPE 20-60X60 MM ANGLED

(also in straight)
Weight: 36.1 oz
Length: 13 ¹/₅ in
Power: 20-60X
Objective Diameter: 60 mm
Exit Pupil: 3-1 mm
Field of View: 114-51 ft @ 1000 yds
Twilight Factor: 34.64-60
Eye Relief: 17-14 mm
Waterproof: Yes
Fogproof: Yes
Unconditional Lifetime Warranty
Features: The Vortex Nomad spotting scope has fully multi-coated lenses with multiple anti-reflective coatings on all air-to-glass surfaces. Optics are sealed with O-rings and nitrogen-gas purged. Eyecup twists up and down. Includes sunshade and a rotating tripod ring for adjusting of the eyepiece to a sideways position.
Manufacturer's Suggested Retail Price:. **$389**
Estimated "Real World" Price:. **$339.99**

RAZOR 20-60X85 MM ANGLED

(also in straight)
Weight: 65.7 oz
Length: 15 ¹/₂ in
Power: 20-60X
Objective Diameter: 85 mm
Exit Pupil: 4.25-1.41 mm

Field of View: 117-60 ft @ 1000 yds
Twilight Factor: 41.23-71.41
Eye Relief: 20-18 mm
Waterproof: Yes
Fogproof: Yes
Unconditional Lifetime Warranty
Features: The large objective Vortex Razor spotting scope features high-density extra-low-dispersion glass with Vortex proprietary XR anti-reflective coatings, and the optics are fully multi-coated on all air-to-glass lens surfaces. The optics are sealed with

O-rings and argon-gas purged. Exterior lenses are protected from scratches, oil, and dirt by Armor-Tek, an ultra-hard scratch-resistant coating. Has dual focus for coarse and fine adjustments. With twist-up-and-down eyecup, sunshade, and rotating tripod ring for varied viewing angles.
Manufacturer's Suggested Retail Price:. **$2000**
Estimated "Real World" Price:. **$1600**

SPOTTING SCOPES

Vortex Optics

www.vortexoptics.com

VIPER HD 20-60X80 MM ANGLED

(also in straight and in 15-45x65 mm angled and straight)

Weight: 67 oz
Length: 17 ½ in
Power: 20-60X
Objective Diameter: 80 mm
Exit Pupil: 4-1.33 mm
Field of View: 110-50 ft @ 1000 yds
Twilight Factor: 40-69.28
Eye Relief: 18 mm
Waterproof: Yes
Fogproof: Yes
Unconditional Lifetime Warranty
Features: The Vortex Viper HD spotting scope features high-density extra-low-dispersion glass with Vortex proprietary XR anti-reflective coatings, and the optics are fully multi-coated on all air-to-glass lens surfaces. The optics are sealed with O-rings and argon-gas purged. Exterior lenses are protected from scratches, oil, and dirt by Armor-Tek, an ultra-hard scratch-resistant coating. Has twist-up-and-down eye-cup, sunshade, and rotates for varied viewing angles. Includes a rail that allows attachment of red-dot type sights.

Vortex Viper 20-60x80 MM

Manufacturer's Suggested Retail Price: $899
Estimated "Real World" Price: $799.99

Weaver

www.weaveroptics.com

CLASSIC SERIES 15-45X65 MM, STRAIGHT EYEPIECE

(also in angled eyepiece)

Length: 15 ⅕ in
Width: 3 ⅓ in
Power: 15-45X
Objective Diameter: 65 mm
Exit Pupil: 4.3-1.4 mm
Field of View: 174-57 ft @ 100 yards
Twilight Factor: 26-54
Eye Relief: 22-21 mm
Waterproof: Yes
Fogproof: Yes
Limited Lifetime Warranty
Features: The roof-prism Weaver Classic Series spotting scope includes a large, fast-focus ocular (eyepiece) lens. With a black matte finish.

Manufacturer's Suggested Retail Price: $388.95
Estimated "Real World" Price: $379.99

Weaver Classic Series 15-45x65 MM

VICTORY 65MM T*FL DIASCOPE

Weight: 56.3 oz
Length: 16 ½ in
Width: 3 ⅕ in
Power: Variable 15-56X
Objective Diameter: 65 mm
Exit Pupil: 4.3mm–1.16mm
Field of View: 156-63 ft @ 1000 yards
Twilight Factor: 31.22-60.33
Eye Relief: 16 mm
Waterproof: Yes
Fogproof: Yes
Transferable Limited Lifetime Warranty
Features: Comes with Dual Speed Focus System (DSF), a rubber-armored exterior over a magnesium-aluminum housing, and a FL lens system.
Manufacturer's Suggested Retail Price: $2649.99
(with Vario 15-56x Eyepiece with other available eyepieces including Vario 20-75X, 15-45X, 20-60X, and 30X and 40X fixed, also in straight body)
Estimated "Real World" Price: $2649.99
(With Vario 15-56x Eyepiece)

VICTORY 85MM T*FL DIASCOPE

Weight: 59.8 oz
Length: 17 ⁹⁄₁₀ in
Width: 3 ⅘ in
Power: Variable 20-75X
Objective Diameter: 85 mm
Exit Pupil: 4.25 mm–1.13mm
Field of View: 120-48 ft @ 1000 yards
Twilight Factor: 41.23–79.84
Eye Relief: 16 mm
Waterproof: Yes
Fogproof: Yes
Transferable Limited Lifetime Warranty
Features: Like the 65 mm DiaScope, comes with a Dual Speed Focus System (DSF), rubber-armored exterior over a magnesium-aluminum housing, and the FL lens.
Manufacturer's Suggested Retail Price: $3149.99
(with Vario 20-75X Eyepiece with other available eyepieces including Vario 15-56X, 15-45X, 20-60X, and 30X and 40X fixed, also in angled body)

Estimated "Real World" Price: $3149.99
(with Vario 20-75x Eyepiece)

DIALYT FIELD SPOTTER

Weight: 42.15 oz
Length: 15 ½ in
Width: 3 in
Power: Variable 18-45x
Objective Diameter: 65 mm
Exit Pupil: 3.6 mm–1.4 mm
Field of View: 120–69 ft @ 1000 yards
Twilight Factor: 34.2–54.08
Eye Relief: 16 mm
Waterproof: Yes
Fogproof: Yes
Transferable Limited Lifetime Warranty
Features: The new ZEISS Dialyt 18-45x65 Field Spotter is lightweight and compact for field use by Western hunters in the U.S. and for mountain hunting elsewhere. The straight, rubber-armored scope comes with a built-in variable eyepiece. The metal body is rubber armored.
Manufacturer's Suggested Retail Price: $1299.99
Estimated "Real World" Price: $1299.99

Zeiss Victory 65 MM T*FL Diascope

Zeiss Victory 85 MM T*FL Diascope

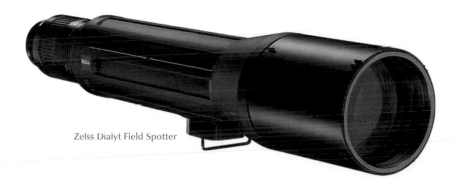

Zeiss Dialyt Field Spotter

SPOTTING SCOPES

Carl Zeiss Optics

www.zeiss.com/sports

VICTORY PHOTOSCOPE 85 T* FL

Weight: 104 oz
Length: 17 ¼ in
Width: 4 ¼ in
Power: Variable 15-45X
Objective Diameter: 85 mm
Exit Pupil: 5.6 mm-1.8 mm
Field of View: 240-81 ft @ 1000 yards
Twilight Factor: 35.70-61.84
Eye Relief: 16 mm
Waterproof: Yes
Fogproof: Yes
Transferable Limited Lifetime Warranty on the optics. Camera Electronics: 2 years.
Features: The PhotoScope integrates panoramic observation optics with a high-power, 7 megapixel digital camera with a 3X optical-zoom lens (the photographic equivalent of 600 mm to 1800 mm).

Zeiss Victory Photoscope 85 T* FL

Manufacturer's Suggested Retail Price: $6499.99
Estimated "Real World" Price: $6499.99

SPOTTING SCOPES

Glossary

Accommodation

The eye *accommodates* to varying focal lengths by relaxing the elastic lens through the tightening of the ciliary body, which in turn reduces the tension on the fibers of the zonule of Zinn attached to the lens. A young human eye can accommodate from distance vision to focus on objects as near as 7 cm in 350 milliseconds by the contraction of the ciliary muscles. As humans grow older their range of accommodation declines, reducing the focal power of the eye and thus leading to presbyopia.

Achromatic Lens

Achromatic means "without color," and the lens is constructed from a convex lens of crown glass and a concave one of flint glass (traditionally a high-dispersion and high-refractive potash-lead glass, now made with nontoxic metals substituting for the lead, and sometimes referred to as "eco glass"), fitted and cemented together in what is known as an *achromatic doublet*. Achromatic lenses work by bringing two different color wavelengths into shared focus.

Adjustment Turret

Adjustment Turret

Holds the knob on the main tube body of the riflescope that adjusts either the *elevation* or the *windage* of the crosshair in the reticle to coincide with the point of impact of the bullet on the target. The windage adjustment moves the point of aim right or left along the horizontal plane, and the elevation adjustment changes it up and down on the vertical plane. Adjustments are made in increments or "clicks" that often equal ¼ MOA.

Anti-Reflective Device (ARD)

A lens filter or cover, that can be viewed through, for reducing the glint from the objective lens of an optical device.

Apochromatic Lens

Originally developed for microscopes, apochromatic lenses focus three (red, green, and blue) or more wavelengths of light on the same point and so create an even sharper image than non-apochromatic lenses. Often designated as *APO*, these lenses may use elements made from the artificial crystal fluorite and are found on high-quality optics.

Aperture Sight

Also called a *peep sight*, it uses an *occluder* (a disk or ring with a center hole of varying sizes depending on the precision of the sight). The shooter's eye centers the front sight in the opening of the rear sight. The most precise aperture sights are competition target models that use a large rear disk, called a *diopter*, with a small sighting hole. The fastest aperture sights, often used on defense shotguns and combat rifles, is the *ghost ring* that uses a thin-ringed rear sight and thicker front post for rapid target acquisition.

Apparent Field of View (AFOV)

As light passes through an eyepiece, the angle is widened. This is the apparent field of view. AFOV is calculated by multiplying the degrees of true FOV by the magnification power:

FOV in degree × Power = AFOV in degrees

Thus for an 8.5×43 mm binocular with a true angular field of view of 6.1 degrees the apparent field of view would be–

$$6.1° × 8.5 = 51.85°$$

Aspheric Lens

A lens, also called an *asphere*, whose profile is neither a portion of a sphere or a cylinder. It's more complex surface profile can reduce spherical and other optical aberrations compared to a simple lens and a single aspheric lens can replace multi-element lenses.

Baffling

This is a black interior coating on an optical device that reduces stray and reflected light inside the device to improve image contrast. With proper baffling the image in the field of view at the ocular should be surrounded by a solid black background.

BaK-4

This is the designation for a superior quality of optical barium crown glass used to make prisms, that produces clearer images. Of lesser quality is BK-7 borosilicate flint glass. If the type of prism glass is not specified on a binocular, it is possible to check by reversing the binocular and looking through the objective: With BaK-4 glass prisms the image will be close to true round which means better light transmission and edge-to-edge sharpness, while through the BK-7 prism the image will be squared off. The best-quality prism glass is SK15 with a minimum of internal reflection for the clearest image. The quality of the glass that goes into the prisms plays a large part in the manufacturing cost of a binocular.

Bases

The part of the riflescope mounting system that attaches to the rifle's receiver and to which the rings are attached.

Bell

The bell-shaped parts at either end of the riflescope. The *objective bell*, on the front, holds the objective lens while the *eye bell* at the rear holds the ocular lens.

Biasing Spring

In a riflescope the reticle is contained in an *erector tube* inside the main tube body is held in position at one end by a pivoting mount known as a *gimbal* and at the other end against the adjustment pads/screws by a *biasing spring*.

Bolometer

A device for measuring incident electromagnetic radiation. From the Greek *bole*, for something thrown, as with a ray of light.

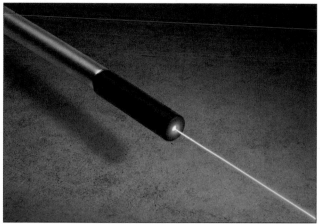

Laser Boresight

Boresighting

Boresighting, as the name implies, involves removing the bolt from a rifle action and looking through the barrel and centering a target in the bore. With the rifle then held in place, the sights are adjusted to align with the target. Devices such as collimators or lasers can also be inserted into the bore and the sights adjusted.

Bridge

The hinge or hinges that connect the two barrels of a binocular. Bridges can be "open" or "closed" in design. In the closed bridge the hinge runs the length of the barrels, while with the open the barrels are hinged at the top and the bottom and there's room in between the two to wrap the fingers which is said to provide a more solid grip. *Bridge* may also refer to that portion of the rifle receiver that arches over the bolt hole, and to which the bases of scope mounts may be attached.

Brightness

The ability of an optical device to gather and transmit enough of the available light to give a sufficiently bright and sharp image.

Buckhorn Sight

Named for its resemblance to deer antlers, this sight's protrusions form a large ring that nearly meets above the V of the notch.

Center Focus

A binocular of this type has a focus wheel or knob on the bridge between the two barrels that simultaneously focuses both oculars of the binocular. Generally there is also a separate dioptre focus ring on one of the of the oculars or as an integrated part of the center focus.

Chromatic Aberration

This is the breaking up of white light into its spectrum of hues, known as *dispersion*, which is seen through a lens as fuzzy "color fringing" in the images being viewed, the varied color wavelengths unable to be brought into focus together.

Close Focus

Please see "Near Focus."

Close Quarters Battle (CQB)

Also called *close quarters combat* (*CQC*), this is a form of fighting in which the enemy is engaged with personal weapons at very short range. Optics for this type of fighting generally use very low or single-power magnification and rapid-target-acquisition reticles.

Collimation

Collimation is the alignment of the optical elements of an optical device to the mechanical axis. Good collimation of binoculars prevents eyestrain, headaches, and inferior and double images while improving resolution. Top quality roof-prism binoculars usually do not require collimation servicing, while over time Porro-prisms may need to be returned to factory or to a qualified repair shop to be re-collimated.

Collimator

An optical instrument that is used to align the optical axes of two or more devices such as the barrels of a binocular or the bore and the sights of a firearm.

Construction

A critical factor in the performance of any optical device is its construction. The security of the barrel alignment and proper internal mounting and alignment of the optics are crucial to producing mechanical reliability, smooth functioning, and long life.

Contrast

The degree to which both dim and bright objects in the image can be differentiated from each other and from the background of the image. High contrast helps in observing fainter objects and in discerning subtle visual details. High quality optical coatings provide better contrast in an image. The other factors affecting contrast are collimation, air turbulence, and the quality of the objective lens, prism, and eyepiece. Some high-contrast lens coating aid in spotting game against leafy or timbered backgrounds.

Crown Glass

One of the earliest low-dispersion glasses made from alkali-lime silicates with approximately 10-percent potassium oxide.

Depth of Field

With an object in focus, the depth of field is the distance in front of and behind it that is also in focus. The higher the magnification of the optical device the shallower the depth of field.

Dioptre

Also *diopter*–a word from the Greek meaning "see through." It is a measure of the refracting or focusing power of a lens. On center-focus binoculars the *diopter eyepiece* is usually on the right. To focus the binocular the right objective is covered by a lens cap and the center-focus wheel is used to make the image sharp and clear. The cap is removed and then placed on the left objective, and only the dioptre focus ring is used to sharpen the image. This accommodates for different vision in each eye. Once the dioptre is properly adjusted the center focus is used to focus the binocular at varying distances. The larger the number of dioptres the greater the range of focusing.

Dispersion

Pleases see *chromatic aberration*.

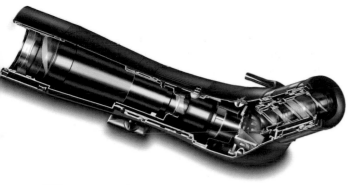

Element

A single lens, or *simple lens*, like a magnifying glass or the individual lenses of eyeglasses, is an "element." Elements can be cemented together to form a *compound lens*. When a series of elements and/or compound lenses are assembled together, one behind the other, in a telescope or another optical device but not cemented together, they are known as *groups*. Groups not cemented together are described as *air spaced*. Assembling groups in this way allows for various quality of different types of glass to work together. An objective lens (or *objective assembly*) made from an air-spaced group of an element and a compound lens could be described as a lens with three elements, or a "three-element lens."

Erector Lens

The erector lens is placed in the housing of a telescopic sight between the objective and the ocular to invert the image that would appear upside down through the eyepiece without an erector.

Exit Pupil

The diameter, in millimeters, of the beam of light that leaves the eyepiece of an optical device is the *exit pupil*. The larger the exit pupil, the brighter the image at the ocular. Having a large exit pupil is an advantage in low light. The maximum dilation of the human pupil in darkness is generally between 5 to 7 mm, decreasing with age. So an exit pupil of 7 mm is near the upper limit of maximum efficiency. The exit pupil is calculated by dividing the diameter of the objective lens in millimeters by the power:

Objective Lens Diameter in Millimeters ÷ Power = Exit Pupil in Millimeters

As an example on a 6×42 mm riflescope, the exit pupil would be–

42 mm ÷ 6 = 7 mm

This is the maximum useful exit pupil.

Express Sight

Used on heavy-caliber rifles for fast acquisition of dangerous game. Has a large V with a white contrast line marking its bottom, with a front sight like a shotgun bead.

Extra Low Dispersion Glass (ED)

ED glass, also called *SLD* ("special low dispersion") or *HD* ("high definition") or something similar, contains rare-earth elements that reduce light dispersion– usually *chromatic dispersion*, which is the separation of light into its spectrum of colors as seen when white light is refracted through a dispersive prism.

Eyecups

The soft rings around the eyepieces of a binocular's oculars. These can be adjusted in several ways, depending on how they are manufactured. Some simply fold out or in to suit those with glasses and those without, or the eyecups can push in or pull out, or turn in or turn out. In the first instance, the synthetic rubber of the eyecup can fatigue and crack in time from the folding as well as from age. Better binoculars seem to use one of the latter two systems.

Eyepiece Focus Ring

A ring on the eyepiece, or ocular, of a riflescope to focus the image to the shooter's eye. Some scopes have a locking ring which when loosened allows the eye bell to be screwed in and out to focus, and then the ring can be tightened to hold the eye bell in position.

Eye Relief

This is the distance that the eyepiece may be held away from the eye and still provide the viewer with the complete field of view. This distance can fall into a range that is sometimes called the *eye box*. Some binoculars may have a very small eye box of 9 to 14 millimeters, which might be comfortable for most people who do not wear eyeglasses. For glasses wearers it is estimated that an eye relief of at least 16 mm is required to see the whole picture. Riflescopes generally have eye relief of 3 ½ to four inches, allowing for recoil, while scopes for handguns may have up to two-feet of eye relief so the gun can be held at arm's length and still provide the complete field of view for the shooter.

Field of View (FOV)

Field of view (FOV) can be described as "true" or "apparent." (see "Apparent Field of View.") True field of view is the angle subtended by the objective lens. An 8.5x43-millimeter binocular may have a true field of view of 6.1 degrees. This is the wedge, or cone, of light entering the objective. Thought of simply as width, this is how wide an area from which the objective is drawing light and accordingly is the physical width, or diameter, of the area that may be observed. The formula for determining this in feet is:

52.5 × FOV in degrees = FOV in feet @ 1000 yards

So for the binocular described above, its FOV in feet at 1000 yards would be:

52.5 × 6.1° = 320.25 feet @ 1000 yards

This is the linear field of view. The angular field of view, if the linear is known, can be calculated by dividing the feet at 1000 yards by 52.5. So, using the same example–

$$320.25 \div 52.5 = 6.1°$$

Finish

The outer surface or coating of an optical device. This can be gloss or blued, matte black, silver, anodized, camouflaged, or rubber armored.

First Focal Plane Reticle (FFP)

The reticle in this position in a riflescope lies on the first lens onto which the focused light from the objective falls, usually in the middle of the main body tube. On FFP variable-power scopes the reticle changes size with the change of power.

Fixed Focus

The lens focus is pre-set from some close distance to infinity. Assumes that a user has both perfect vision and vision that is perfectly matched in both eyes and that those eyes are young and flexible enough to do a great deal of accommodating.

Flint Glass

An optical glass with a relatively high refractive index. Fashioned into a concave lens, flint glass is joined to a convex crown-glass lens to form an *achromatic doublet* which reduces *chromatic aberration* due to the two glasses's compensating refractive properties.

Focus Mechanism

The three types are *fixed focus, individual eyepiece focusing* (IF), and *center focus*.

Gating

The switching on and off of circuits to reduce the loss of electric power.

Gen I

The light-intensification systems of night-vision devices advance through various generations, a classification introduced by the US Government. The first, Generation 0, dates back to the 1930s and involved the projection of infrared light. Gens I through III (or Generations 1 through 3), initially referred to as "Starlight" scopes, are advancements of a passive system that intensifies the available light. Advancements beyond Gen III have been made, but so far there is no official Gen IV classification.

Housing

Also called *body*, *chassis*, *barrel*, or sometimes the *tube* or *main tube body*, especially the main housing of a riflescope. It holds the lenses, mechanicals, and if the device has them, the electronics. Housings before the 20th century were made primarily from brass. Now they can be titanium, magnesium, aluminum, or even polymer. Binoculars and scopes can be rubber-armored. The housing holds the internal parts of the optical device in place and protects them from dust and moisture. Most devices today are purged of atmospheric air and then filled with inert gas such as argon or nitrogen to prevent internal fogging due to temperature changes.

Index Match

Each type of glass has a particular refractive index that describes how much it bends and disperses light waves passing through it. By matching the indices of glasses that complement one another (such as *crown glass* and *flint glass*) it is possible to improve the clarity and brightness of light transmission over that through a single type of glass.

Individual Focus (IF)

An *IF* binocular can be adjusted for the vision in each eye; but once that is accomplished, it is fundamentally the same as a fixed-focus.

Interpupillary Distance (IPD)

Interpupillary distance is a term for describing how far apart someone's pupils are. For most adults this is between 58 and 72 millimeters; most binoculars can be adjusted within this range so that the eyepieces are the right distance apart in order for the centers of the eyes to coincide with the centers of the eyepieces, creating a single round sight picture rather than two overlapping ones. Some individuals can, though, have extremely narrow- or extremely wide-set eyes. If a hunter believes he fits into one of those categories, then he does need to try a binocular before buying it to determine if it can be adjusted to the proper degree of spread. One of the several virtues of the Porro-prism binocular over the roof prism is that it can in general offer a more generous range of hinge adjustments.

IR

"Infrared" light lies in the wavelength longer than that of visible light, measured from the edge of visible red light at 0.74 μm to 300 μm, and includes the thermal radiation emitted by objects.

Lens Coatings

The elements of an optical device are coated to reduce external and internal reflection, light loss, and glare, which in turn ensures even light transmission, resulting in greater image sharpness, brightness, color fidelity, and contrast. Anti-reflective coatings are based on a 19th century discovery that the optical glass of the time, which tended to develop a tarnish on its surface with age due to chemical reactions, was found to transmit more light than new, clean glass. Today, lens coatings–transparent thin films with alternating layers of contrasting refractive index–range in quality or applications as follows: *Coated*–a single layer of coating has been lavishly slapped on at least one lens surface, somewhere; *Fully Coated*–a single layer has been applied to all the "air-to-glass" surfaces, which includes the two sides of any air-spaced elements inside the optics ("air" being a term of art because most good optics will be purged of atmospheric air and filled with an inert gas such as nitrogen to prevent internal fogging); *Multi-Coated*–several layers of antireflective coating have been applied to at least one lens surface; *Fully-Multi-Coated*–all air-to-glass surfaces have received multiple layers of anti-reflective coating.

Light Transmission

A certain percentage of light passing through an optical device is lost through absorption and reflection at each air-to-glass surface or inside the prism system itself. The amount of original light available to the observer by the time it exits the eyepiece will vary from as low as 50 percent to over 90, depending on the quality and number of optical glass elements used in the lenses and prisms, configuration and size of the prisms, collimation of the optical system, and type and amount of anti-reflection coatings present. Some manufacturers will underscore the fact that the layer of anti-reflective coating they apply will permit something like "99.8 percent" of the available light to pass through, which may be perfectly true. Yet, what they often fail to mention is how many layers of coating are applied to each surface, how many air-to-glass surfaces are contained in their binocular (light loss being multiplied with each of those surfaces), and that a 0.2 percent loss of light is probably a reference to what is lost by the best (and most costly) layer of anti-reflective coating being used and not for all the other (cheaper) ones put on in order to call the lenses "multi-coated" without being accused of false advertising. If a binocular manufacturer can guarantee anywhere from 90 to 92 percent transmission of light through the binocular, that is about as good as it gets.

Magnification (Power)

Magnification is the degree to which an object is made to appear closer by an optical device than it does to the naked eye. In scopes and binoculars this is expressed as a *power,* designated by a numeral and the symbol *X,* such as "8X" or "10X," and thought by many to represent a factor of enlargement in which the image is made eight or ten times bigger. Making

an image larger, as a 6-foot-tall man projected onto a movie screen becoming 20 feet tall, is called *linear magnification.* With a telescope, etc., images seen through the eyepiece are actually no bigger than a few millimeters, yet the way they appear to the eye is the result of *angular magnification.* The image is not bigger, the way a person projected onto a movie screen is, but is seen as if the viewer had reduced the distance to it. In the case of an 9X scope, the image is as it would appear nine-times closer: A deer at 360 yards, seen through a 9X scope, would appear as it would at 40 yards to an unaided eye.

Manufacturer's Suggested Retail Price (MSRP)

This is the price published by an optics maker—often in product literature—at which the maker says a product should be sold.

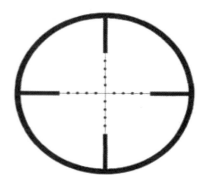

Mil Dot

A *mil* is a unit of measure for a circle, like MOA. *Mil* is an abbreviation of *milliradian,* a *radian* being the angle that subtends an arc of a circle that is equal in length to the radius of that circle (e.g., a 10-inch-diameter circle would have a radius of 5 inches, and therefore the angle of a radian of that circle would subtend 5 inches of the circle's circumference). Put another way, a mil is approximately 1/6283rd of a circle, or about .057 degree. By definition one mil subtends one meter at 1000 meters. Mil-dot reticles, developed for military snipers, use dots on the reticle for range estimation and calculating holdover for the trajectory. At a particular power setting in a scope, usually the highest, the distance between the centers of two mil-dots on the reticle post is proportioned to subtend 3.375 MOA, or slightly less that 3.6 inches at 100 yards. Snipers use known lengths, such as the average shoulder width of a human of about 21 inches, and compare it to the *subtension* of the mil-dots to approximate the range—if a mil-dot increment covers half the entire chest area of a target, then that target would be almost 300 yards away. The calculation is made by taking the target width or height in yards, multiplying by 1000 and dividing the sum by the number of mil-dot increments needed to subtend it. In this case, if it took two mil-dot increments to subtend a 21-inch-wide chest (21 inches equal to .583 yards), the distance to the target would be calculated as–

(583 yards × 1000) ÷ 2 mils = 292 yards.

Similar ranging and trajectory correction can be done by hunters knowing the approximate sizes of most game animals as follows (these are the heights in inches from the bottom of the brisket to the top of the withers–if measuring from the top of the back instead of the withers, a few inches, such as 2 inches for a whitetail, may be deducted)–

White-Tailed Deer: 18 inches (mule deer may be slightly larger)
Elk: 24 inches
Sheep: 22½ inches
Black Bear: 18 inches
Pronghorn Antelope: 14 inches
Coyote: 9 inches
Rockchuck (standing, i.e., measured from head to foot): 18 inches
Prairie Dog (standing): 9 inches

Minimum Advertised Price (MAP)

This is a price figure approved by the manufacturer that retailers may show in their published or broadcast advertising. The MAP will be less than MSRP, sometimes considerably.

Minute of Angle (MOA)

Also called *minute of arc*, it is a 1/60th division of one degree of arc, known as a "minute." As the total piece of a full circle, a minute would amount to roughly .0046 percent of it, or .0166 degree. If mathematical formula for determining field of view at 1000 yards is modified slightly, it can be calculated that a single minute of arc subtends about 1 inch at 100 yards:

52.5 X .0166° X 1.2 = 1.05 inches @ 100 yards

The fractional divisions on the adjustment knobs for each "click" or each graduation on the dial can be from one-tenth to one MOA, but on most scopes it will be one-quarter.

mK (millikelvin)

A unit of temperature measurement based on the Kelvin scale.

µm

The symbol for a micrometer or *micron*, one-millionth of a meter (1/1000th of a millimeter or 0.001 millimeter).

Near Focus

Also called *close focus*, this is the minimum distance at which an object will still appear sharp in an optical device. It is of more importance to birders who want to be able to focus down to 15 feet or less for detailed observation of birds. For some "butterfliers" a near focus of four feet may be desirable.

Night Vision Device (NVD)

These optical devices intensify the ambient light down to total darkness through the use of an image-intensifier tube. They may also include infrared illuminators and telescopic sights and can be used as independent weapons's sights or as an attachment to a daylight weapon's sight for nighttime use.

Objective Lens

The objective is the front lens of an optical device–the lens closest to the object being viewed–the "big one." The diameter of the objective in millimeters will be the second number describing a particular optical configuration. An 10×40 mm binocular, for example, has an objective lens 40 mm in diameter. Doubling the size of the objective quadruples the light-gathering ability of the binocular. This means that a 7×50 binocular will gather four-times the light of a 7×25.

Ocular Lens

The viewing lens in the eyepiece of an optical device. Or simply the "small one."

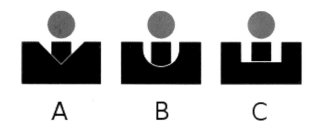

Open Sight

A sight using a *post* or *bead* front sight and a rear sight notch. The shooter aligns the front sight in the notch and rests the target on the aligned sights. The various types of open sights include V(A) and U notches *[B]*; *Partridge sights [C]* that use a rectangular post and a square rear notch; and *buckhorn*, *semibuckhorn*, and *express*.

Parallax

The word derives from the Greek for "alteration" and is defined as an "apparent shift of an object against a background caused by a change in observer position." In a riflescope, parallax is caused by the inability of the scope to remain focused at all distances, particularly farther ones. Parallax can be seen in a riflescope by the shooter's holding the reticle on a target and then moving his eye around the ocular and noting whether or not the target moves in relation to the reticle. In the worst-case scenario, parallax can seriously affect the accuracy of the scope. Not all scopes, though, will come with parallax adjustments. Most scopes that might reasonably be used for big-game hunting will come from the factory already adjusted to be parallax-free at 100 yards (and sometimes at 50 yards for scopes intended for use on shotguns and muzzleloaders), and they shouldn't be substantially bothered by parallax for at least 200 yards beyond that. But for scopes higher than 10X and at extreme ranges, a parallax adjustment can be critical, and a band or knob will carry graduations for adjusting out to 400 or 500 yards or more and to infinity.

Phase Coating

A treatment applied to *roof prisms* to correct different light waves's being out of phase with one another and so causing a degradation in resolution and contrast–more apparent at higher powers of magnification, this fault might be thought of as a timing problem in light transmission, like a timing problem in a car's engine.

Picatinny Rail

Named for the Picatinny Arsenal in New Jersey where it was originally tested, it is a bracket "tactical rail"–a standardized optical mounting platform with spacing slots–for firearms like the AR-15. Similar to the Picatinny is the *Weaver-style* rail mount.

Picket

The top point of the heavy-post portion of a *duplex reticle*.

Receiver

The receiver is the part of a rifle that houses the operating parts such as the bolt and trigger mechanism.

Porro Prism

A retired Italian artillery officer and surveyor Ignazio Porro (1801–1875) invented the optical prism that bears his name in 1854 in Paris. Traditional binoculars with large objectives use this "dogleg" prism (actually two 180-degree prisms cemented together) which permits the offsetting of the oculars, as compared to the straight-through viewing with a Galilean binocular.

Prisms

Prisms are used to invert the image between the objective and the ocular without the need of a long tube. Prisms allow binoculars to have a shorter, more compact housing.

Real World Price

The average price a consumer can expect to pay when purchasing an optical device from a retailer.

Reflex Sight

An aiming device that reflects a *reticle* off a curved mirror or slanted glass plate and keeps that reticle in alignment with the target whatever the eye position of the viewer, making it effectively *parallax* free.

Refraction

The bending of light when it passes through a medium, such as glass or water, that reduces its speed; expressed as the *refraction index* or *index of refraction*. By bending the light, a refracting lens can focus it on a point.

Relative Brightness Index (RBI)

The *RBI* is calculated by squaring the exit pupil (e.g., an exit pupil of 4 mm would work out to a relative brightness of 16). A minimum relative brightness of 25, the square of a 5-millimeter exit pupil, is considered the optimum in all light conditions; but for present-day optics, this and other indices of brightness such as *twilight factor* and, to a lesser extent, *relative light efficiency* are of real value only as comparisons between optics with lenses and anti-reflectivity of equal quality.

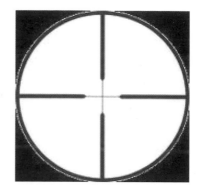

Relative Light Efficiency

An arbitrary value some optics manufacturers employ by boosting the *relative brightness* (which is a calculable number) of their optical devices by 50 percent, claiming that this takes into account the higher light transmissions achieved by coated optics over uncoated, ignoring the fact that almost no optics anymore come without lenses that have at least some coating.

durable and less likely to transmit stray light, as an etched reticle might.

Resolution

Resolution is a measurement of and optical device's ability to distinguish fine detail and produce a sharp image. In general a larger objective lens will deliver more detail to the eye than a smaller objective lens, regardless of magnification. Actual resolution is determined by the quality of the optical components, the type and quality of the optical coatings, atmospheric conditions, collimation, and the visual acuity of the user. Theoretically, a perfect human eye's acuity should be able to resolve objects, such as two lines, separated by 0.4 minute of arc or 0.0066 degrees, which would be the equivalent of 20/8 vision.

Rings

Hold the main tube body of riflescope and are attached to the bases attached to the rifle's receiver.

Reticle

From the Latin word for "net" and related to "reticule" which is a woman's knitted handbag; the *crosshair* in telescopic sight. The shapes of reticles can be described as "fine" to "dot" to "duplex," and with thick-and thin posts that can be further categorized from "fine" to "heavy duplex." Some reticles may be a pointed post. Reticles may also be illuminated. The earliest reticles or crosshairs were actual hairs. In other cases strands of spider web were used. Today most reticles are wire which can be flattened to various thicknesses. Another type of reticle is engraved or etched onto a thin glass plate. Etched reticles can take an almost infinite range of shapes and can have "floating" components, such as circles. Wire crosshairs, though, are said to be more

Roof Prism

Called *roof* or *Dach*, the German word for roof, because of its supposed resemblance to a house roof, this prism erects the image in a straight line, allowing for the objective and ocular to remain basically in line. Physically, roof prisms are not as bright as *Porro prisms*, but modern phase-coatings and glass make the difference negligible, and they produce a more compact binocular. The types of roof prism include the shallow-V-shape *Abbe-Koenig* and the cube-like, less bulky *Schmidt-Pechan*, named for their developers.

Second Focal Plane Reticle (SFP)

The reticle in this position in a riflescope lies on the second lens onto which the focused light from the objective falls after passing through the erector assembly, usually toward the ocular bell of the scope. On SFP variable-power scopes the reticle size remains constant with the change of power.

Spectral Response

The sensitivity of a photosensor to optical radiation of different wavelengths.

Spherical Aberration

This a blurring of the image at the margins of a lens. It can appear as a doughnut with the image in the center of the lens being sharp and clear and the edges increasingly out of focus. It is caused by the light from the outer circumference of the lens having a shorter focus than the light from the middle. Also called *dioptric aberration*.

Stadia

The fine wire portion of a duplex reticle.

Stray Light

Light in an optical device that is not intended in the design. The sources of such light may be leakage in the housing, diffuse reflection from faulty mirrored surfaces, scattering from the unbaffled surfaces of supporting structures within the optical system, and reflections from lens surfaces.

Subtension

The number of degrees of arc covered by an object in the field of view. As an example, the full moon *subtends* 0.54 degrees of arc in the night sky, which is about the same amount of the sky a thumb will subtend if held at arm's length. In a rifle scope, *reticle subtension* is the amount of the target covered by the reticle. This is commonly expressed in inches at 100 yards—in the case of a *mil-dot* reticle the increment between the center points of each dot effectively works out to 3.54 inches. This subtension can be used to estimate the range to the target and determine holdover for the shot.

Twilight Factor

A comparative value of the relative usefulness of different configurations of optical devices in low light, assuming equal quality of lenses and coatings. Twilight factor is calculated by multiplying the diameter, in millimeters, of the objective by the power of magnification and determining the square root of the product:

$$\text{Twilight Factor} = \sqrt{(\text{Power} \times \text{Objective})}$$

As an example, an 8.5×43 mm binocular would have a Twilight Factor of

$$\sqrt{(8.5 \times 43)} = 19.1$$

Compare that to the twilight factor of an 8×56 mm binocular:

$$\sqrt{(8 \times 56)} = 21.1$$

So based solely on the twilight factor, the 8×56 would as might be expected perform better in low light than a 8.5×43, although low-light performance is not the only factor to consider when selecting a binocular or other optical device.

Variable Magnification Band

Also called the *power selector ring*, the knurled or rubbered ring at the front of the ocular bell that is used to change the magnification on variable-power scopes.

OPTICS MANUFACTURERS

ALPEN OPTICS
10329 Dorset Street
Rancho Cucamonga, California 91730
909-987-8370

BROWNING
One Browning Place
Morgan, Utah 84050-9326
800-333-3288

BRUNTON
2255 Brunton Court
Riverton, Wyoming 82501
307-857-4700

BSA OPTICS, INC.
3911 SW 47th Ave. Suite 914
Ft. Lauderdale, Florida 33314
954-581-2144

BURRIS COMPANY
920 54th Avenue
Greeley, Colorado 80634
970-356-8702

BUSHNELL
9200 Cody
Overland Park, Kansas 66214
800-423-3537

C. SHARPS ARMS
100 Centennial Drive
Big Timber, Montana 59011
406-932-4353

CABELA'S
1 Cabela Drive
Sidney, Nebraska 69150
800-237-4444

DAVIDE PEDERSOLI & C.
Fabbrica d'armi
Via Artigiani, 57
25063–Gardone Val Trompia
Brescia ITALY
011-39-030-8915000

HENSOLDT
c/o Carl Zeiss Sports Optics
13005 N. Kingston Avenue
Chester, Virginia 23836
800-441-3005

HUSKEMAW OPTICS
115 W. Yellowstone Avenue
Cody, Wyoming 82414
307-586-1878

KONUS USA
7530 NW 79th Street
Miami, Florida 33166
305-884-7618

KOWA SPORTING OPTICS
20001 S. Vermont Avenue
Torrance, California 90502
310-327-1913

KRUGER OPTICAL, INC.
251 W. Barclay Drive
Sisters, Oregon 97759
541-549-0770

LEATHERWOOD—HI-LUX, INC.
3135 Kashiwa Street
Torrance, California 90505
310-257-8142
888-445-8912

LEICA CAMERA INC.
1 Pearl Court, Unit A
Allendale, New Jersey 07401
800-222-0118

LEUPOLD & STEVENS, INC.
Post Office Box 688
Beaverton, Oregon 97075-0688
800-LEUPOLD

LUCID
235 Fairway Drive
Riverton, WY 82501
307-840-2160

MILLETT

c/o Bushnell Outdoor Products
9200 Cody
Overland Park, Kansas 66214
800-423-3537

MINOX USA, INC.

438 Willow Brook Road
Meriden, New Hampshire 03770
603-469-3080

NIGHT OPTICS USA, INC.

15182 Triton Lane, Suite 101
Huntington Beach, California 92649
800-30-NIGHT

NIGHTFORCE OPTICS, INC.

336 Hazen Lane
Orofino, Idaho 83544
208-476-9814

NIKON, INC.

1300 Walt Whitman Road
Melville, New York 11747-3064
631-547-4200

NITEHOG SYSTEMS, LLC

10500 Metric Drive, Suite 120
Dallas, Texas 75243
972-213-0162

PENTAX IMAGING COMPANY

600 12th Street, Suite 300
Golden, Colorado 80401
303-799-8000

PREMIER OPTICS, LTD.

173 Commonwealth Court
Winchester, Virginia 22602
540-868-2044

QUIGLEY-FORD SCOPES

209 Side Street
Box 300
Stayner, Ontario L0M 1S0
CANADA
705-428-4428

REDFIELD

c/o Leupold & Stevens, Inc.
Post Office Box 688
Beaverton, Oregon 97075-0688
800-LEUPOLD

SCHMIDT & BENDER INC.

741 Main Street
Claremont, New Hampshire 03743
800-468-3450
603-287-4836

SHEPHERD ENTERPRISES, INC.

P.O. Box 189
Waterloo, Nebraska 68069
402 779-2424

SIMMONS

c/o Bushnell Outdoor Products
9200 Cody
Overland Park, Kansas 66214
800-423-3537

STEINER OPTIK

920 54th Avenue, Suite 200
Greeley, Colorado 80634
970-356-1670

SWAROVSKI OPTIK NORTH AMERICA LTD.

2 Slater Road
Cranston, Rhode Island 02920
800-426-3089

TRIJICON, INC.

49385 Shafer Avenue
P. O. Box 930059
Wixom, Michigan 48393-0059
248-960-7700

U.S. OPTICS INC.

150 Arovista Circle
Brea, Calfornia 92821
714-582-1956

VORTEX OPTICS

2120 West Greenview Drive
Middleton, Wisconsin 53562
800-426-0048

WEAVER

Onalaska Operations
N 5549 County Trunk Z
Onalaska, Wisconsin 54650
800-635-7656

CARL ZEISS SPORTS OPTICS

13005 N. Kingston Avenue
Chester, Virginia 23836
800-441-3005